Eternal ZOE

What did Jesus really say about Life,

Death, the Soul, and Immortality?

Second Edition

2.1

Mark C Elmore

Acknowledgments

I must begin by thanking my sweet wife, Laura.

There is absolutely no way I could have completed
this book without Laura's encouragement,
sacrifice and incredible patience.

Thank you, Sweetheart!

Next, I want to thank Amber Helt, my initial editor.
Amber's insights, advice and editing were huge.

Lisa Thompson with Write By Lisa was also a
major help with editing revisions.

Lian Mudd conducted the final round of edits,
particularly focusing on content that was super helpful.

Thank you all for your contribution
to this book in so many ways!

What did Jesus really say about Life,

Death, the Soul, and Immortality?

EternalZoe.com

Mark C Elmore

First Edition © 2019, Second Edition © 2022

Contents

Copyrights - Permissions

Greek-English Interlinear New Testament verses are from:
http://www.scripture4all.org

Sublinear texts in the Greek-English Interlinear can include:

GNT-C: The Concordant Greek Text 1975

© 1975 Concordant Publishing Concern

std-1.en: Standard-Level_1, Version 1.0

© 2015 Gernot R. Frey

CGTS: Concordant Greek Text Sublinear, Version 1.5
© 2009 Concordant Publishing Concern
Adapted for Scriveners Textus Receptus 1894—Scripture4All Foundation

Scriveners Textus Receptus 1894

CGES_id: Concordant Greek-English Sublinear -idiomatic-
For Scriveners Textus Receptus 1894
Version 2.3, Interlinear Format

© 2009 Scripture4all Foundation.

Parsing for ScrTR, Version **1.1**

Adapted from Robinsons (Scrivener Textus Receptus 1894)

Strong's numbers for ScrTR

Strong's Exhaustive Concordance
by James Strong, STD, LLD, 1890

DISCLAIMER

The statements made in this book regarding correct translation and interpretation of the Bible are my opinion (the author) and not a declaration of fact.

Strong differences of opinion as to how the original Greek or Hebrew should be interpreted have existed for millennia. My opinion on the correctness of any interpretation or translation are focused on particular words or phrases at any given point in this book and merely reflect my viewpoints.

From time to time throughout this book, I will disagree with certain words used in many English Bible translations. These disagreements or criticisms reflect my opinion and are not statements of fact.

I am actually very thankful for the English translations that exist, for they have been the basis of my faith and growth as Christian and a means of spreading the good news of eternal life that comes through Jesus to millions of people throughout the world for centuries.

It is my hope that some future translations will transliterate the words that I focus on in this book, and let the educated reader decide for themselves what God's Word is saying.

DISPLAY OF WORDS

In many Bible verses throughout this book, I will display the original Greek word (or its root) next to the translated English word in parentheses.

These Greek words do not appear in any English translation that I am currently familiar with. Rather, I have displayed the Greek word as a teaching aid. I also incorporate some screen-captures from a Greek-English Interlinear New Testament, where the original Greek words can be seen and read.

RESOURCES AND REFERENCES

At the end of this book, I provide a list of resources and references.

Preface

I believe the views that I have expressed in this book regarding the interpretation of the Greek words *psuche* and *zoe* are true.

However, I don't believe that my salvation (nor anyone else's) is dependent upon having a totally accurate understanding of how Jesus used *psuche* and *zoe* in his teaching. We are saved by belief in who Jesus is and what he has done for us. Holding to that truth is essential.

Even when Jesus taught small groups of people, they usually did not understand everything he said. But those who laid hold to who he was and held onto their belief, even in spite of their questions, became children of God.

If we make "absolute correctness" a gauge of our walk with God and our spiritual maturity, then we have missed the point about the gift of salvation that comes only through Jesus, not through any works of our own.

Having said that, I do believe an accurate understanding of Jesus' teaching will clarify his message and purpose. The importance of this clarity cannot be overstated. Without clarity, our doctrine and our emphasis will be out of step with Jesus' message.

But make no mistake about it. My salvation is based on wholeheartedly believing that Jesus is who he claimed to be—the Messiah, the Son of God—and counting on the fact of his death and resurrection.

Note: This book is intended to be a catalyst for dialogue.

Comments are welcome on the Eternal Zoe YouTube channel,
or at the website EternalZoe.com

Part One

The Clear Difference

1

Just 5 Minutes

If I only had 5 minutes of your time and we were never to cross paths again, what could I say to help you understand the importance of reading this book?

Let's say that you and a friend are playing a game of darts. You are throwing darts at a target with a bullseye in the middle worth 100 points.

Then imagine some guy walks up to you and tells you that the true bullseye is missing from the target. He tells you and your friend that the bullseye you are focusing on actually has no value at all, in fact the target you are using for your game is flawed.

After looking at this guy a bit suspiciously at first, you might then humor him by suggesting that maybe you should just replace the whole target. He then replies that is not necessary, that indeed the target areas outside of the bullseye are mostly fine, only the bullseye is heavily flawed. He then suggests once you get the correct bullseye in place, any remaining issues with the rest of the target would likely correct themselves. At this point your suspicion of this guy increases to the point of wondering whether this conversation really needs to continue.

Well, I am that guy. And you are probably going to look at me a bit suspiciously, but that's okay. I expect that. However, it is my hope that you will continue this conversation with me.

As Christians in today's world, I believe we have failed at correctly identifying the bullseye. We have focused on a bullseye that never actually existed, at least with respect to our current understanding of the bullseye.

The current prevailing understanding of the bullseye is that Jesus came to save us from hell, so that we can go to Heaven. My hope is that after reading this book you will see that the true bullseye has very little to do with hell, at least with respect to the traditional view of hell.

In fact, the bullseye that Jesus focused on was man's sentence of death that has existed since Adam's sin, and God's solution to this sentence of death. God's solution is Jesus' gift of **Eternal Zoe**, which he bequeaths to wholehearted believers.

I believe mainstream Christianity began to lose focus on Jesus' stated purpose, over 1600 years ago. We have tragically substituted the core teaching of Jesus with a false narrative. I invite you to take a fresh look at what Jesus said 2,000 years ago, unencumbered by powerful paradigms that have likely played a part in shaping what you understand and believe.

You will come to see how several key words used extensively by Jesus and the New Testament authors are almost impossible to recognize in our Bibles or in today's mainstream Christian teaching, in part due to these influential paradigms. On the other hand, you will see how Jesus' consistent and deliberate use of these original words actually clarify and define his powerful message of salvation.

Join with me as we unwrap Jesus' and the New Testament authors' use of these key words. Come see the clarity that Jesus intended.

Let's focus on the true bullseye.

Ready to get started?

2

Seeking Clarity

CUTTING TO THE CHASE

As it turns out, what Jesus did *not* say has become a significant portion of mainstream Christianity's doctrine. To be frank, part of what we have believed is simply false.

At the risk of oversimplifying the situation just let me say this: "immortality" as most Christians understand it is just not reality. There are two prevailing views on this topic: the traditional view and the conditional view. I happen to hold to the conditional view. I believe in conditional immortality.

I held to the traditional view for most of my life. It was not until I began a long study on Jesus' use of the words "life," "death," "soul," and "eternal" that I began to question my beliefs and eventually came to see that Jesus was talking about something very different than what I had believed most of my life.

TRADITIONAL VIEWPOINT

The "Traditional" view is associated with the belief that hell is a place of endless torment, burning, being eaten by worms, darkness, and separation from God where unbelievers will spend eternity. The traditional view believes the second death (mentioned several times in the Book of Revelation) is not speaking of physical death but rather is symbolic or referring to spiritual death, signifying eternal spiritual separation from God. The traditional view believes this separation also includes everlasting torment and excruciating suffering.

CONDITIONAL IMMORTALITY

The "Conditional" view holds to the belief that man is mortal. The Conditional view believes the Bible clearly teaches that man does not "have an immortal soul", but rather that man "is a soul" and that the soul is mortal. Immortality is not an innate aspect of mankind's nature. Conditionalists have the understanding that a person receives immortality via the gift of eternal life (eternal zoe) when that person wholeheartedly believes the truth about Jesus' identity.

Conditionalists believe a person's immortality is "conditional" upon this gift of salvation. Immortality comes only from the impartation of the Holy Spirit into the believer. This deposit of the Holy Spirit imparts eternal zoe unto the believer.

Conditionalists believe that the unsaved are destroyed (perish) in the lake of fire. This means that the unbeliever dies and ceases to exist at some point after being thrown into the lake of fire. The lake of fire and the second death are both mentioned several times in Revelation, and in two instances the lake of fire is defined as the second death. (Revelation 2:11; 19:20; 20:6,10,14,15; 21:8).

Conditionalists hold to the belief that when any person dies (passes away from their earthly life), that is their first death.

Several of the reformationists that played highly significant roles in the Reformation were Conditionalists. These men risked their lives for proclaiming the truth they saw in the original teachings of the New Testament. However, their conditionalist views are basically unknown or ignored by most traditionalists who otherwise hold these men in high esteem for their other contributions to the reformation movement.

Four of these important reformers who were Conditionalists are:

- John Wycliffe
- John Huss
- William Tyndale
- Martin Luther

There have been many others since then. I will go into more detail on these men's beliefs in Part 3 of this book.

Note: To learn more about early church leaders who stuck to the New Testament's original teaching on Conditionalism, go to EternalZoe.com/links and click on the links under 'Early Church Beliefs on the Mortality of Psuche.'

CORRUPTION OF THE GOSPEL

There is a serious lack of understanding today as to what Jesus meant when he talked about life, death, the soul, eternity, hades and Gehenna. This divergence from what Jesus really said began to appear within 2 centuries of his resurrection. Jesus' message began to be corrupted by secular beliefs regarding man's nature that slowly infiltrated into Christian doctrine and eventually transformed Jesus' original true message.

This incorrect redefinition of the gospel became the predominant belief and doctrine of the Christian world by around 500 AD and remained as the heavily protected belief for almost 1000 years, until the rumblings of the Reformation began.

This divergence from Jesus' original clear message stemmed from changing Jesus' emphasis on life, death and the resurrection to instead make it appear that his focus was on saving souls from hell.

There were several early church leaders who knew the true message was "conditional immortality" and it is apparent in their writings. However, over the course of several centuries the incorrect belief that man was innately immortal (that man has an immortal soul) prevailed. This false belief was eventually sanctioned as "official" church doctrine in the early centuries of the Catholic church. This notion of the immortality of man's soul continues to be heavily guarded by the Catholic church and most protestant churches as part of their fundamental belief.

This lack of clarity about what Jesus really said about life, death, the soul, hell (Gehenna), resurrection and immortality has continued to prevail to this day. Were it not for the fact that these words form the very foundation of Jesus' and the New Testament's teaching, I would not feel the need to write this book.

MY ENCOUNTER WITH PSUCHE AND ZOE

My journey began over twenty years ago, when I started doing a word search on the English word "life". In some instances, the way the word "life" was used in the New Testament just didn't make sense to me. I began my study using *The NIV Exhaustive Concordance*. It quickly became evident that the single English word "life" had been translated from two different Greek words: psuche and zoe. These two words account for most of the instances where *life* appears in English translations of the New Testament.

It also became obvious to me that there was a very clear pattern in the way Jesus used the words *psuche* and *zoe*. As I progressed in the study it became apparent that psuche and zoe were in fact very different in their meaning, especially in the manner that Jesus and the New Testament authors used these words.

The fact that these two original Greek words are not visible to English readers of the New Testament generates several critical problems. The first problem is that using the single word life for both psuche and zoe actually *obscures* what Jesus, Paul, and others in the New Testament originally said. Secondly, the English words that have been inserted in lieu of psuche and zoe have literally *changed* what Jesus and Paul said. There are other serious problems that are intertwined with this, which we will examine in detail as we progress through the book.

Psuche is translated into English as "life" about 30-40% of the time it appears in the Greek New Testament. (This varies among English translations). Approximately 50-60% of the time psuche is translated into the English word "soul!" Please don't miss this fact! Over a third of the time psuche is translated into English as "life" and over half of the time it is translated as "soul".

This was confusing to me and appeared to be a somewhat arbitrary choice of words. Especially in light of my understanding of the word "soul" at that time in my life, the insertion of these significantly different English words "life" and "soul" for the single Greek word "psuche" seemed to introduce ambiguity into what was originally a singular word.

In order to truly know what Jesus emphasized in his teachings, it is imperative that we identify how Jesus defined psuche and zoe by examining how he consistently used these two very different words.

The English words life and soul, which have been inserted in lieu of

psuche and zoe, have actually changed Jesus' original teachings.

I did not come to my understanding of Jesus teaching on immortality initially by studying his teaching on hell. Rather, it was his teaching on life and death (which as you will see was Jesus' bullseye or primary focus) that drew me into this in-depth study. It is this study on Jesus' teachings on psuche, zoe and death that I am going to share with you in parts 1 and 2.

As we go through these first two parts of the book you may naturally grapple with questions like, "if Jesus really said these things about psuche, zoe and death then what am I to do with my current understanding of topics like hell and hades?"

These are the same questions I grappled with for many years. As I studied the concepts that I cover in parts 1 and 2, I became convinced that Jesus' primary focus was indeed different than what I had believed for most of my life.

I began to do deeper studies on hades and hell, and eventually came across the teachings of Edward Fudge, Chris Date and many others who had exhaustively studied the topics of hades, hell and perishing. Their teaching helped to fill in the gaps of my understanding. It is in Part 3 that we will delve into these topics, because that is the sequence that I followed as my understanding developed.

I also want to emphasize that it is indeed Jesus' teaching on psuche, zoe and death that characterized his focus and ultimate purpose.

While hell does hold a roll in the finality of mankind, it was not Jesus' primary focus. In addition, Jesus' teaching on hell (Gehenna) was nothing like the definition conveyed by mainstream Christianity today.

HISTORY OF TRANSLATIONS

English translations are a fairly recent occurrence in the history of the New Testament. Since I speak English, I can only comment on what I see in the English translations. However, this is significant because over the last five centuries English translations have had a major shaping effect on church doctrines worldwide.

In my opinion the misunderstanding of these words in the last millennium (not just in English) has contributed to the distortion of Jesus' original clear message.

3

Intro: Psuche & Zoe Defined

When you see the word "life" in an English New Testament, most of the time it is being translated from one of two Greek words. These two words are *psuche* and *zoe*. Zoe is almost always translated into English as "life." Psuche is also translated as "life" around 30-40% of the time it occurs in the New Testament, depending on the English translation.

DEFINITION OF PSUCHE - A LIVING BEING

A psuche is a living being. If you are human, then you are a human being. Psuche can also be translated as "creature". A human psuche is a person. Your psuche is you. It is your *self*, it is your own distinct identity. Your psuche is the totality of your mental, emotional, and *conscious existence*.

Psuche includes all of your inmost thoughts and feelings such as your affections, yearnings, angst, will, emotions, memories, and experiences.

Psuche is never indicated in the Bible as being immortal. Rather, psuche is your mortal life, it is your mortal personhood. It is quite capable of dying.

The Bible differentiates psuche from the body. The two go together when your psuche is alive. However, your psuche is your conscious existence as opposed to your body which is physical.

ENGLISH WORDS TRANSLATED FROM PSUCHE

In addition to psuche being translated into life and soul, it is also translated (a few times) into the words self, us, heart, and mind.

To see a complete listing of how psuche is translated in all 104 instances where it occurs, you can go to the online link below to see a list of all these verses and their English translations of psuche. This list is helpful in gaining an understanding of the how the word psuche was used by Jesus and the New Testament authors.

https://biblehub.com/greek/strongs_5590.htm

IS THE WORD "SOUL" A GOOD TRANSLATION OF THE WORD PSUCHE?

As mentioned psuche is translated into the English word "soul" around 60% of the time it occurs in the New Testament. There is some variation between English versions of the NT, as the decision to translate psuche into life or soul depends on which word the English translator felt best fit the context of a particular verse. However, it must be understood that the decision on which word to use was simply a choice. There was no biblical imperative to choose between life or soul in any given case. It appears to have been purely a choice on the part of the translator. When Jesus and the NT authors used the word psuche, the word was not divided up in their mind into two different components of a person, such as we have ended up with in our English bibles... with the words *life* and *soul*.

When most English readers encounter the word "soul" they understand this word as representing two things. First, it seems to emphasize the inner self of a person. The aspect of a person's thoughts and emotions that is very deep and personal: their psyche. In that respect, I think "soul" made sense to the translators when they wanted to emphasize this aspect. But there is a huge complication that comes with this choice.

The complication comes from the second thing that is associated with the word soul. Most English readers, particularly Christians, associate immortality as being one of the primary characteristics of the "soul". This idea of the immortal soul has played a major role in distorting and changing the message from the original gospel. This will be explained in a later chapter, but as previously mentioned a person's psuche is mortal, not immortal. It can die, and in fact scripture says it can be destroyed forever. The Bible teaches that God alone is immortal.

Most Christians believe the word "soul" is an essential and foundational word to the gospel, when in fact the word never existed in the original Greek New Testament as a unique word! Please do not miss this important fact, the word "soul" as you probably understand the meaning of the word, (including the belief of the immortal soul) does not exist in the Bible.

On the other hand, the word "psuche" is indeed foundational to the message of the gospel! In fact, psuche is a key word that is at the core of Jesus' teaching. By using the term "key word" I mean that having a clear understanding of how Jesus and the New Testament authors consistently used the word psuche is essential to understanding the rest of the Bible.

The word "soul", as you likely understand the

meaning of the word, does not exist in the Bible

The use of the word psuche should influence and shape how we understand and apply scripture. Yet due to psuche being translated into two very different words, (one of which actually derails Jesus' message), it's virtually impossible to understand the core focus of Jesus' teaching.

One other thing to note at this point about the idea of "soul". You do not have psuche as some component of yourself. In other words, you don't "have" a soul, but rather you "are" a soul (you are a psuche). And your soul or your life - whichever term you prefer to use - is mortal.

Psuche is the sum-total of your existence. You do not have a life in the here and now, and then a separate soul that lives on in the afterlife. Your psuche is simply you. It is the entirety of your conscious existence.

10

The understanding that psuche is merely mortal was an implicit but fundamental part of the gospel. Misunderstanding this simple but vital piece of information inevitably leaves the reader no choice but to rearrange Jesus' message into something quite different than what he intended.

Believing in the "immortality" of the soul compels us to rearrange

Jesus' message into something quite different

DEFINITION OF ZOE

Primary Definition: The state or condition of being alive.

At it's core, zoe simply means the state of being physically alive, as opposed to being dead. It's pretty simple. Zoe just means being alive. Zoe is the exact opposite of death. In most cases in the New Testament it is referring to being physically alive. When it is used to refer to Jesus and God it is often referring to their intrinsic nature of having zoe (the capacity for being alive) within themselves. In other words, they have life as part of who they are, and are not dependent upon anyone or anything else to sustain their life. They are immortal as part of their intrinsic nature. As humans we are merely mortal by nature.

The traditional view tries to explain zoe in some instances by saying it is referring to believers being spiritually alive. While this is partially true, it is not true to Jesus' focus and the New Testament's intent with the word. Humans certainly have the spirit of God living within them when they are born again. But the use of zoe does not focus on this, it is focusing on the end game, which is eternal life, eternal zoe. More on this later. In an upcoming chapter we will focus on the use of zoe in the New Testament.

So how are zoe and psuche to be understood in their relation to each other?

RELATIONSHIP BETWEEN PSUCHE AND ZOE

Anytime you see the word "psuche" it is referring to the life of a person.

Anytime you see the word zoe, at it's core it is referring to the "state of being alive".

So, how are they are related?

Your psuche can be said to have zoe if your psuche is alive. If your psuche is dead, then it does not have zoe.

Zoe and death are polar opposites. Zoe cannot die because by definition zoe means "the state of being alive".

On the other hand the words psuche and death are not polar opposites, because your psuche can be alive or it can be dead. If your psuche is alive, it exists in the state of zoe.

> Zoe cannot die, because by definition zoe means "being alive."
>
> Zoe is the exact opposite of being dead.
>
> On the other hand, psuche can be alive or dead.

I would like to go on the record saying that it actually does make sense to translate both of these Greek words into the same English word *life*. That is, if you look at each word individually, either word can reasonably be translated into *life*. The English word *life* does indeed encompass the meaning of both of these words. The problem occurs however, with the fact that *life* has a very broad meaning. On the other hand, zoe and psuche each have a more specific definition than the expansive meaning of the English word *life*.

Thus, the broad stroke of the paint brush "life" ends up blurring the precise, important differences that existed in psuche and zoe. The use of life actually conflates these two *key* words, injecting obscurity instead of conveying clarity.

These two words provide the framework of Jesus' message. Yet due to how they have been translated, it is impossible to see their differences. We also miss the vital relationship that existed between these two words.

Again, if your psuche is alive, it is said to have zoe. This is simple to understand in Greek, but this relationship translates poorly into English because this basically translates as "your life has life", which is redundant and confusing. The English word life is actually broader than psuche and zoe combined. I have heard many sermons where the speaker goes off in some unintended direction with a verse because they take the word life and portray it in whatever manner they think it fits.

A CLEAR EXAMPLE OF THE PSUCHE-ZOE CONNECTION

A good example of how zoe and psuche are connected can be seen in 1 Corinthians 15:45. I've listed both the LEB and ESV versions of this verse. Notice how one version translates psuche as "being" and the other as "soul".

> Thus also it is written, "The first man, Adam, became a living (zosan) soul (psuche)"; the last Adam became a life (zoe)-giving spirit. (LEB)

> Thus it is written, "The first man Adam became a living (zosan) being (psuche)"; the last Adam became a life (zoe)-giving spirit. (ESV)

The image below is from the Scripture4All.org website. It is a bit small to look at here. If you want to look at it in detail the link is:

https://www.scripture4all.org/OnlineInterlinear/NTpdf/1co15.pdf

The phrase "living being" or "living soul" is a combination of the adjective form of *zoe* (zosan) and the word *psuche* (sometimes spelled in English as *psyche*). Zosan means "living" or "to live" as in "being physically alive".

Whereas psuche just means "a being", or "a creature", or soul if you prefer to use the word soul, but only in a mortal sense.

This combination of words results in "living being". That is, Adam became a psuche that was alive. It is just that simple.

Notice the last part of the verse, where Paul contrasts Adam to Jesus. Adam was merely a <u>living being</u>, whereas Jesus is the <u>spirit-making-live</u>. This "making live" phrase comes from the verb form of zoe. In other words, Adam was merely a man (a being) that God created, thereby making Adam alive. Adam's source of life came from God. The stark contrast comes from the fact that Jesus has this "life giving source" within himself. Zoe (being alive) is an intrinsic aspect of Jesus' nature as the son of God. The traditional view basically overlooks the phrase "Jesus is the zoe-giving-spirit" because it cannot fathom its significance. This is a huge miss, as this phrase plays a huge part in what Paul is saying here.

First, it is Jesus's spirit (indwelling the psuche of the believer) that assures believers in this age that they will live again (in the age to come) upon their resurrection from the dead. Secondly, (and the primary focus of this verse), is that the spirit of Christ will resurrect believers from the dead giving them eternal zoe.

This resurrection is only possible due to Jesus (the zoe-giving-spirit) imparting life to dead believers, raising them from the dead.

THE IMPORTANCE OF KEY WORDS

Key words are like switches on a train track. If you correctly understand the meaning of a key word, then your comprehension gets started on the right track and stays on the right track. On the other hand, if you have the wrong understanding of a key word, then the trajectory of understanding veers off in the wrong direction, and any truth you encounter from that point on is shaped by an incorrect paradigm. The dangerous thing about incorrect paradigms is that they anesthetize you from realizing you are on the wrong course, so that you blissfully continue on the course of incorrect understanding.

Let me illustrate one more facet of this particular key word problem. There are several key word problems that we will cover in this book, but in this instance let's focus on the fact that zoe and psuche are both translated into the word "life".

Let's say I am a boss, and I am explaining an important task to an employee about using a truck to take a boat onto the lake. Let's say that I am forced to translate these two words into just one word. So maybe I use the word "craft" to represent both words. A truck and a boat are both a type of a craft so that makes sense, right?

So I explain to this employee that the task requires them to use the craft to take the craft onto the lake. Would the employee be able to clearly understand what I was telling them, without me drawing them a picture or them asking me a lot of questions? What if I just left it at that without any further explanation? Would the employee figure out what I wanted them to do, or would they give up, or do something totally different than what I expected?

Such is the problem that occurs when translating both key words "psuche" and "zoe" into the single English word "life". This obscures the critically different roles these two words play in the New Testament. If we miss their individual meanings, and the connection between them, there is no way we can understand what we are being saved from, or what we are being saved to.

If psuche and zoe were not such critical words to begin with, then this effect probably would not be significant. But as it stands, it prevents us from having a clear understanding of Jesus' purpose in his teaching, his death on the cross, and his resurrection. The resurrection has subsequently been relegated to an unclear role, while in fact it is the pinnacle of the Bible. Jesus' resurrection assures all believers that their own psuche will be resurrected from the dead to live again, this time forever, also known as Eternal Zoe.

The current traditional view believes that both believers and unbelievers already have eternal zoe. The only difference is the quality of that eternal life. The saved person lives in a paradise, while the unsaved are tortured forever. The usual explanation that the traditional view provides for the resurrection is that those who are already in heaven or hell, get a body back at the point of the resurrection, and then essentially resume their places in paradise or torment. There are numerous inconsistencies with this understanding, that the traditional view is rarely pressed upon to explain.

One way the traditional view explains this, is to say that the phrase "eternal life" is not speaking of being physically alive, but is rather speaking about "being spiritually alive ", where the saved person has the spirit of God while the unsaved does not, the unsaved are spiritually dead. In reality, eternal zoe is never used to speak of spiritual life. It is always referring to resurrection of the dead to live forever, in an imperishable body. The resurrection occurs because of the power of the Holy Spirit, but zoe is being used to speak of being physically alive. We will cover this in more detail later.

INTERESTING QUOTE

A powerful quote attributed to Mark Twain goes like so...

> "The difference between the almost right word and the right word is really a large matter. 'tis the difference between the lightning bug and the lightning"

IMPORTANT FACTS ABOUT ZOE & PSUCHE

➢ The majority of the time when *zoe* is used in the New Testament it is referencing the assurance of "immortal life" (*eternal zoe*) that God gives as a gift of salvation to the believer, saving them from permanent death.

➢ *Psuche* on the other hand, is never directly depicted as the gift of immortal life (salvation). Rather it is a person's *psuche* that is clearly the beneficiary of this gift of *zoe,* assuring and enabling psuche's resurrection from the dead to live forever.

➢ *Zoe* is frequently contrasted as the opposite of death, perishing or destruction. This makes sense, because zoe (being alive) is the opposite of being dead. It is also the opposite of not existing. Before Adam was created and God breathed life into him, he did not exist. He did not become a living psuche until God breathed life into him.

➢ *Psuche* is never contrasted as the opposite of death or perishing, rather the New Testament teaches that death or perishing is the death or perishing of that person's *psuche*. We will cover several scriptures throughout this book that make this very clear.

➢ A person is a "*psuche*" (a being) as part of their nature as a human *being*. Their human *psuche* is merely mortal.

➢ *Zoe*, on the other hand is depicted as part of God's inherent nature. This inherent nature of God includes "immortality". Just to clarify, God is indeed a being (psuche). The bible clearly refers to God's and Jesus' psuche. We will see Jesus referring to his own psuche later in this chapter. But their psuche is immortal! Our psuche (as human beings) is not.

It is important to understand that psuche is not replaced by zoe. These words are not mutually exclusive. A person's psuche has zoe if their psuche is alive. Eternal zoe is the phrase that represents a person's psuche "being alive for eternity".

Note: The Greek word "bios" is used 10 times in the NT and is sometimes translated as "life". But bios is <u>never</u> used to refer to the type of life that the believer receives as salvation. This is the only time I will mention bios in this book, as it has no bearing on our discussion.

Every time the New Testament speaks of the **life** that we enter as believers, it **never** uses the word psuche, it **always** use the word zoe

---

EXAMPLES OF ZOE AND PSUCHE BEING USED TOGETHER

Let's take a look at a verse where Jesus uses psuche and zoe in the same sentence. The English word "life" appears here 3 times. See if you can guess (based on what you have already learned at this point), which words were originally psuche and zoe.

> **John 12:25** Whoever loves his **life** loses it, and whoever hates his **life** in this world will keep it for eternal **life**. (ESV)

Now let's look at this with the original Greek words listed next to the English words:

> **John 12:25** Whoever loves his **life (psuche)** loses it, and whoever hates his **life (psuche)** in this world will keep it for eternal **life (zoe)**.

To briefly paraphrase, the person who lives unselfishly, (even unto the point of sacrificing their psuche under persecution) seeking God first before themselves will keep (save or preserve) their psuche so that it will live forever. This is referring to resurrection of their psuche from the dead, to live again, this time forever. This is much simpler to understand when you can see the original words.

On the other hand, that person who loves his psuche, so much that they follow their own ways, instead of following God, will end up losing their psuche. At the resurrection, they will be judged and cast into the lake of fire, which is the second death. They will lose their psuche. It will no longer exist, they will be dead forever, after the second death.

Next, we are going to look at a powerful narrative in John 10, where Jesus explains his purpose. This passage becomes difficult to understand due to the single word "life" that is used to translate both psuche and zoe.

Let's read this section from John 10 first, and then we can discuss it. As you read it, notice the different but critical roles these two words play in conveying Jesus' message.

> **John 10:7-18** Then Jesus said to them again, "Truly, truly, I say to you, I am the door of the sheep. 8 All those who came before me are thieves and robbers, but the sheep do not listen to them. 9 I am the door. If anyone enters through me, he will be saved, and will come in and will go out and will find pasture. 10 The thief comes only so that he can steal and kill and destroy; I have come so that they may have **life (zoe)**, and have it abundantly (perisson).
>
> 11 "I am the good shepherd. The good shepherd lays down his **life (psuche)** for the sheep. 12 The hired hand, who is not the shepherd, whose own the sheep are not, sees the wolf approaching and abandons the sheep and runs away—and the wolf seizes them and scatters them— 13 because he is a hired hand and he is not concerned about the sheep.
>
> 14 "I am the good shepherd, and I know my own, and my own know me, 15 just as the Father knows me and I know the Father, and I lay down my **life (psuche)** for the sheep. 16

And I have other sheep which are not from this fold. I must bring these also, and they will hear my voice, and they will become one flock—one shepherd. 17 Because of this the Father loves me, because I lay down my **life (psuche)** so that I may take possession of **it** again. 18 No one takes **it** from me, but I lay **it** down voluntarily. I have authority to lay **it** down, and I have authority to take possession of **it** again. This commandment I received from my Father." (LEB)

There is a lot to say about this section, but let's focus on our current discussion of psuche and zoe. As the good shepherd, Jesus is going to lay down his psuche for the sheep. He says this three times, denoting the importance of this fact. Jesus is speaking of the fact that his pusche is going to die. He then mentions he has the authority to take possession of "it" (his psuche) again. In fact, the word "it" refers to Jesus' psuche 5 times in verses 17-18.

When he says he will take possession of "it" again, he is referring to his own resurrection from the dead. Jesus' psuche will rise from the dead.

In v10 Jesus says that he has come so that his sheep might have zoe. Zoe is referring to the resurrection of the believer's psuche to live again, this time to live forever. Remember, zoe at it's core means "being alive". Thus, the word "abundantly" may be primarily referring to "quantity" of time of being alive, not a quality of life as is so often portrayed in mainstream Christianity.

The Greek word "perisson" which has been translated into English as "abundantly" could just as easily be translated into the word or phrase "immeasurably", "going past the expected limit", "beyond measure", or "exceeding some number or measure".

In other words, Jesus could just be using another expression here to declare his purpose of coming to give believers eternal life. This fits the entire narrative of John 10, and in fact the entirety of the gospel of John.

Notice what Jesus says about the thief immediately prior to saying he comes to give his sheep zoe. The thief comes to steal, kill (the Greek word means sacrifice) and destroy. Jesus comes to do the opposite. He comes to rescue the sheep from death, by dying in their stead (by sacrificing his own psuche), then rising from the dead and subsequently giving his sheep eternal zoe (being alive without measure). Eternal zoe is frequently contrasted against being "destroyed" or "perishing" (both words come from the Greek word apollumi). Destroy and perish are speaking of permanent death. On the other hand, the traditional view tries to say that the word perish means "ruin" of a person's "quality" of life, such as experiencing eternal torture in hell.

We will cover this in more detail later in the chapter on John 10.

4

Nuances of Zoe

UNIQUE USE OF ZOE IN THE NEW TESTAMENT

At its core, zoe is defined as "the state of being alive". Jesus contrasts zoe against death throughout his teaching. Zoe is the opposite of death.

However, zoe's use by Jesus and the New Testament authors in most instances give zoe an additional nuance. These nuances can be broken down into various points of emphasis. Any given instance of the word zoe in the New Testament may convey one or more of these points of emphasis. These nuances occur in about 90% of the instances of zoe in the New Testament.

These nuances condense down to a single major theme running throughout the New Testament, which is this:

The believer has complete assurance of being resurrected from the dead to the state of being alive again, this time to live forever. This is known as Eternal Life (Eternal Zoe). Most of the time when zoe is used by itself (not as part of the phrase - eternal zoe), it is still implicitly referring to this future eternal zoe.

There are 3 essential facts that are vital to understand going forward:

Fact #1: Zoe is an intrinsic attribute of God, Jesus and the Holy Spirit. The Gospel of John makes this very clear. The Godhead has zoe inherent within themselves. They are not dependent on anyone or anything for "being alive".

Fact #2: On the other hand, God, Jesus and the Holy Spirit are the source of zoe (life) for all creatures. This holds true for the initial creation, as well as all creatures who have been born since then. It also holds true for the resurrection from the dead. Those humans whose names are written in the book of life (book of zoe), will be resurrected by the Holy Spirit to physically live again, this time to live forever. They will be resurrected with physical, but imperishable bodies.

Fact #3: Mankind is not immortal by nature. The Bible makes this clear. Immortality is a gift given to believers upon their resurrection. Believers have this assurance of being raised from the dead to immortality, due to the Holy Spirit (aka the Spirit of Christ) indwelling them.

Jesus imparts the immortal zoe of God into the psuche of the believer via the gift of the indwelling Holy Spirit. This process is known as being born again, this time being born of the spirit of God. While the resurrection from the dead to live forever does not occur until the future, the believer receives the zoe of Jesus living within them in this present age due to the presence of the indwelling Holy Spirit (aka the Spirit of Christ).

There are many current blessings associated with the Holy Spirit living within the psuche of the believer during their present temporal life on Earth. The believer can be said to be spiritually alive, due to this indwelling Spirit of God and the restoration of a personal intimate relationship that now exists for the believer directly with the Godhead.

Yet the focus of the New Testament is <u>not</u> on spiritual life. Don't miss this point! The focus is not on spiritual life but rather physical life, specifically <u>resurrection</u> from the dead to physically live again. Jesus's focus was on the end-game. The ultimate end game that Jesus focuses on is the resurrection of believers from the dead to physically living again forever – aka Eternal Zoe.

NUANCE # 1: ZOE IS USED TO EXPLAIN GOD'S INTRINSIC IMMORTALITY

When zoe is used to refer to Jesus, God or the Holy Spirit's nature, it means that zoe is inherent within them. That is, they are self-existent and not dependent upon anyone or anything else for their state of being alive. In this aspect they are said to be intrinsically immortal. Their source of "being alive" is within themselves.

The New Testament also clearly says that Jesus and God are psuche (they are living beings). But due to their immortal nature their psuche cannot die.

In fact, it is this immortal nature of God that is imparted into the believer's psuche when they believe. This occurs via the Holy Spirit indwelling the believer, thereby assuring the believer of being resurrected from the dead to eternal life. At the future resurrection, this same Holy Spirit will raise the believer's psuche from the dead to live forever (eternal zoe).

Examples:

John 1:4 In him was **life (zoe)**, and the **life (zoe)** was the light of humanity. (LEB)

John 5:26 For just as the Father has **life (zoe)** in himself, thus also he has granted to the Son to have **life (zoe)** in himself. (LEB)

NUANCE # 2: PHRASE - ETERNAL ZOE

Zoe is frequently paired with the Greek word "aionian" in the New Testament. Aionion means "unto the age". Jesus came to give believers "zoe unto the age". This phrase is best known by the way it is commonly translated in English bibles as "Eternal Life".

This means "being alive forever". This is not exactly a nuance, but rather is an explicit statement, since "eternal zoe" is the exact wording. But it is very important that we understand what this phrase really means.

Eternal zoe is an explicit reference to resurrection from the dead to physically live forever. It is not an awkwardly worded reference about going to heaven.

Example:

> **John 3:16** For in this way God loved the world, so that he gave his one and only Son, in order that everyone who believes in him will not perish, but will have **eternal life (zoe)**. (LEB)

> **John 12:25** The one who loves his **life (psuche)** loses it, and the one who hates his **life (psuche)** in this world preserves it for **eternal life (zoe)**.

Comment: In John 12:25 (above) notice that psuche appears twice in this verse and zoe appears once. Although we are currently focused on the nuances of zoe, I want to point the critical importance of the different use of these two words, which is not a nuance at all, but a stark difference in meaning. We will cover this verse in other chapters, but to put it simply, this verse is saying that the person who hates his psuche (himself) preserves his psuche for eternal zoe. In other words, that person will be preserved or saved by resurrection from the dead to live forever. On the other hand, the one who loves his psuche, will lose his psuche. His psuche will die, forever.

NUANCE # 3: ASSURANCE OF ETERNAL ZOE (SOLO IMPLICIT USE OF ZOE)

Frequently when zoe is used by itself (without the paired Greek word aionion) it is implicitly referring to eternal zoe. When zoe is used in this way, it is pointing to the assurance that the believer has of being raised from the dead, to live forever.

This solo use of zoe implicitly refers to eternal zoe in the following ways:

1. Sometimes it is obvious, due to the phrase eternal zoe being used in the same context.
2. Sometimes it is implied expectation, by language that depicts the expectation of eternal zoe.
3. Sometimes it is used proleptically to refer to eternal zoe.
4. Sometimes it is used to describe the state (or status) of the believer's position of assurance of eternal life.
5. Sometimes it points to Jesus as being our eternal zoe.

FIVE DIFFERENT USES OF THE WORD "ZOE" IN ITS SOLO FORM

Solo use of Zoe # 1: Obvious reference to Eternal Zoe

In several instances where zoe is used by itself, it occurs within a context where the phrase eternal zoe has already been used. So, it is obvious that the single use of zoe is merely circling back as a reference to eternal zoe. This usually occurs when eternal zoe is mentioned first, then zoe is used immediately afterward clearly referring back to eternal zoe.

Examples:

> **John 3:36** The one who believes in the Son has **eternal life (zoe)**, but the one who disobeys the Son will not see **life (zoe)** —but the wrath of God remains on him (LEB)

> **1 John 5:11-12** And this is the testimony, that God gave us **eternal life (zoe)**, and this **life (zoe)** is in his Son. 12 Whoever has the Son has **life (zoe)**; whoever does not have the Son of God does not have **life (zoe)**. (ESV)

Solo use of Zoe # 2: Implied Expectation of Eternal Zoe

Several times zoe is used in a context where it is depicted as being in the future. This use is clearly not speaking of someone's present day life. This generally includes a leading phrase which depicts the future, such as "leads to" or "will" or "may". Zoe is depicted as being in someone's future due to saving faith. Sometimes this depiction occurs simultaneously while zoe is contrasted against future death (or destruction). Life and death are both used in these instances to depict the end game. Neither is referring to the first life nor the first death. They are being used to refer to the future resurrection to eternal life, or resurrection to judgment and the subsequent second death (eternal death).

Examples:

> **Matthew 7:13-14** "Enter through the narrow gate, because broad is the gate and spacious is the road that **leads to destruction**, and there are many who enter through it, 14 because narrow is the gate and constricted is the road that **leads to life (zoe)**, and there are few who find it! (LEB)

> **Acts 11:18** And when they heard these things, they became silent and praised God, saying, "Then God has granted the repentance **leading to life (zoe)** to the Gentiles also!" (LEB)

> **Romans 5:17** For if by the trespass of the one man, **death reigned** through the one man, much more will those who receive the abundance of grace and of the gift of righteousness **reign in life (zoe)** through the one, Jesus Christ.

> **2 Corinthians 5:4-5** For indeed we who are in this tent groan, being burdened for this reason, that we do not want to be unclothed, but to be clothed, in order that **what is mortal may be swallowed up by life (zoe)**. 5 Now the one who has prepared us for this very thing is God, who has given us **the down payment, the Spirit**. (LEB)

> **2 Timothy 1:1** Paul, an apostle of Christ Jesus through the will of God, according to the **promise of life (zoe)** which is in Christ Jesus

Solo use of Zoe # 3: Zoe is used Proleptically to refer to Eternal Zoe

"Proleptic" is a pretty good word to describe the way that Jesus and the New Testament authors use zoe as a direct reference to eternal zoe.[1] It is presented as if it is a state (or status) that the believer enters into or is already in possession of at this time.

Proleptic (broad definition): The representation or statement of something that will occur in the future as if it already exists.

In reality, eternal zoe (resurrection from the dead to live forever) is yet to come. But the assurance of eternal zoe exists now. Zoe is a guaranteed hope and expectation for the believer.

We have already seen several examples of the solo use of zoe referring to eternal zoe, when there are leading words such as "will", "leads to" or "may', etc. When zoe is used proleptically these leading phrases do not occur, but the end result is the same, the single word zoe still refers to eternal zoe.

The proleptic use sometimes includes the word "enter" or "has". Each is speaking of entering or possessing zoe now. This proleptic use points to several aspects of zoe that a believer currently possesses.

- Although the believer has not been resurrected from the dead (this is obviously a future event), they do already *have* the indwelling zoe of God living within them.
- The believer currently possesses *assurance* of being resurrected from the dead to eternal zoe. This expectation of resurrection to live forever is a certainty they enter into, even if they are currently suffering from some physical ailment. We won't receive new imperishable, perfect bodies until this expectation is fulfilled at the resurrection.
- Thus, the believer enters or possesses "zoe" now. In summary, this proleptic use includes the indwelling Spirit of Christ (the source of zoe), and the *assurance* of "being alive forever" upon the resurrection from the dead.

In the following examples, zoe is referring (proleptically) to the assurance of eternal zoe. However, there may be other nuances that can be seen in these verses as well.

> **John 5:24** Truly, truly I say to you that the one who hears my word and who believes the one who sent me **has eternal life (zoe)**, and does not come into judgment, but **has passed from death into life** *(zoe)*.

> **John 6:53** Then Jesus said to them, "Truly, truly I say to you, unless you eat the flesh of the Son of Man and drink his blood, **you do not have life (zoe) in yourselves!** (LEB)

> **Matthew 19:16-17** And behold, someone came up to him and said, "Teacher, what good thing must I do so that I will **have eternal life (zoe)**?" 17 And he said to him, "Why are

---

[1] Chris Date "Rethinking Hell Live 026: What the Bible Really Says About What 'Life' Means." Podcast video, *YouTube*.com. https://www.youtube.com/watch?v=HgtG2XGkULI&t=7s

you asking me about what is good? There is one who is good. But if you want to **enter into life *(zoe)***, keep the commandments!" (LEB)

1 John 5:16 If anyone should see his brother sinning a sin ***not leading to death***, he should ask, and he will ***grant life (zoe)*** to him, to those who sin not leading to death.

2 Timothy 1:9-10 who saved us and called us with a holy calling, not according to our works but according to his own purpose and grace that was given to us in Christ Jesus before time began, but has now been disclosed by the appearing of our Savior Jesus Christ, who has ***abolished death and brought to light life (zoe) and immortality*** through the gospel (LEB)

1 Peter 3:7 Husbands, in the same way live with your wives knowledgeably, as with the weaker female vessel, showing them honor as fellow heirs also of the grace of **life (zoe)**, so that your prayers will not be hindered (LEB)

Note: The believer enters "life (zoe)" when they are born again. Although they have the assurance of immortality upon their resurrection from the dead, and they have the immortal Holy Spirit living within them, they are not themselves immortal – yet. They will be raised from the dead to immortality at their resurrection.

Solo use of Zoe # 4: Jesus is our Zoe

In the verses below Jesus is portrayed as "zoe" in several ways:

- Jesus is your life
- Jesus is the life
- Jesus is the eternal life
- Eternal Life is in Jesus (the son)
- The one who has the son, has life
- The one who does not have the son, does not have life
- Jesus is the one true God and eternal life

The gist of all these verses comes down to this. Jesus is the source of eternal zoe. It is the spirit of Jesus (aka the Holy Spirit) that indwells all believers assuring them of being resurrected from the dead to live again, this time to live unto the ages (aka eternal zoe). At the resurrection, this same Spirit of Jesus will give life (zoe) to believers, bringing them back to life (zoe).

When these verses say something like Jesus is "the life" or is "the eternal life", they are being profoundly accurate. Jesus is the source of our resurrection to eternal zoe.

Note: In all the verses below where you see the word "life", it is translated from "zoe".

1 John 1:1-2 What was from the beginning, what we have heard, what we have seen with our eyes, what we have looked at and our hands have touched, concerning the **word of life**

(zoe) — 2 and *the **life (zoe)*** was revealed, and we have seen and testify and announce to you *the* **eternal life (zoe***)* which was with the Father and was revealed to us (LEB)

1 John 5:11-13 And this is the testimony: that God has given us **eternal life (zoe), and this life (zoe)** is in his Son. 12 The one who has the Son has the **life (zoe)**; the one who does not have the Son of God does not have the **life (zoe)**. 13 These things I have written to you who believe in the name of the Son of God, in order that you may know that you have **eternal life (zoe)**. (LEB)

1 John 5:20 And we know that the Son of God has come and has given us understanding, in order that we may know the one who is true, and we are in the one who is true, in his Son Jesus Christ. This one is the true God and **eternal life (zoe)**. (LEB)

John 14:6 Jesus said to him, "I am the way, and the truth, and the **life (zoe)**. No one comes to the Father except through me. (LEB)

Solo use of Zoe # 5: Describes status of a person's assurance of Eternal Life

Jesus occasionally uses zoe by itself to depict the state or status of a person. Such as when Jesus says the believer crosses over from death to zoe. It is a status change, from the current sentence of certain death to one of certain life.

In the last phrase of John 5:24 Jesus speaks proleptically about the destiny of believers versus non-believers. The believer passes from a status (or sentence) of death, to a status of zoe. The unbeliever remains in the state (or assurance) of future death.

Obviously, the unbeliever is currently physically alive, yet he lives under the sentence of death which will be carried out on the day of judgment. Jesus uses both death and zoe proleptically, i.e., he is speaking of these future events as if they are already a fact.

1 John 3:14-15 We know that *we have passed over from death to* **life (zoe)** because we love the brothers. The one who does not love *remains in death*. 15 Everyone who hates his brother is a murderer, and you know that every murderer does not have **eternal life (zoe)** residing in him.

John 5:24 Truly, truly I say to you that the one who hears my word and who believes the one who sent me has **eternal life (zoe***)*, and does not come into judgment, but has passed from death into **life (zoe)**.

Traditional Twist

The traditional view sometimes explains John 5:24 by insisting that Jesus is speaking here about spiritual death and spiritual life. It is true that the believer receives the indwelling Holy Spirit upon their conversion (being born again of the Spirit). It is also true that the Holy Spirit can produce fruit in the Christian, along with wisdom, insight (the light of zoe) and other benefits. It is common for Christians to say that the believer has spiritual life or is spiritually alive at this point. From the standpoint of God's spirit *living* within that person, these phrases seem to make sense. However, it should be noted that the phrases *spiritual life* and *being spiritually alive* are not actually found anywhere in the bible.

The Spirit of Christ (aka Holy Spirit) will ultimately be the force of God that raises the believer from the dead to live forever. The focus of John 5:24 is not on spiritual life, but physical life! The focus is on being resurrected from the dead to physically live forever (eternal zoe).

NUANCE # 4: THE SOURCE OF ETERNAL ZOE FOR MANKIND

Jesus is the only *source* of eternal zoe (immortality). Jesus imparts zoe into the believer's psuche via the gift of the indwelling Holy Spirit when they are born again. (Note: the Spirit of God, Spirit of Christ and Holy Spirit are used interchangeably in the New Testament). The Trinity works seamlessly to impart zoe unto the believer. We briefly touched on this in the solo use of the word zoe, pointing to Jesus as being our zoe.

Examples - Source of Eternal Zoe for Mankind

> **John 5:39-40** You search the scriptures because you think that you have **eternal life (zoe)** in them, and it is these that testify about me. And you are not willing to come to me so that you may have **life (zoe)**. (LEB)

> **John 6:32-33** Then Jesus said to them, "Truly, truly I say to you, Moses did not give you bread from heaven, but my Father is giving you the true bread from heaven! For the bread of God is the one who comes down from heaven and gives **life (zoe)** to the world." (LEB)

> **John 6:61-63** But Jesus, because he knew within himself that his disciples were grumbling about this, said to them, "Does this cause you to be offended? Then what if you see the Son of Man ascending where he was before? The Spirit is the one who gives **life (zoe)**; the flesh profits nothing. The words that I have spoken to you are spirit and are **life (zoe)**. (LEB)

> **John 14:6** Jesus said to him, "I am the way, and the truth, and the **life (zoe)**. No one comes to the Father except through me." (ESV)

NUANCE # 5: THE LIGHT OF ZOE

The "Light of Zoe" can refer to other benefits the believer receives from zoe indwelling the believer's psuche during their temporal life in this age.

This zoe makes the light of Jesus available to the believer, as well as the fellowship of the trinity, the fruit of the spirit, the precious relationship of a child with God the Father, etc. This occurs at the point of being born again, and the believer can abide in these benefits during the remainder of their temporal lifetime in this present age.

This light may be referring to the insight, understanding and illumination that comes from the Holy Spirit guiding us as to how we live our lives in this dark world.

Darkness may also refer to looming death. It is possible that these verses are also referring to Jesus zoe being the solution to this looming, overshadowing death.

Examples - The Light of Zoe

> **John 1:4** In him was *life (zoe),* and the **life (zoe)** was the *light* of humanity. (LEB)

> **John 8:12** Then Jesus spoke to them again, saying, "I am the light of the world! The one who follows me will never walk in darkness, but will have the **light of life (zoe)**." (LEB)

NUANCE # 6: LIVING WATER

In the following verse we see the phrase "living water". This is talking about water that is alive and makes alive (same root as zoe). In other words, the water is living (a direct metaphor referring to the indwelling Holy Spirit). It is the Spirit that conveys the zoe of God unto a person.

> **John 7:37-39** Now on the last day of the feast—the great day—Jesus stood and cried out, saying, "If anyone is thirsty, let him come to me, and let him drink, 38 the one who believes in me. Just as the scripture said, 'Out of his belly will flow rivers of **living water**.'" 39 Now he said this concerning the **Spirit**, whom those who believed in him were about to receive. For the **Spirit** was not yet given, because Jesus had not yet been glorified.) (LEB)

The Greek word for "living" is the adjective form of zoe. The Holy Spirit will flow from within the believer, bringing many benefits to the believer in this current life. However, while the fruits and benefits of this living water during our present life on earth are very important, this is not the ultimate purpose of the living water.

The *end game* or *ultimate purpose* of the living water is to well up unto *eternal life* (as seen below) which is speaking about being *resurrected to physical life*. That is, the believer will raise from the dead to live again, this time forever with a new immortal body.

> **John 4:10** Jesus answered and said to her, "If you had known the gift of God and who it is who says to you, 'Give me water to drink,' you would have asked him, and he would have given you *living water*."... (LEB)

> **John 4:14** But whoever drinks of this water which I will give to him will never be thirsty for eternity, but the **water which I will give to him** will become in him a well of water **springing up to eternal life**. (LEB)

In the following verse from Revelation, Jesus makes a stark contrast between the spring of the water of zoe, and the lake of fire, which he aptly describes as the second death. The end game depicted repeatedly throughout the Old and New Testaments is a contrast between life (zoe) and death.

> **Revelation 21:6-8** And he said to me, "It is done! I am the Alpha and the Omega, the beginning and the end. To the one who is thirsty I will give water from the **spring of the water of life (zoe)** freely. 7 The one who conquers will inherit these things, and I will be his God and he will be my son. 8 But as for the cowards and unbelievers and detestable persons and murderers and sexually immoral people and sorcerers and idolaters and all liars, their share is in the **lake** that burns with fire and sulphur, **which is the second death.** (LEB)

GENERIC USE OF ZOE (WITHOUT NUANCE)

Zoe is used about 10% of the time it occurs in the NT to merely refer to the basic "state of being alive". When zoe is used in this manner (i.e. with no connection to the eternal life theme) it can be referring to:

- A person's lifetime (the time they are alive).
- The course of a person's life
- Their life journey, experiences, or their character during this lifetime.

Example:

> **James 4:13-15** Come now, you who say, "Today or tomorrow we will travel to such and such a city and spend a year there, and carry on business and make a profit," 14 you who do not know what will happen tomorrow, what your **life (zoe)** will be like. For you are a smoky vapor that appears for a short time and then disappears. 15 Instead you should say, "If the Lord wills, we will live and do this or that."

Note: Zoe does not refer to the person themselves, but as in the verse above is speaking of the person's life journey, or their lifetime. Psuche is the word that is used to directly refer to a person. A person is a psuche. A person's psuche can be alive, or it can be dead. If a person is alive, their psuche can be said to have zoe.

5

Unrecognized Key Words

There are 7 words that permeate the New Testament that are basically unrecognized in mainstream Christian teaching. These 7 words form the very foundation of Jesus' message of salvation, yet they remain essentially unseen, or unrecognized or misunderstood.

The first two key words that we have already talked about are psuche and zoe.

In addition, the Greek words *Hades* and *Gehenna* are not clearly differentiated in English translations of the New Testament, nor in mainstream Christian teaching. *Hades* and *Gehenna* are directly tied and contrasted to psuche and zoe, but these important connections are also obscured.

Gehenna is always translated as "hell" when in reality the concept of "hell" that most Christians believe is not at all what Jesus was teaching about when he referred to Gehenna. Gehenna was actually a valley with an infamous history (involving an apocalyptic judgment) from the Old Testament, located just outside of Jerusalem.

Hades and Gehenna are two completely different events (or venues) that people may face after their earthly death, but their differences are impossible to see in some English Bibles as both are translated as "hell". Jesus and the New Testament authors would have never used these two words interchangeably. Yet that is exactly what takes place on a regular basis in mainstream Christian teaching.

Indeed, many sermons heard today will use the words *Hell, Gehenna,* and *Hades* interchangeably and inconsistently, which distorts and confuses Jesus original teachings.

Another word is "apollumi" which means "utterly destroy" or "perish". The frequent use of this word throughout the New Testament is directly connected to all 6 of the other key words. However, the widespread misunderstanding of the other 6 words results in the inevitable twisting of the word "apollumi" to fit the paradigm of the traditional view.

Although the English word "perish" does indeed appear in the English Bibles, the traditional view often twists this word in an attempt to explain that it means "ruin" as opposed to the original meaning of "kill or utterly destroy". The concept of 'ruin' fits the traditional narrative in describing the ruined life of the unsaved in hell.

The traditional view also understates the significance of the 'resurrection', and twists the word 'death' into meaning something different than what it actually does.

Having a clear comprehension of these 7 words is essential to understanding Jesus's message of salvation. Without clarity, our understanding will be vague and misinformed.

As a baseline, if you understand psuche and zoe, you will be more likely to interpret the other 5 words correctly. They will fall into place so to speak. For this reason, it is very important to understand Parts 1 & 2, prior to digging into Part 3.

Important Note: Jesus frequently used words and phrases that were directly tied to Old Testament words and phrases. Without understanding these connections that Jesus is making (when he refers back to scriptures and prophecies in the Old Testament), we will indeed misinterpret many of the scriptures that we discuss in this book.

Jesus was 100% tied into the Old Testament in his teaching. His teachings on psuche, zoe, death, destruction, eternity, Hades and Gehenna can only be correctly understood by seeing the direct connections that Jesus makes to Old Testament scripture, concepts and imagery.

There are 7 key words in the New Testament, that are basically

unrecognizable in current mainstream Christian teaching

CLARITY IS VITALLY IMPORTANT

Using the metaphor of a rudder on a ship, if we do not have clarity in our understanding of Jesus' message we will be like a ship without a rudder. We may continue sailing in a generally correct direction yet be waving in obscurity and ambiguity. We will be unable to give straight, clear answers to those who depend on us for truth, like our children, family, and friends. Without an accurate understanding, we will also portray lies about the character of God and his plan for the unsaved.

Without clarity we will never have a full grip on Jesus' true message. We will never be completely in sync with God's ultimate purpose.

If you believe in Jesus as Lord, Savior, and the Son of God then you are saved. Perhaps you have shared that message with others who have believed and are saved. So, as far as your salvation is concerned you are good to go. But wouldn't you like to be able to clearly understand what you are saved *from*, and be able to convey that to those you share the gospel with?

EMOTIONAL EFFECT

There are some holding to the traditional view that use the accusation of "emotion" to discredit those who hold to the "conditional" view. This is not only unfair, but inaccurate. It's also irrelevant. The totality of verses that support the conditional view dwarf those used by the traditional view. In fact, all of the verses that the traditional view uses for support, upon closer inspection support the conditional view.

Some Traditionalists infer that Conditionalists don't have the "stomach" to hold onto the view of eternal suffering of the unbeliever. Again, this is totally irrelevant to this entire discussion. To insult conditionalists by saying they are primarily driven by emotion is being dismissive of their earnest and biblical approach.

It is indeed truth that conditionalists seek to bring to light. Believers on both sides need to be able to show grace to those we disagree with on this issue. This is not an issue of salvation, nor an issue that should divide fellowship.

Wouldn't you like to be able to accurately understand what you are

saved **from**, and be able to clearly convey that to others?

Lack of Clarity Obscures Vital Details

When I was about five years old, my family spent a summer in Colorado. My dad was finishing up some course work on a degree at a Colorado university. On weekends, we would occasionally drive to see some of the beautiful country that was within driving distance. I don't remember much about the weekend excursions, but I do remember seeing the photos that my dad took. They were black and white and clearly showed our family as well as the beautiful mountains.

My dad had an old camera that looked like a small box. It was a typical family camera of that time and only had a single fixed lens. At that time, the photos looked great. But, as decades went by and camera technology improved, it became clear that the old black and white photos were actually not clear. That is, you could make out pretty much everything in the photo, but nothing was really crisp. None of the leaves on trees in the photo could be individually seen, and there were no distinct edges on anyone or anything in the photo. The old photos were . . . somewhat blurry.

Now, if I had really needed to see some fine detail in the photos, I would have been out of luck. With today's technology, no one would think a blurry photo is acceptable. Blurry photos lack important details that are vital to having a clear picture.

In a similar manner, I believe that most Christians lack a clear understanding of the core message of Jesus' teachings. I believe you will see Jesus' message about life and death is not only foundational, but *central* to all his teachings. Not having this understanding will prevent you from having the clarity that Jesus intended. You will indeed go through your journey with a blurry interpretation of scripture.

Comparison to Agape and Philos

As shown in earlier chapters, the distinct differences between *psuche* and *zoe* have been obscured in mainstream Christian teaching. The conflation of these two key words has resulted in significant loss of meaning and lack of clarity as to what Jesus said.

We can see this translation/conflation issue as well, in the Greek words *agape* and *philos*. Both words are often translated into the single English word "love." Each word had a unique intent and definition as the author or speaker used them. *Agape* describes unconditional love, like a parent would have for their child. *Philos* describes a love that is loyal and committed, like a friendship. Yet in the English translations, we usually just find the English word "love." As you can see, some of the original intent is lost.

However, the loss of intent in the words psuche and zoe is much more significant because they are *foundational* key words in Jesus' teachings. If we don't clearly see how he used them, the rest of our doctrine will be an improvisation, held together by a disarray of assumptions.

Failing to have a clear understanding of

key words creates obscurity and ambiguity.

This leaves us to form our doctrine based on false assumptions.

6

Clarifying *Psuche*

PERPLEXITY OF *PSUCHE* IN THE NEW TESTAMENT

The common language of the Roman Empire during the first century AD was called *Koine'* Greek (*Koine'* means "common"). The New Testament (written during the first century) was originally written in *Koine'* Greek. In order to best understand what Jesus and the New Testament authors were saying, translators have sought to go back to the oldest Greek manuscripts of the New Testament books that are available. (Koine' Greek is considered an ancient language, and is different from modern Greek).

As previously mentioned, *Psuche* appears 104 times in the New Testament. It is overwhelmingly translated into the English words "life" or "soul." On a few occasions, it is translated as "heart," "mind," "person," or "self."

STRONG'S DEFINITION OF *PSUCHE*

Let's look at the definition for *psuche* from *Strong's Concordance*. *Strong's* is a widely accepted concordance and dictionary of the Bible. Strong's definition of *psuche* is given as:

Short Definition: the soul, life, self

Definition: (a) the vital breath, breath of life, (b) the human soul, (c) the soul as the seat of affections and will, (d) the self, (e) a human person, an individual.

On the following pages, you will see several verses in which the word *psuche* has been used by New Testament authors. The English words translated as "life" or "soul" are shown in bold next to the original Greek word, *psuche*.

SPLITTING UP PSUCHE

As you read these verses, keep in mind that each time you see the word "life" or "soul," these two words have been translated from the single Greek word *psuche*.

The following verse comes from Jesus' Sermon on the Mount.

> **Matt. 6:25** For this reason I say to you, do not be anxious for your **life (psuche)**, what you will eat, and not for your body, what you will wear. Is your **life (psuche)** not more than food and your body more than clothing? (LEB)

It makes sense that the English word "life" was chosen here. As an English-speaking person, my life would seem to be closely associated with such things as food and clothing, certainly more so than my soul.

But this is strictly due to the fact that as an English-speaking person, my definition of the word "soul" is much different than my definition of the word "life". Whereas Jesus made no distinction between the two concepts of "soul" and "life". Jesus simply used the single word psuche. It was a singular concept to him, there was no dual aspect to his definition of psuche.

Rather it has been mankind that has introduced the inaccurate, dualistic idea of "life" and "soul". This is due to powerful, secular paradigms that infiltrated into Christian thought during the first 5 centuries of the church and have dominated Christian doctrine ever since.

> **Matt. 10:28** And do not be afraid of those who kill the body but are not able to kill the **soul (psuche)**, but instead be afraid of the one who is able to destroy both **soul (psuche)** and body in hell (Gehenna). (LEB)

In all honesty, if the word "life" were to be used here (instead of "soul"), would this verse make any sense to you?

In the English translation, we get the distinct impression that the word "soul" is a unique word when in fact, it does not exist in the Greek New Testament as a unique word. By saying unique, I mean in the sense that we would expect there to be a unique Greek word whose sole definition would match the popular English understanding of the word soul.

So, the question arises: Is Jesus talking about a person's soul being destroyed in hell (*Gehenna*), or their life being destroyed?

What exactly is Jesus cautioning us about?

In the English translation we get the impression that the word "soul" is a unique, foundational word when in fact, the word "soul" as we have traditionally defined it does not exist as a unique word in the Greek New Testament.

This next verse comes from a session of Jesus' teachings.

> **Luke 14:26** "If anyone comes to me and does not hate his own father and mother and wife and children and brothers and sisters, and furthermore, even his own **life (psuche)**, he cannot be my disciple. (LEB)

At first glance, it certainly makes sense that the English word "life" was chosen in this verse. Certainly, the idea of hating your own *soul* would not make sense to most people. But my point is this, the choice should never have been made.

Splitting up *psuche* into the *divergent* concepts of "life" and "soul" has injected ambiguity and confusion in lieu of the clarity that Jesus spoke on that day. As Christian readers we end up coming away from these verses thinking that there are two different narratives flowing through the New Testament. One about a person's life and a different narrative for a person's soul. In reality, Jesus was concisely speaking about your psuche. If we don't get a handle on the critical importance of this clarity, we will continue to read our Bibles with a fuzzy understanding, leading to conclusions that are not only wrong, but actually change Jesus's original message.

> **Matt. 10:39** The one who finds his **life (psuche)** will lose it, and the one who loses his **life (psuche)** because of me will find it. (LEB)

How would the context of the above verse change if the English word "soul" had been used here instead of "life?"

Perhaps exchanging "soul" for "life" in this verse does not make sense because the definitions of *life* and *soul* are so firmly entrenched in our minds as separate concepts. Thus, it is difficult for us to think of them as the same thing.

But in Jesus' mind, they were exactly the same . . . they were *psuche*.

Would the meaning of the following verse change if the word "soul" had been used instead of the word "life"?

> **Mark 10:45** For even the Son of Man did not come to be served, but to serve, and to give his **life (psuche***)* as a ransom for many. (LEB)

I have a big question for you: What did Jesus come to give?

His life? His soul? Or his *psuche*?

You may be asking yourself, "Why do I have to choose?" I would in turn ask you, "Would you prefer someone else to choose for you?"

Because in effect, someone else already has.

Someone else has chosen the words you have come to know and understand, and they do *not* accurately reflect what Jesus said!

> **Matt. 16:26** For what will a person be benefited if he gains the whole world but forfeits his **life (psuche)**? Or what will a person give in exchange for his **life (psuche)**? (LEB)

Is there a difference in forfeiting one's life versus forfeiting their soul? If so, what is the difference? Several English Bible versions actually translate both instances of the word psuche as 'soul' (instead of life) in the verse above.

But in reality, the use of *psuche* in the New Testament never distinguishes between life and soul in any way! There was no divergence originally. A person's *psuche* was simply who they were.

In other words, your psuche is you.

But, let's get back to Jesus' question, what exactly is he asking?

Please keep this question in the back of your mind as we progress. What exactly does it mean to forfeit your psuche?

WHERE DID THE AMBIGUITY COME FROM?

The ambiguity crept in when a single, clearly defined word was later arbitrarily interpreted into two highly divergent concepts that fit the belief system of the prevailing Roman culture.

This ambiguity was initiated and perpetuated by the prevailing Greek paradigm that the *soul is immortal* when in fact, the Bible **never** associates immortality with the word *psuche*.

The cultural paradigm of the "immortality of the soul" was a firm belief of the Hellenistic culture that the Jews found themselves in. This paradigm of the "immortality of the soul" began to permeate into Christian circles during the period from around 180 AD to 500 AD. This incorrect but powerful paradigm drove the divergence of *psuche* into the separate concepts of *life* and *soul*. This paradigm of the "immortal soul" became the foundational belief of Christian doctrine by around 500 AD, supplanting Jesus' original teaching. The notion of the immortal soul has remained a powerful influence in Christianity ever since.

Heb. 10:39 But we are not among those who shrink back to destruction, but among those who have faith to the preservation of our **souls (psuche)**! (LEB)

What is it that those who have faith are preserving? What happens to those who shrink back? If they are destroyed, then just exactly what is destroyed? On the other hand, what is preserved for those who have faith? Their lives or their souls?

And just exactly how does this *preserving* take place? What is the nature of this process?

As you will see later, this is one of many verses that clearly portrays conditional immortality.

---

1 John 3:16 We have come to know love by this: that he laid down his **life (psuche)** on behalf of us, and we ought to lay down our **lives (psuche)** on behalf of the brothers. (LEB)

Did Jesus lay down his life for us? Or his soul?

The fact is, Jesus laid down his *psuche* for us.

This theme of Jesus giving his *psuche* for mankind is replete throughout the New Testament! Understanding this key concept is fundamental. But this theme is basically hidden in current versions of the English Bible because ambiguity and conflation have replaced the original clarity of Jesus's words.   As a result, we fail to see the true significance of Jesus death.

For the moment we are focusing in on *psuche*. We will look at *zoe* shortly. While these two words are very different, they work together in tandem, synergistically explaining God's plan of salvation. In current English Bibles we are left clueless about the existence of these two words, because they have been replaced with two other words (which we are about to discuss) which have actually hijacked Jesus' original message.

In current English bibles we are left clueless about the existence

of psuche and zoe, because they have been replaced with

two other words which have hijacked Jesus' original message

7

Focusing on Jesus' Use of *Psuche*

We are now going to look at three different conversations in the gospels where Jesus uses the word *psuche* multiple times during each conversation. As you will see in this chapter, something very alarming occurs in each of these texts.

In each case, *psuche* is translated into two different words ("life" and "soul") within a few sentences of each other. When Jesus used the word psuche, he never intended for us to carve it up into two different words with such devastating consequences!

Life and *soul* have *become* two of the most important key words in the Bible, but they are *false* key words! These two false key words have *supplanted* the original two key words used by Jesus and the New Testament authors.

Life and soul (false key words) have supplanted

Jesus' original key words, psuche and zoe.

This action has radically distorted his teaching.

The original narrative conveyed by the intentional use of psuche and zoe in the New Testament, has been lost. It has been replaced by a totally different narrative conveyed by the use of life and soul. This has resulted in a 'new and different' gospel that has radically changed what Jesus originally said.

THE PARABLE OF THE RICH FOOL

These verses contain one of Jesus' parables. In this parable, Jesus uses the word *psuche* five times. Yet, it is translated as "soul" twice and "life" three times. (There is some variation of this between different English versions).

> **Luke 12:16-23** And he told a parable to them, saying, "The land of a certain rich man yielded an abundant harvest. And he reasoned to himself, saying, 'What should I do? For I do not have anywhere I can gather in my crops.' And he said, 'I will do this: I will tear down my barns and build larger ones, and I will gather in there all my grain and possessions. And I will say to my **soul (psuche)**, "Soul (psuche), you have many possessions stored up for many years. Relax, eat, drink, celebrate!"' But God said to him, 'Fool! This night your **life**

(psuche) is demanded from you, and the things which you have prepared—whose will they be?' So is the one who stores up treasure for himself, and who is not rich toward God!" And he said to his disciples, "For this reason I tell you, do not be anxious for your **life (psuche)**, what you will eat, or for your body, what you will wear. For **life (psuche)** is more than food, and the body more than clothing. (LEB)

Why were the first two occurrences translated as "soul" but the last three as "life?" Most likely, the translator felt like this made the most sense based upon his or her paradigm. However, due to the fact that most people believe the soul is immortal, inserting the word "soul" in these verses injects and reinforces this false notion of the innate immortality of "man's soul". Jesus never implied this, nor taught this, nor is the "immortal soul" taught anywhere in the Bible.

In addition, using the word *life* in the phrase 'this night your *life* is demanded from you,' understates the importance of what Jesus is teaching here.

Use of the word *life* makes it appear that the consequence *is less* than what Jesus actually taught. Due to *psuche* already being translated as *soul* in the previous sentence, the narrative implies that the person's soul is not going to die, only the person's life is going to be taken.

Since most English-speaking people would associate a much more serious and permanent consequence with the loss of a *soul,* in comparison to the loss of a *life*, the reader gets the impression there are two different narratives taking place here.

But Jesus is not speaking about two different outcomes. He is not suggesting the outcome for the soul and for a person's life are any different. Jesus uses the single word psuche throughout these verses and he is only speaking of one outcome. Only one narrative is being presented - the loss of that person's psuche.

When Jesus says, "this night your psuche will be demanded of you", he is speaking of the death of that person's psuche.

Since most English-speaking people associate a much more serious

and permanent consequence with the loss of a soul, in comparison

to the loss of a life, the reader gets the impression there are

two different narratives taking place in Luke 12:16-23

DESTRUCTION OF AND LOSING ONE'S *PSUCHE*

In Matthew 10, Jesus sends out his apostles to proclaim that the kingdom of heaven has come near. He encourages them not to be afraid of those who might kill them for their message.

In fact, in the decades to follow, ten of these twelve men would indeed be killed for sharing their message about Jesus.

Matt. 10:28 And do not be afraid of those who kill the body but are not able to kill the **soul (psuche)**, but instead be afraid of the one who is able to destroy both **soul (psuche)** and body in hell (Gehenna). (LEB)

A moment later in this conversation Jesus circles back this statement with his apostles, with an emphasis on the willingness to follow him.

Matt. 10:38-39 And whoever does not take up his cross and follow me is not worthy of me. The one who finds his **life (psuche)** will lose it, and the one who loses his **life (psuche)** because of me will find it. (LEB)

In 10:28, psuche has been translated twice as "soul." A few seconds later in the conversation (10:39), psuche has been translated twice as "life." Why?

Read these verses a second time and ask yourself: "If I exchange the English word "soul" for "life" and visa-versa, how would that affect my understanding of these verses?"

Based on your own current paradigm if you had been forced to choose between using these two words, would you have done anything differently? Perhaps you can see how powerful a paradigm can be.

To Jesus, the word psuche was a single concept.

A person's psuche, simply put "was" that person.

But was it the best choice? More importantly, do the words chosen accurately convey what Jesus was saying? Or do they obscure his original message?

Or, even worse...

could the words *chosen* actually *change* his message?

SAVING YOUR *PSUCHE*

In Matthew 16, Jesus explains to his disciples that he is going to Jerusalem and will be betrayed, killed, and raised from the dead. It is in the context of this conversation where Jesus again emphasizes the importance of being willing to lose your *psuche* in order to gain your *psuche*.

Psuche is used four times in these verses and is translated into both "life" and "soul" in the English translation.

Let's play a bit of a game. This time, I am replacing the words "life" and "soul" with the Greek word *psuche* in the following verses. Which instances do you think would read as "soul" or "life" in the typical English translation?

Matt. 16:24-26 Then Jesus said to his disciples, "If anyone wants to come after me, let him deny himself and take up his cross and follow me. For whoever wants to save his *psuche* will lose it, but whoever loses his *psuche* on account of me will find it. For what will a person be benefited if he gains the whole world but forfeits his *psuche*? Or what will a person give in exchange for his *psuche*? (LEB)

Well, how did you do?

The Lexham English Bible (LEB) translates all four instances as "life". But most English translations use a mix of both life and soul in this passage.

Previously, we discussed the paradigm of the "immortal soul." Notice how natural it would be (if you are influenced by that paradigm) to insert the word "life" into the first two sentences and "soul" into the last two sentences.

Summary

The translation of psuche into the divergent words 'life" and "soul" has introduced heavily damaging ambiguity into the New Testament. This action has replaced two of the most important key words used by Jesus and the New Testament authors (psuche and zoe) with false key words which have ended up conveying a very different message. Jesus' and the New Testament authors' original consistency and clarity have been lost. Their original teaching has been replaced by a similar but distorted narrative.

8

Three Problems with *Psuche*

At first glance, we might think that in each of the previous examples, translating *psuche* into the English word "life" or "soul" seems fairly innocent. These words might initially seem suitable for use in the context in which they are used.

On the other hand, there are three significant problems with this.

PSUCHE PROBLEM 1: AMBIGUITY

First, the words "life" and "soul" have very different meanings to the typical English-speaking person.

Typical English understanding of the word "life": A person's life consists of who they are, what they are doing with their time on earth, their attitudes, their personality, their relationships, the period from their birth to their death, the process of living, and so on. Your definition might vary from mine a bit, but it is probably similar.

The typical English understanding of a persons "life" consists of who they are, what they are doing with their time on earth, the process of living — from birth to death, their attitudes, personality, relationships, and so on

On the other hand, the typical English understanding of the word, "soul", implies a spirit-like, ethereal component of the person that has an immortal nature to it. The soul is thought of as transcending a person's "life" on earth. The soul is commonly thought of as the "inner person" that lives on after that person dies an earthly death. Again, your definition might vary from mine a bit, but it is probably similar.

We have ended up with two distinctly different words when in fact, there was originally only one word. Splitting up *psuche* into these two divergent words has garbled what Jesus originally said, injecting *ambiguity* and false narratives that did not exist in the original Greek texts. These false narratives have a subtle but powerful influence on how we process what we read in the Bible.

Jesus' focus was on saving a person's psuche from death,

by resurrecting them to eternal zoe. Disastrously, this message is

essentially hidden due to the conflation of psuche and zoe

43

PSUCHE PROBLEM 2: IMMORTALITY

The second problem occurs specifically with the word "soul." Most English-speaking people believe the Bible teaches that the soul is immortal.

In reality, the Bible *never* teaches this nor implies this, either directly or indirectly.

The idea that man has a soul is not biblical. Furthermore, there is not a unique word in the Greek New Testament that specifically means *soul*. Yet, in the English translation that is exactly what we have ended up with!

The idea of *psuche* being immortal originated (at least within the Hellenistic culture) with Socrates and Plato, centuries before Jesus' time. These two ancient philosophers believed in a dualistic nature of a person's psuche. But Jesus and the New Testament authors never used the word *psuche* with this understanding.

This falsely held notion of the "immortal soul" has significantly distorted the context of Jesus' teachings. Indeed, it is this very notion of the "immortal soul" that has driven much of traditional Christian doctrine and belief.

IS A SOULISH PERSPECTIVE OKAY?

Psuche can refer to the inner person in regard to their thoughts, emotions, and will. In that sense it could be considered to be the *soul* of that person. Therefore inserting "soul" for *psuche* could be seen as a fairly *innocent* translation if done with this understanding.

However, due to the prevailing belief that the soul is immortal, this ends up being anything but *innocent*. Instead, it has tragically undermined Jesus' clear message of salvation.

How many times have you heard the phrase "immortal soul?" This phrase does not appear anywhere in the Bible - period. This notion is strictly an innovation of man and is not in the scriptures.

It might be best to avoid using the word "soul," since this word carries such strong connotations. But if it is necessary to use the word then just think of it this way: you do not have a *soul,* but rather, you are a *soul*. And most importantly you are merely *mortal*.

Due to the prevailing belief that the soul is immortal, inserting the English word "soul" in the Bible ends up being anything but innocent

---

In Paul's first letter to Timothy, he tells us something very unique about God with respect to immortality. Paul clearly indicates that only God is immortal.

1 Timothy 6:14-16 that you observe the commandment without fault, irreproachable until the appearing of our Lord Jesus Christ, which he will make known in his own time, the blessed and only Sovereign, the King of those who reign as kings and Lord of those who rule as lords, **the one who alone possesses immortality,** who lives in unapproachable light, whom no human being has seen nor is able to see, to whom be honor and eternal power. Amen. (LEB)

PSUCHE PROBLEM 3: OBSCURING *ZOE*

Inserting the word "life" for *psuche* creates another serious problem.

The third problem that occurs with inserting the word "life" for psuche is that it conflates the vitally important differences of psuche and zoe. This obscures the critical roles that each word uniquely plays in the New Testament. Psuche and zoe are no longer recognizable as having these distinct roles.

Let me explain. The word *zoe* is one of the most influential words in the New Testament, especially and explicitly because of the way Jesus and the NT authors consistently used *zoe*.

Here is where the problem begins. Zoe is translated as "life" about 99% of the time in English bibles. Psuche is also translated as "life" about 30-40% of the time. The obscurity and conflation occur because the English reader cannot see that Jesus used two very different words in his teaching, because both words have been translated as "life."

As a result, we are left unaware of the critically different definitions of these two words and their profound impact on the clarity of Jesus' message.

This third problem has resulted in *severe consequences* that extend throughout Christian doctrine, heavily obscuring and distorting the profound truth that Jesus taught.

This masking of *zoe* is the biggest of the three *psuche* problems, but each problem has enormous implications and is entangled with the other two.

Inserting the word Life for Psuche, covers up

Jesus' focus on Zoe (also translated as Life)

FOCUS

As you will see, *psuche* is not the main focus of our study. While it is very important to remove the confusion that the dissection and divergence of *psuche* has created, it is not as important as zeroing in on what Jesus did say.

Jesus' focus was not primarily on *psuche*. While he was very concerned about a person's psuche, it was because he came to give zoe to a person's psuche. His focus was on saving a person's psuche from death, by resurrecting them from the dead to give them eternal zoe.

However, Jesus' focus is almost impossible to see in our current English translations, due to the conflation of "psuche" and "zoe". This conflation has covered up the original clarity these two words conveyed in concisely explaining the gospel.

AN AVALANCHE OF MISUNDERSTANDING

The fact that it is impossible to differentiate these two words in English bibles prevents us from seeing Jesus' primary message, the reason for his death and the huge implications of his resurrection.

In addition, the lack of understanding of how Jesus consistently used these two words has resulted in several other words also not being accurately understood. It's as if *psuche*'s divergent translation started an avalanche of ambiguity (like a contagious virus) that spread to other highly influential words of Jesus, resulting in a serious distortion of Jesus' original teaching.

This is known in any system of study as misunderstanding "key words". Anytime a person fails to understand "key words", the downstream effect of that can be disastrous. Misunderstanding key words always generates subsequent misunderstandings that rely on the key words.

A clear understanding of psuche and zoe is a vital prerequisite for

understanding critical concepts dependent on these key words

USING A METAPHOR OF THEATER

Here is where we stand at this point. There are two key words that are highly visible in the English New Testament, that *never* existed in the original Greek New Testament!

These "key words" are the English words *Life* and *Soul*.

Using a metaphor of theater, we could call these two key words "impostors." Imagine a play in which impostors have taken center stage over the two real (original intended) key words that Jesus used.

Life and *Soul* are counterfeits, mimicking *Psuche* and *Zoe* but delivering a completely different message.

As we have already seen, the original single Greek word *psuche* has been translated into two very different English words, which has culminated in these two key words *Life* and *Soul* becoming the focal point of the whole show. Consequentially, the audience focuses on these phony actors *Life* and *Soul,* even though they never existed in the original script.

Jesus' intended main character *Zoe*, is never recognized by the audience, because *Zoe* has been hidden backstage. The original script has been revised so that *Life* and *Soul* have been given all the speaking roles. The pinnacle of the show was originally intended to occur with the introduction

46

and demonstration of *Zoe*. But *Zoe* is never heard from in the English version of the show, even though *Zoe* was originally the leading character throughout Jesus' teachings!

Instead, *Zoe* has been dressed in the same clothes and makeup as *Life but is not allowed to speak*. As a result, the most important character in the script has been relegated to the status of an unrecognizable extra in the crowd!

Are you tracking with me?

Psuche and *Zoe* were supposed to be the main characters in the show, but we have ended up with a show that has substituted two impostors: *Soul* and *Life*. The voices of the original intended characters are muted in the background, where they cannot be heard. In addition, the original script for Psuche and Zoe has been altered to accommodate the fake actors Soul and Life.

The impostors have stolen the show! The audience has missed the real plot, as the important message of the true characters has been totally transformed by the impostors.

The audience walks away satisfied thinking they have seen the real show when tragically, the original lifesaving, empowering message has been relegated to obscurity without the audience having a clue as to what they missed.

Psuche and **Zoe** were originally scripted as the main

characters in the show, but we have ended up with

a show that has substituted two impostors! - **Soul** and **Life**

A THOUGHT ABOUT SATAN'S INFLUENCE

Satan is a master of deceit. Jesus tells us in John 8 that Satan is the father of lies. Rarely does Satan use outright lies, because that is easy to see through. Rather, he twists truth, distorts it, making the deformed message seem legitimate, even making sense and capable of being attractive to the listener.

Satan uses diversion. He seeks to destroy man by getting them to believe a lie, by diverting our attention from what is true to false narratives that blind us as to what is real. Satan is the prince of this world in this present age. Though Jesus has overcome death by his own resurrection, and has defeated the power of Satan's accusations of man deserving death by taking our death sentence for us, Satan's power of distorting truth is as strong today as ever.

If Satan could change, distort and impede the effectiveness of the message of Christ by injecting ambiguity and twisting the message over centuries, do you think he would? Of course, he would.

The question is... did he?

Satan's first lie began with "you shall not surely die". One of his most powerful lies today is a copy of this first lie but with a different twist.

LINKS TO WORD STUDIES

Going forward, you can easily view the original Greek text for yourself by viewing the interlinear Greek-English New Testament.

From the website EternalZoe.com, if you click on *Recommended Links*, you will see links to the Interlinear New Testament, as well as links to Strong's definitions for psuche and zoe.

The psuche and zoe links provide a complete listing of every verse where these words are found in the New Testament. You can learn a lot from seeing how these words were used in the original Greek by just reading these lists. You could easily read through either list in 30 minutes.

I have no affiliation or influence with any of these resources. They are just great Bible study resources that anyone can access.

BEFORE WE MOVE ON

Look at this section from 1 John. Notice how the English translation uses the word life or lives 4 times in these verses. The first two instances use zoe, which makes sense. We are passing from death to zoe. Passing from death to psuche wouldn't make any sense. Same for eternal life. Eternal zoe means being alive forever and is specifically referring to your psuche resurrecting from the dead to live forever. The last part of this section speaks of the fact that since Jesus laid down his psuche for us, we ought to lay down our psuche for the brothers. Zoe would not work in these last two instances. This is just one example. There are many more. It is more than just a matter of semantics. A correct understanding of the gospel message hinges upon having a clear understanding of these two words and how they are consistently used throughout the New Testament.

> **1 John 3:14-16** We know that we have passed over from death to **life (zoe)** because we love the brothers. The one who does not love remains in death. 15 Everyone who hates his brother is a murderer, and you know that every murderer does not have **eternal life (zoe)** residing in him. 16 We have come to know love by this: that he laid down his **life (psuche)** on behalf of us, and we ought to lay down our **lives (pusche)** on behalf of the brothers. (LEB)

9

Understanding Zoe

Over the years, I have taken my kids and their friends to several waterparks. One of my favorites has a lazy river that meanders in a loop through the park. There are four or five entrances with steps where one can get in or out of the lazy river. Now, the largest entrance is near the front of the park, and most people get in there, but you can get in or out at any of the entrances.

Once you see how zoe is consistently used in the New Testament, the scriptures will make more sense to you virtually anywhere you open them up and begin reading. The hard part for me is deciding where to begin this study with you. We could get into the water anywhere along the river and do just fine. But what makes the most sense?

I certainly did not begin my study at the beginning. My study began with questions I had over a twenty-year period regarding several scattered scriptures that just didn't seem to make sense. It was only after a long struggle with comparing and studying that it slowly came together like a puzzle for me. That's not an optimal way to teach or train, so I have decided to use the Gospel according to John as a map for this journey.

As we embark on this journey through John's gospel, I would like to point out something that is particularly unique to John. I think of the four gospels as narratives that describe Jesus' life, teachings, miracles, etc. in a timeline, so to speak.

Each author seemed to record the events that they thought would be of importance to their particular audience as they occurred. A typical sequence of events included Jesus' birth, selecting his apostles, his teachings, betrayal, death, resurrection, etc.

But in John's gospel, something significantly different occurs. John intentionally and progressively reveals a multi-nuanced use of zoe, that becomes the centerpiece of Jesus' teaching. John's record revolves around Jesus' teaching on zoe.

John introduces *zoe* during his introduction of Jesus, then gradually reveals more and more about *zoe* as he progresses through his gospel. It is comparable to an artist gradually revealing a magnificent sculpture as he chisels away the stone chip by chip. The sculptor already knows what the final image is, but it is unveiled in stages for the observer. John records Jesus' own teachings about *zoe* progressively, thereby revealing Jesus' unique application of *zoe* in steps.

Jesus spoke of *zoe* many times and in many different venues. But John selectively and methodically reveals *zoe* so that we can grasp it in small bites. As we see Jesus reveal this truth, we begin to understand that *zoe* is the most powerful underlying theme in the gospel according to John.

You may be asking, "If this focus on zoe does exist, why hasn't it already been explained and taught?"

My answer is that there is significant evidence that this emphasis is exactly what the church taught for approximately the first two to three centuries of its existence.

UNTANGLING KNOTS, ONE AT A TIME

Having ambiguous and conflated wording in the English translation has perpetuated tangled misconceptions that have lasted for centuries.

Have you ever had to untangle a fishing line, an extension cord, necklace, or maybe the wires to your earbuds? It's a pain, isn't it? Imagine having to untangle a long string with many tangled knots that have been tightly pulled together. You must decide where to begin untangling and then gradually untangle each knot, until you have a string free of tangles.

We are going on a journey through the New Testament, untangling knots one a time. After we untie a few knots, it will gradually become clear where John is leading us with Jesus's teachings on *zoe*.

SEEING THINGS IN FULL COLOR

When I was a kid, our family had a black-and-white television. My friends and I would spend hours watching our favorite TV shows. We thought black & white TV was the coolest thing ever! I can't remember how long we had our black & white TV, but I do remember the excitement that all the kids in our neighborhood shared when we heard about the new color TVs that were soon to be available at the department store. We couldn't even imagine what that would be like!

Eventually one of the neighboring kids' parents purchased one of these new, amazing TV sets. All the kids could not wait to hang out at the friend's house and watch a TV show in full color. I can clearly recall the amazement that we all felt at being able to see our favorite TV show in vibrant color.

We had no idea how much vibrancy we had been missing! These colors obviously existed when the show was originally filmed, but they were muted in the background in the black & white display.

But with the new color TV, the shows seemed so much more exciting to watch. Seeing the shows in full color changed the whole experience. Things just popped off the TV screen that were previously monotone in appearance.

As you begin to understand what Jesus actually said in the original Greek, this may be how you start to feel. Important details that you never noticed before will become vibrant and powerful. Old familiar phrases from the Bible (both Old and New Testaments) will take on new depth and meaning as you see the original intent that was there all along but had subsequently been obscured.

Part Two

Jesus Defines Zoe

10

Following the Gospel of John

This chapter of Eternal Zoe covers several chapters 1-5 of the Gospel of John. As we move into John chapters 6, 8, 10 and 11 there is so much material to cover in each of these chapters, that each will be covered by one or more "book" chapters.

JOHN 1

John introduces Jesus by saying several things about him, but the key concept we are focusing on is what John says about *zoe*.

> **John 1:4** In him was **life (zoe)**, and the **life (zoe)** was the light of humanity. (LEB)

John points out that "In Him was Life". This introductory statement about Jesus "having zoe within himself", is only one of two times that John inserts his personal comments about *zoe*. Toward the end of the gospel, he does this again by making a closing statement about Jesus and *zoe* (John 20:30-31). The rest of the *zoe* scriptures in John are taken directly from Jesus' teachings and conversations (and one from John the Baptist).

John introduces Jesus, emphasizing "In Jesus was Life (Zoe)"

REFLECTION

Please take a minute and write down what you think John meant by this statement:

"In Jesus was life . . ."

A few questions, are appropriate:

➢ Why did John emphasize that Jesus had life in himself?
➢ How is it possible that this life could be the light of mankind?
➢ Maybe the biggest question we should be asking ourselves is this: Is the fact that Jesus had *zoe* in himself somehow different than you and me?

If you are a Christian, how influential has this part of John's introduction of Jesus been in your understanding of who Jesus is? Maybe you haven't given it much thought. I just used to pass over this verse, giving it little to no thought, because I didn't really know what it was talking about.

As an illustration, when I was a young man, I worked for a company selling concrete brick. Most people don't know the difference between a concrete brick and a clay brick.

However, if you know what to look for you can easily tell the difference between clay and concrete brick. Occasionally, when I am driving around with my wife in the car, I'll see a house with concrete brick. I'll point it out to my wife, and she will look at me like, "Really...Okay... I am pretending to be interested..."

But we are all like this in one way or another. We go through life not noticing certain things around us, until one day we learn about something new at school or work. We then begin to notice that 'new thing' we learned about, is all around us. We never noticed it before because we didn't know enough about it to appreciate it.

This illustration is similar to what is about to take place with John's statement in John 1:4.

You may have not paid much attention to John's statement, "In Jesus was life," because you didn't know its *implications.*

I pray that is about to change.

KEY CONCEPTS DEFINED IN GOSPEL OF JOHN

What we have learned about life (*Zoe*) thus far:

➢ In Jesus was *Zoe.*
➢ *Zoe* was the light of mankind.

What we don't know yet:

➢ What exactly is *Zoe*?
➢ Why is this so important that John felt he needed to introduce Jesus in this way?
➢ Do I have *Zoe*?

JOHN 3

In John 3:1-22, Jesus is approached by a man named Nicodemus. I encourage you to read this narrative in its entirety, as it is a very powerful dialogue. But, for now, let's zero in on just the verses that contain *zoe*.

About halfway through this narrative, Jesus tells Nicodemus the following:

> **John 3:16** For in this way God loved the world, so that he gave his one and only Son, in order that everyone who believes in him will not perish, but will have **eternal life (zoe)** (LEB)

By believing in Jesus, a person can have *eternal zoe*. Notice that Jesus did *not* use the word *psuche*. Trust me, this is no insignificant detail. The term "eternal p*suche*" **never** occurs in the Bible.

Every time you see the phrase "eternal life" in your English New Testament, it comes from the combination of the Greek word *zoe (which means being alive)* and another Greek word *aionion*, which means "unto the ages" and is generally translated as "everlasting," or "eternal."

Let's pause for a second and ask ourselves a few questions:

- ➤ Why did Jesus use *zoe* instead of *psuche* for this phrase?
- ➤ Is there a connection between John's introduction in verse 1:4 and this opening statement in 3:16 that Jesus has just made about eternal zoe?
- ➤ Jesus uses *opposites* frequently in his teaching. In this case the opposites are eternal zoe (being alive forever) and perishing. What do you think perishing means? This is a very important question and is actually a primary focus of the gospel. The traditional view cannot give a straight answer on this. As for that matter, the traditional view cannot provide a reasonable definition as to what eternal life means either. We will delve into the word *perish* in part 3 of this book.

The term "Eternal Psuche" never occurs in the Bible

FURTHERMORE

If the statement, "In Jesus was Life," is true, and this can't be said about you and me . . . then the statement that Jesus made to Nicodemus becomes that much more interesting.

Because Jesus just told Nicodemus he can have *zoe* . . . and he can have it for *eternity*!

JOHN THE BAPTIST UNDERSTOOD THE CONCEPT OF *ZOE*

In John 3:22-36, John (the apostle and author of the gospel according to John) records an interaction between John the Baptist (a different John, not the author) and some of John the Baptist's disciples.

During this conversation, John the Baptist explains several important things to his disciples about Jesus. He proclaims that Jesus is the Son of God. Then, in the very last verse of this conversation, John the Baptist states the following:

> **John 3:36** The one who believes in the Son has **eternal life (zoe)**, but the one who disobeys the Son will not see **life (zoe)** —but the wrath of God remains on him (LEB)

In the first half of this verse, John the Baptist essentially says the same thing that Jesus told Nicodemus.

> The one who believes in the Son has **eternal life (zoe)**

But it's the second part of the verse that answers one of the questions we were pondering.

> but the one who disobeys the Son **will not see life (zoe)** —but the wrath of God remains on him.

John the Baptist points out that anyone who disobeys or rejects the Son (Jesus) will not see life (*zoe*).

This clearly indicates that John is using the word zoe with a unique perspective, because these people that Jesus is speaking to are clearly *already alive*. One helpful key to understanding this verse is John's use of the word "see". He is speaking of *being alive* in the future. (Jesus's focus is on the end game, resurrection from the dead to live forever).

Notice that John did not use the word *psuche* here. Using psuche would not have made any sense.

The last section of this verse indicates that in order for us to receive *zoe*, we must get out from under God's wrath. How does God's wrath figure into all this? It sounds as though we are already under God's wrath, and we need to remove it by believing in Jesus.

Somehow removing his wrath is a prerequisite for me receiving *zoe*.

Every time the phrase **Eternal Life** appears,

it comes from the combination of the Greek word

zoe (which means being alive) and another Greek

word **aionion**, which means "unto the age"

JOHN 4

In John 4:1-26, Jesus encounters a Samaritan woman who comes to draw water at a well outside of the town she lives in. Jesus uses a conversation about getting water as a segue into his purpose for meeting this woman.

Jesus wants to give her eternal zoe, just like he wants to give eternal zoe to you and me.

John 4:13-14 Jesus answered and said to her, "Everyone who drinks of this water will be thirsty again. But whoever drinks of this water which I will give to him will never be thirsty for eternity, but the water which I will give to him will become in him a well of water springing up to **eternal life (zoe)**." (LEB)

John 4:36 The one who reaps receives wages and gathers fruit for **eternal life (zoe)**, in order that the one who sows and the one who reaps can rejoice together (LEB)

KEY CONCEPTS DEFINED IN GOSPEL OF JOHN

What we have learned about Zoe thus far:

➢ In Jesus was *Zoe*.
➢ *Zoe* was the light of mankind.
➢ If I believe in Jesus, I will receive eternal *Zoe*.
➢ On the flip side, if I reject Jesus, I will not see life (*Zoe*).
➢ If I reject Jesus, I will remain under God's wrath.
➢ I do not have *Zoe* as an inherent part of my nature.

What has not been identified yet in John:

➢ What exactly is *Zoe*?
➢ Why is this so important that John felt he needed to introduce Jesus in this way?
➢ How does God's wrath fit into this?
➢ What exactly is the difference between *psuche* and *zoe*, in the way that Jesus uses these two words.
➢ What is the significance of zoe's exclusive use in the phrase "eternal life" (zoe aionion)?

JOHN 5

As we move into John 5, Jesus begins to expand his teaching on zoe.

> **John 5:21** For just as the Father raises the dead and makes them **alive**, thus also the Son makes **alive** whomever he wishes. (LEB)

The word "alive" comes from the root word zoe. Jesus is speaking proleptically about the resurrection from the dead to zoe (being alive again). As mentioned in chapter 4 of this book, multiple nuances can often be seen in any instance where Jesus is speaking about zoe. In this instance, in addition to the *assurance* of being raised from the dead to live forever, a believer is *made alive* in their present time on earth by being born again, by the indwelling Holy Spirit. This second birth bestows the life (zoe) of Jesus into the psuche of the believer.

> **John 5:24** Truly, truly I say to you that the one who hears my word and who believes the one who sent me has **eternal life (zoe)**, and does not come into judgment, but has passed from **death into life (zoe)**. (LEB)

What did Jesus just say about believers?

They cross over from *death* to *zoe*!

It is not until we wholeheartedly believe in Jesus, that we receive the assurance of *zoe*. We then cross over from death to zoe. At that point, our status changes from "death" to "zoe." Jesus just used both of these words (death and zoe) proleptically.

As mortals we initially start out under the curse of death. We do not have an assurance of future zoe. Unlike Jesus who has zoe intrinsically (he is immortal) our only future expectation would be death unless we are saved from this permanent death sentence.

We can deduce that no one besides the Father and Jesus have zoe intrinsically as part of their nature. Any other creature that has zoe has it because it has been bestowed upon them by the Father or Jesus.

> **John 5:25-29** "Truly, truly I say to you, that an hour is coming—and now is here—when the dead will hear the voice of the Son of God, and the ones who hear will **live**. 26 For just as the Father has **life (zoe)** in himself, thus also he has granted to the Son to have **life (zoe)** in himself. 27 And he has granted him authority to carry out judgment, because he is the Son of Man. 28 "Do not be astonished at this, because an hour is coming in which all those in the tombs will hear his voice 29 and they will come out—those who have done good things

to a **resurrection of life (zoe)**, but those who have practiced evil things to a resurrection of judgment. (LEB)

Those who believe in Jesus cross over from a

status of Death to a status of Life (Zoe)

Let's focus in on 5:26 for a moment.

> **John 5:26** For just as the Father has **life (zoe)** in himself, thus also he has granted to the Son to have **life (zoe)** in himself. (LEB)

5:26 is an insightful verse that *defines* the *source* of zoe. Zoe comes from God the Father and Jesus himself, as zoe (the state of being alive) is inherent within them. Being immortal is part of their nature.

As Jesus continues this difficult conversation with the Jewish leaders, he reiterates that they must come to him to receive *zoe*. Jesus is very direct with them, confronting them about their stubbornness of heart.

> **John 5:36-40** But I have a testimony greater than John's, for the works which the Father has given to me that I should complete them—the very works which I am doing—these testify about me, that the Father has sent me. And the Father who sent me, that one has testified about me. You have neither heard his voice at any time nor seen his form. And you do not have his word residing in yourselves, because the one whom that one sent, in this one you do not believe. You search the scriptures because you think that you have **eternal life (zoe)** in them, and it is these that testify about me. And you are not willing to come to me so that you may have **life (zoe)**. (LEB)

Jesus chastises the Jewish leaders because they assumed that by searching the scriptures, they would somehow find eternal life, yet they failed to recognize that the scriptures were actually pointing to Him. As a result, they refused to come to Jesus for *zoe*.

This is terribly unfortunate, for Jesus is the only source for *zoe*.

However, it is very interesting that Jesus infers that the Jewish leaders knew what the real issue was - *death*. Jesus points out that they searched the scriptures to understand God's solution to death. Yet their hard hearts prevented them from recognizing that the scriptures indeed pointed to God's solution – Jesus himself.

Today, while those holding to the traditional view recognize Jesus as their savior, their paradigm prevents them from recognizing that death is the main issue, not "hell" as they perceive it. The Jews that Jesus is chastising knew that death was the primary issue. They did not hold to some notion of eternal torture in the afterlife. In fact, the idea of "hell" as perceived by the traditional Christian view today, did not exist in the minds of Jews in Jesus's day, nor did it cross Jesus's mind.

CONSISTENT USE OF ZOE

In chapter 4 of this book (*Nuances of Zoe*) I described several ways that zoe is used with a distinct nuance. *Zoe* is consistently used with these nuances 35 out of the 36 times that zoe occurs in the gospel of John.

Note: Eternal zoe (explicit use of the word using zoe and aionion) and the solo use of zoe (used implicitly) are referring to resurrection from the dead to physical life, with physical bodies. The only time zoe is used in John where it is not directly referring to physical life, is when Jesus says the Father and himself have zoe within themselves. In this case, it is saying that God and Jesus have "the state of being alive" as an inherent part of their nature. As already mentioned, they are immortal and are not dependent upon any source outside of themselves for being alive or staying alive.

PSUCHE - ON THE OTHER HAND

On the other hand, *psuche* is used 10 times in the gospel of John, in an entirely different context. *Psuche* is clearly depicting the mortal life of a human. In John, *psuche* is depicted as being killed, and as capable of being lost (as in dying). In fact, Jesus repeatedly emphasizes that he is going to lay down *his psuche*. In other words, Jesus is going to be killed, his *psuche* is going to die.

Note: A psuche is a being. God and Jesus are both presented as psuche (beings) in the Bible. But they are inherently immortal. Man was not created immortal, he is mortal, and dependent on God for zoe (being alive). Jesus became a mortal man so that he could die. That is, so his psuche could indeed be killed, as a substitute for our death sentence. This is the core truth of the New Testament. If you miss this essential, fundamental truth about Jesus, then you have missed the very core of Jesus' purpose and message.

There is absolutely no way that the word *zoe* would make any sense if you were to try to substitute it for psuche in this context, since it is impossible for *zoe* to die. This is due to the fact that zoe means the "state of being alive". Zoe is the exact opposite of death.

If you were to randomly switch out the words *psuche* and *zoe* throughout the gospel of John, the gospel would no longer make any sense. It would be total chaos, hijacking the vital message delivered in the original context. Reading it in such a way would lead to other confusing conclusions.

But chaos is exactly what has occurred in our English bibles. In current English bibles (that I am aware of) there is no way to distinguish the use of psuche from zoe (when you encounter the word "life").

For example, Jesus makes a vital connection between *zoe* and *psuche* in John 12:25 (see below). But this is impossible to discern in English bibles because both words have been translated into the ambiguous word "life". This has rendered the verse incapable of conveying its original clear message.

> **John 12:25** The one who loves his **life (psuche)** loses it, and the one who hates his **life (psuche)** in this world preserves it for **eternal life (zoe)**. (LEB)

This verse actually sums up the gospel. Jesus came to preserve (some versions use the word "save") our psuche for eternal zoe. He will keep our psuche secure, by the assurance that comes from being born again. This second birth of the believer is not of the flesh, but of God's holy spirit (aka spirit of Christ). It is the Spirit that conveys zoe (John 6:63). It is has always been the spirit of God that has conveyed zoe (being alive), beginning at the creation when God breathed into man and he became a living being.

Believers can die in confidence knowing that God has assured us that he will raise us from the dead by his Spirit, this time to live forever (eternal zoe).

Resurrection from the dead was the main thing promised to believers. Instead, we have changed Jesus' primary message from resurrection to a false narrative involving heaven and hell.

We are going to go into John chapter 6 next. This is one of my favorite chapters of John because the statements that Jesus makes about zoe are so powerful and defining. What Jesus says in John 6 can change your life.

11

John 6 – Bread of Zoe

NOTE ABOUT JOHN 6

This is an important chapter in understanding Jesus' teaching about Zoe. Jesus is going to weave two separate narratives together throughout John 6. Each narrative alludes to different historical events that took place in the days of Moses. He will go back and forth in his references to these two legacies of Jewish history, tying each legacy to his unique use of zoe.

The first historical narrative that Jesus discusses with the crowds is "manna". He draws a stark contrast between manna and himself. The second, and even more important narrative that he alludes to is Passover. He doesn't mention Passover directly like he does the manna, but it becomes obvious that he is drawing a direct parallel with the Passover lamb and himself. When I say obvious, it becomes obvious (later) to readers of John. But it was not at all obvious to his Jewish listeners on this day of teaching. In fact, many in the crowd will become offended by what he says.

Jesus is having this conversation with the Jewish crowd a few days before the annual Passover memorial meal. The Passover memorial lasted approximately one week, culminating on the last day with the sacrifice of the Passover lamb and the subsequent Passover meal when the flesh of the lamb is eaten. This particular Passover week is taking place exactly one year before Jesus's crucifixion. Jesus uses the timely context of this highly important memorial as the basis for the strong metaphors he uses in this chapter. Jesus will make very powerful allusions to himself in direct parallel with the Passover lamb.

It is crucial to see the connections that Jesus builds in this chapter. It all began with a miracle the previous day, which was merely a setup for Jesus' extremely important teaching about Zoe. We begin by looking at Jesus' contrast with manna.

Buckle in, this is going to be a bit of a roller coaster ride, just as it was for those listening to him on that incredible day of life saving metaphors from the Son of God.

JESUS DECLARES, "I AM THE BREAD OF ZOE"

As we move into John 6, Jesus' teaching and miraculous healings attract a very large crowd that follows him as he travels through the countryside. Jesus feeds this crowd of thousands with five barley loaves and two small fish. This miracle amazes the crowd so much that many of them perceive that this miracle was a sign of the *prophet* who was to come into the world.

Some thirteen hundred years earlier, Moses foretold of a prophet (that would be like himself) that God would raise up from the midst of the Israelites. God would put his words in the mouth of this prophet, and the prophet would speak unto them all that God should command him. God foretold through Moses that anyone who did not hearken unto the words that the prophet spoke would be judged (see Deuteronomy 18:15-19).

Now, many in this crowd suspect that Jesus is this anticipated prophet. One of the noteworthy things that transpired while Moses led the Israelites through the wilderness for forty years was the miraculous "manna" that God provided each morning for the people to eat (see Exodus chapter 16).

In Exodus 16:4, God said to Moses,

> "Look, I am going to rain down for you bread from the heavens, and the people will go out and gather enough for the day on its day." (LEB)

This manna-bread (along with quail in the evening) sustained the food needs of the Israelites for forty years as they wandered through the desert. The Israelites associated this miracle with the leadership of Moses.

Now that the crowds have seen Jesus miraculously feed the thousands, they interpret this event as a sign that he is the prophet that Moses spoke of. They are in fact, correct in interpreting this sign. However, they are incorrect in that they assume Jesus intends to be an earthly king.

Even so, the crowd becomes intent on making Jesus their king. Jesus must elude the crowd and withdraws to a nearby mountain by himself. The fact that Jesus can miraculously feed them has them determined to follow him. After all, if this prophet can do miracles including feeding thousands, how much more could he do for them if he were indeed inaugurated as king? The excitement among the thousands that pursue him is palpable.

During the night, Jesus crosses the sea to Capernaum along with his disciples. This is in itself a miraculous event but has nothing to do with *zoe*, so we are going to skip discussing this journey. The next morning, the crowd realizes that Jesus and his disciples have left so they commandeer several boats and cross the sea to follow Jesus to Capernaum. When they find Jesus, they begin to question him about when he managed to get to this side of the sea. Jesus' reply (as we shall see) was not what they were expecting.

This sets up the crowd for "paradigm shift" teaching by Jesus. Jesus uses the miraculous feeding done the day before as a metaphor to lead them into deeper instruction. In this encounter, just as in John 5, most of his listeners will not accept his teaching.

I would encourage you to read all of John 6. It is very informative and powerful. But again, in the interest of staying on course in this section I am focusing on the verses that have to do with *zoe*.

We are going to pick up in John 6:25, the day after Jesus has fed the thousands.

> **John 6:25-27** And when they found him on the other side of the sea, they said to him, "Rabbi, when did you get here?" Jesus replied to them and said, "Truly, truly I say to you, you seek me not because you saw signs, but because you ate of the loaves and were satisfied! Do not work for the food that perishes, but the food that remains to **eternal life (zoe)**, which the Son of Man will give to you. For God the Father has set his seal on this one." (LEB)

Jesus confronts this crowd that followed him to Capernaum and tells them that they are seeking him not because they were convicted by the miracles, but because they ate the bread and were filled. He challenges them not to work for food that perishes but for food that remains unto eternal *zoe*.

Important: Notice the contrast that Jesus introduces here. He is contrasting food that perishes with food that remains, providing eternal zoe. He is just getting started with this contrast.

Jesus uses the crowd's focus on food to segue into that which is of vital importance. This is much like the segue that Jesus used with the woman at the well in John 4. If you recall, she was drawing water from the well which was a daily burden for her when Jesus challenged her to ask him for "water that wells up to eternal zoe." Now back to Jesus' current conversation:

> **John 6:28-29** So they said to him, "What shall we do that we can accomplish the works of God?" Jesus answered and said to them, "This is the work of God: that you believe in the one whom that one sent." (LEB)

The crowd asks Jesus what they must do, in order to accomplish the works that God requires. Jesus' reply is simple and to the point: "The work of God is this: believe in the one that he has sent."

Secondly, the Greek word for "sent" implies a commission. God has commissioned Jesus for a mission. He has not been randomly sent out. Jesus has a clear purpose. We will see Jesus gradually reveal his mission in its entirety by John chapter 10.

> **John 6:30-31** So they said to him, "Then what sign will you perform, so that we can see it and believe you? What will you do? Our fathers ate the manna in the wilderness, just as it is written, 'He gave them bread from heaven to eat.' (LEB)

The crowd then replies, "What sign will you show us that would give us reason to believe in you?" They go on to challenge Jesus, "Can you do what Moses did and provide us with manna from heaven to eat?" This is a two-fold challenge. First, they are asking Jesus to do something miraculous that compares with what Moses did. They are seeking confirmation. Jesus has already performed multiple miracles, including healing the diseased and feeding the five thousand. This should be adequate proof for them.

Jesus exposed their ulterior motive earlier in 6:26. Ultimately, they are looking for a king who can be a provider. They want someone to feed them. So, they are not only looking for confirmation. They want to see if he can continue to miraculously feed them.

> **John 6:32-33** Then Jesus said to them, "Truly, truly I say to you, Moses did not give you bread from heaven, but my Father is giving you the true bread from heaven! For the bread of God is the one who comes down from heaven and gives **life (zoe)** to the world." (LEB)

Jesus replies to their question about manna by correcting them. He instructs them that it wasn't Moses who gave them manna but it was his Father who provided for them.

He also says that now his Father is giving them "true bread from heaven" (Jesus uses this metaphor to allude to himself). Jesus uses the phrase "true bread from heaven" to emphasize the surpassing value of this true bread (compared to manna) that will give *zoe* to the world.

At this point the conversation between Jesus and the crowd becomes strained. First, they question how he can claim to come down from heaven. Then a little later in this conversation Jesus will say some very bizarre things in relation to the metaphor about him being the bread of life.

The first bread (manna) perished and so did the people who ate it.

In contrast, this true bread (referring to himself) will

give zoe (life forever) to the world.

Next, we see the crowd's response:

John 6:34 So they said to him, "Sir, always give us this bread!" (LEB)

Jesus's segue into the true bread that gives *zoe* to the world has gotten the crowd's attention. Jesus will now introduce a second and stronger metaphor as he transitions from the contrast with manna, to a timely parallel with the Passover dinner (these Jews will be eating the flesh of the Passover lamb later during this week of Passover).

Jesus continues to build on the powerful **contrast** between the "manna" that the Israelites ate in Moses day, and the "true bread" from heaven:

➢ He identifies himself as this bread of *zoe*.
➢ Jesus then uses *eating* as a metaphor for believing in Him.
➢ The effect of eating this "true bread" is quite different from the manna that the Israelites ate some 1300 years before.

THE BREAD OF ZOE SURPASSES MANNA

Jesus is going to emphasize himself as being the bread of zoe, to show it's surpassing greatness over the bread-manna. The reason the bread of zoe surpasses manna is because those who ate the manna *are now dead.* Jesus is going to explain that those who eat his flesh (a direct parallel with the Passover lamb) will not die, in fact he says they will live forever.

Living forever happens to be the major theme of John chapter 6.

Note: Each of these narratives have to do with consuming Jesus (metaphorically) and thus receiving zoe. This is the reason Jesus fluidly moves back and forth between these two metaphors (contrasting himself with manna while also paralleling himself with the Passover meal).

> The reason Jesus surpasses the manna is because those who ate the manna are now dead. Jesus is going to explain that those who eat his flesh will not die, in fact, he says they will live forever.

JESUS' "I AM" STATEMENTS

This sets up the first of the seven famous "I Am" statements that Jesus makes in John's gospel. Would it surprise you to know that every one of the "I Am" statements is directly tied to *zoe*?

I Am the Bread of Life (Zoe).
"I Am" Statement 1

John 6:35 Jesus said to them, "I am the bread of **life (zoe)**. The one who comes to me will never be hungry, and the one who believes in me will never be thirsty again. (LEB)

In John 6:35 Jesus introduces himself as the bread of zoe. He will continue by expanding upon this parallel with the Passover meal throughout the rest of John 6.

John chapter 6 simply boils down to this: a believer "eats and drinks" Jesus by coming to him for zoe, putting their trust (belief) in him as the son of God, and in what he did for them in his death on the cross, and his subsequent resurrection to zoe.

At this point Passover is only a few days away, so the sacrifice of the lamb, the significance of it's blood, and the eating of it's flesh, which would take place during the Passover meal would already be on the minds of the Jewish crowd. However, the crowd will fail to make this connection with the parallel that Jesus is making with the Passover lamb. They are going to be offended by what Jesus says as they take what he says literally. Jesus knows this, and apparently doesn't intend for them to understand all the contrasts and parallels he is making at this time. Later, after Jesus is resurrected from the dead and the Holy Spirit comes upon the disciples, the Spirit will give the disciples clear understanding of these teachings.

Jesus often spoke in parables and metaphors which were sometimes difficult to understand. Nowhere is this more apparent than in John 6.

Meanwhile this exchange with the crowd becomes more challenging as it goes back and forth. Let's pick up about halfway through the conversation in 6:47, where Jesus repeats, "I am the bread of life."

67

John 6:47-51 Truly, truly I say to you, the one who believes has **eternal life (zoe)**. I am the bread of **life (zoe)**. Your fathers ate the manna in the wilderness and they died. This is the bread that comes down from heaven so that someone may eat from it and **not die**. I am the **living** bread that came down from heaven. If anyone eats from this bread, **he will live forever**. And the bread that I will give for the **life (zoe)** of the world is my flesh." (LEB)

TWO BENEFITS FROM EATING THE BREAD OF ZOE

➢ You will not die

➢ You will live forever

Living forever (and not dying) happen to

be the main focus of John chapter 6.

Jesus is referring to the second death.

Living forever and not dying go together like a hand and glove. We will clearly see Jesus's perspective on death in the next few chapters in John's gospel, as Jesus ramps up this contrast of death versus eternal life. When Jesus says, 'you will not die', he is referring to the second death. Jesus is focused on the end game. Those individuals who were present that day, that had saving faith or would eventually come to have saving faith, have already died an earthly death. This was their first death. But they died with the assurance that their psuche was safe in Christ, that some day they will be resurrected from the dead to live again, this time forever. Those that are unsaved will be raised to judgment and will ultimately perish (die) in the second death. This is the death that Jesus is speaking of in 6:50.

Second look at John 6:50

> **John 6:50** This is the bread that comes down from heaven so that someone may eat from it and **not die** (LEB)

As Jesus mixes this metaphor of being the bread of zoe with the parallel of the Passover lamb, he takes this narrative about eating his flesh to another level. The crowd will see this as a bizarre statement. Since the parallel of the Passover lamb is based on Jesus's own bloody death on the cross a year later, there is no possible way for them to grasp what he is saying now. But Jesus was planting seed. He was sowing ideas that would come back to yield fruit in the days and years after his resurrection. He knew that most in the crowd this day would leave bewildered. We will see in a moment where even his closest disciples struggled with this teaching. This was a direct challenge to their tenacity. There was just no way they could connect the dots at this time. But this was Jesus's intent.

There were two aspects to this statement that this crowd struggles with.

First is the concept that Jesus wants the people to eat him. This gets even more bizarre in the next few verses. Jesus will extend this metaphor of eating himself to include drinking his blood.

Second, Jesus tells them that if they do eat him, they will not die. The crowd gets so hung-up taking Jesus' statement about "eating" him literally, that they fail to see the significance of the purpose of the statement . . . *that they can avoid death.*

> ➤ **Question:** What did the sacrifice of the Passover lamb 1300 years earlier save the firstborn Jews from?
> ➤ **Answer:** Death
> ➤ **Question:** What was the purpose of Passover week?
> ➤ **Answer:** It was an annual remembrance of God's deliverance of Israel, and the sacrifice of the Passover lamb to save the firstborn from death. This original event involved painting the blood of the lamb over the doorposts of their homes and eating the flesh of the lamb. Jesus's parallel to this is symbolic. The lamb was a fore-type of Jesus. It is Jesus flesh that died on the cross, and his blood that was spilled. This was done to save us from the second death. When in faith, we count on his death for us, to atone for our own death sentence, we can rest assured that we will not be judged but will be resurrected from our first death to eternal life. We will not be affected at all by the second death. (Revelation 2:11, 20:6,14,15)

WHOEVER EATS THIS BREAD WILL LIVE FOREVER

I am the living bread that came down from heaven. If anyone eats from this bread, he will live forever.

Jesus emphasizes that he is the "living bread" that came down from heaven. He goes on to explain that whoever eats this bread will live forever. Again, he is contrasting this living bread (himself) with manna. Those that ate the manna are all dead. Those that eat him (living bread) will live forever.

FURTHER DEFINING THE BREAD OF LIFE METAPHOR

When Jesus tells them that the bread he would give them to eat was his flesh, the Jews began to argue among themselves: "How can this man give us his flesh to eat?"

John 6:53 Then Jesus said to them, "Truly, truly I say to you, unless you eat the flesh of the Son of Man and drink his blood, you do not have **life (zoe)** in yourselves!" (LEB)

As the crowd begins to murmur about eating his flesh, Jesus emphatically restates what he just said. He prefaces the statement this time with, "Truly, truly I tell you." Then, he goes on to say, "Unless you eat the flesh of the Son of Man and drink his blood you have no life (zoe) in you." In addition, he now adds the part about drinking his blood.

John 6:54-55 The one who eats my flesh and drinks my blood has **eternal life (zoe)**, and I will raise him up on the last day. For my flesh is true food, and my blood is true drink. (LEB)

Just when his disciples were probably hoping Jesus would say something like, "Wow, did I just say that? What I really meant to say was something less offensive." But that doesn't happen. Instead, Jesus doubles down on this highly intentional metaphor about eating his flesh and drinking his blood.

RESURRECTION IS THE MAIN THING

Be sure to notice that Jesus defines eternal life in verse 55 by adding the details... "and I will raise him up on the last day".

Friend, this is what eternal zoe is all about, it is being raised from the dead on the resurrection day, to live forever.

This is the definition of eternal zoe:

It is being raised from the dead

on the resurrection day, to live forever.

John 6:56 The one who eats my flesh and drinks my blood resides in me and I in him. (LEB)

This concept of residing in Jesus comes from the Greek word *meno*, meaning "abide," "remain," or "reside." We abide in Jesus by always trusting in his identity as the son of God, and what he has done for us through his death upon the cross. Jesus then resides in us, via the indwelling Holy Spirit. The Holy Spirit indwells the believer, conveying immortal zoe unto the believer's psuche.

John 6:57 Just as the **living** Father sent me, and I **live** because of the Father, so also the one who eats me—that one will **live** because of me. (LEB)

If you recall from John 5:26, Jesus said that just as the Father has zoe within himself, thus he has granted to the Son to have zoe in himself.

John 5:26 For just as the Father has **life (zoe)** in himself, thus also he has granted to the Son to have **life (zoe)** in himself.

This is referring to Jesus having zoe as an intrinsic part of who he is. God and Jesus are immortal. There is some aspect of Jesus having zoe, that is dependent on the Father granting this to him. Don't ask me to explain it beyond that, because I don't know what else to say. Jesus has now alluded to this fact twice, here in 6:57 and previously in 5:26. But the takeaway here is that Jesus has zoe in himself, and he is going to give life (eternal zoe) to those who believe in him.

What Jesus is saying here in 6:57 is that just as the living Father sent me, so also the one who eats me, that one will live because of me. Jesus is again speaking of the future resurrection here. Notice he says "<u>will</u> live". He is not speaking of the here and now, but the future resurrection. The word live here is the verb form of zoe.

Also don't miss the fact that Jesus emphasizes "the <u>living</u> Father". I missed this significance before I learned about how zoe is being used. Now I see this "living God" concept being used throughout the New Testament. It is highly significant, keep an eye out for it's use.

All of these variations of zoe are still based on the fact that at it's core the word zoe means, "the state of being alive".

Note: Zoe is the opposite of death. Psuche on the other hand can die, and in fact will die forever, if that person rejects Jesus. A person's psuche is not inherently immortal. Immortality only comes from the gift of eternal zoe.

So, when Jesus says that person <u>will live</u>, he is specifically speaking of that person (their psuche) being raised from the dead to live again, this time forever.

Zoe and death are opposites.

Psuche on the other hand can die, and in fact

will die forever, if that person rejects Jesus.

A person's psuche is mortal.

Immortality only comes from Eternal Zoe.

12

Prelude to Passover

I'd like to call your attention to the following verses from earlier in John 6. If you recall, this chapter started with Jesus feeding the 5,000. Notice the mention of the impending Passover.

> **John 6:2-6** And a large crowd was following him because they were observing the signs that he was doing on those who were sick. So Jesus went up on the mountain and sat down there with his disciples. (Now the Passover, the feast of the Jews, was near.) Then Jesus, when he looked up and saw that a large crowd was coming to him, said to Philip, "Where can we buy bread so that these people can eat?" (Now he said this to test him, because he knew what he was going to do.) (LEB)

This particular Passover will take place exactly one year before Jesus will be crucified. This is very significant, and as you have already seen is directly tied to what Jesus is saying here in John 6. For the entire account of the Passover, see chapter 12 in the Old Testament book of Exodus.

The annual Passover meal that the Jews observed was a memorial of what God had done to deliver the Israelites from slavery to Egypt, some 1300 years earlier. At that time, God commanded that they commemorate this Passover deliverance in the future as a feast.

> **Exodus 12:14** And this day will become a memorial for you, and you will celebrate it as a religious feast for Yahweh throughout your generations; you will celebrate it as a lasting statute. (LEB)

This deliverance ultimately required the sacrifice of the Passover lamb during the 10th and final plague that God wrought on Egypt. This last plague was known as the "death of the first born".

As we see in the verses below, this deliverance required the Israelites to slaughter a lamb and then paint the blood of the lamb on the doorposts and lintel of the doorway of their home. During the night as the plague of the "death of the firstborn" was wrought on Egypt, any home that had the blood of the lamb covering their doorway was protected from the destroyer. The destroyer would "pass over" that home, not killing any of the first born in that home.

> **Exodus 12:21-27** Then Moses called all the elders of Israel and said to them, "Go and select lambs for yourselves according to your clans, and kill the Passover lamb. Take a bunch of hyssop and dip it in the blood that is in the basin, and touch the lintel and the two doorposts with the blood that is in the basin. None of you shall go out of the door of his house until the morning. For the Lord will pass through to strike the Egyptians, and when he sees the blood on the lintel and on the two doorposts, the Lord will pass over the door and will not allow the destroyer to enter your houses to strike you. You shall observe this rite as a statute for you and for your sons forever. And when you come to the land that the

Lord will give you, as he has promised, you shall keep this service. And when your children say to you, 'What do you mean by this service?' you shall say, 'It is the sacrifice of the Lord's Passover, for he passed over the houses of the people of Israel in Egypt, when he struck the Egyptians but spared our houses.'" (ESV)

The annual *memorial* of the Passover that the Jews in Jesus day were observing incorporated a meal in the evening, after the Passover lamb had been slain and roasted during the afternoon. This meal focused on eating the meat of the lamb, along with bitter herbs and unleavened bread. The bitter herbs signified the bitter suffering that the Jews had endured under slavery to Egypt. The unleavened bread memorialized the haste in which the Jews left Egypt after the 10th plague of "The Passover" had been wrought on Egypt. The roasted "flesh" of the lamb recalled the lamb that was sacrificed.

In John 6, as Jesus is telling the Jews that they must eat his flesh and drink his blood, he is making a direct parallel to the Passover lamb. This was the most important feast and memorial that the Jews held every year, and their minds would have already been dwelling on this impending important sacrifice. They were accustomed to eating the flesh of the Passover lamb. Each time they did, they would recall how the lamb was sacrificed to protect the Jews on that day from the death of their firstborn, and subsequent delivery from slavery.

When Jesus speaks of eating his flesh, he is making a direct connection to the Passover lamb. When he speaks of drinking his blood, he is making a direct connection to the blood of the lamb that was spread around the doorway.

Most of the Jews listening to Jesus certainly did not put these connections together at that time. They struggled with what Jesus was telling them. As we will see, even his disciples struggled with understanding this. It would not be until after Jesus' resurrection that his disciples would understand these connections.

JESUS IS OUR PASSOVER LAMB

Jesus has become the Passover lamb for all who will put their trust in his sacrifice. His death will be a substitute for ours. His blood will cover our sins and protect us from the sentence of death. The first Passover lamb was a "type" or "shadow" of who Jesus would ultimately be.

Jesus is seen as the "lamb of God", throughout the New Testament. In John 1, John the Baptist called Jesus the "Lamb of God."

> **John 1:29** On the next day he saw Jesus coming to him and said, "Look! The Lamb of God who takes away the sin of the world! (LEB)

Paul calls Jesus the "our Passover lamb" in his first letter to Corinth.

> **1 Corinthians 5:7** For Christ, our Passover lamb, has been sacrificed. (ESV)

Peter refers to the precious blood of Jesus, like that of lamb without spot or blemish.

1 Peter 1:19 but with the precious blood of Christ, like that of an unblemished and spotless lamb

---

Jesus has become the Passover lamb for all who

will put their trust in his sacrifice.

His death will be a substitute for ours.

His blood will cover our sins and

protect us from the sentence of death.

Additional Significance of the Blood of Jesus

Note: The focus of this book is not on the significance of the "blood" of Jesus, but I would like to share a couple more verses regarding this. The blood of Jesus has covered the believer's sins, (forgiving them). This action then imputes Jesus' righteousness to the believer, declaring them righteous solely by the blood of Jesus.

Standing in this righteousness, it is Jesus' resurrection from the dead to zoe, that gives the believer assurance of their own resurrection. The power behind this sure hope for the believer is in the zoe of Jesus that lives within the believer. It is the zoe of Christ that will ultimately raise the believer from the dead to live forever.

> **Rom. 5:9-10** Therefore, by much more, because **we have been declared righteous now by his blood**, we will be saved through him from the wrath. For if, while we were enemies, we were reconciled to God through the death of his Son, by much more, having been reconciled, **we will be saved by his life (zoe)**. (LEB)

Throughout the Old Testament, there is a strong connection of the shedding of blood with forgiveness (in addition to the Passover). The priests would make annual sacrifices of animals for the forgiveness of sin. (See Leviticus 4).

In Hebrews 9, the author goes into historical detail about how Jesus' sacrifice of his own blood was superior to the animal sacrifices performed by priests. I would recommend reading Hebrews 9:11-28 for an in-depth understanding of this concept, but for brevity I am only showing 9:22 below.

> **Heb. 9:22** Indeed, nearly everything is purified with blood according to the law, and **apart from the shedding of blood there is no forgiveness**. (LEB)

FINAL NOTE ABOUT PASSOVER

There are so many "types" of Jesus from the Old Testament and so many fulfillment of prophecies about him from the OT as well, that at any given moment in the gospels, there may be more than one fulfillment going on. This is basically what is occurring here in John 6. Jesus makes a direct contrast between himself and manna in this chapter, while at the same time draws a parallel of himself to the Passover lamb.

Both of these "types" that Jesus fulfills here are very powerful, and both directly point to Jesus saving mankind from _death_. In addition, the Bread of _Zoe_ then provides man with eternal life (_zoe_). Of course, this is only available to those who wholeheartedly believe in Jesus' identity.

Manna & the Passover Lamb

Both of these "types" that Jesus fulfills in John 6 are very powerful.

Jesus being the Bread of Zoe is in direct contrast to the manna that was incapable of saving the Jews from dying. In contrast, Jesus said that anyone who eats of the Bread of Zoe will not die.

The eating of Jesus' flesh and drinking his blood is a direct parallel to the Passover lamb that saved the Jews from death.

Jesus says that anyone who (metaphorically) eats his flesh and drinks his blood will be raised from the dead to Eternal Zoe.

Don't miss the fact that both of these "types" are used by Jesus to emphasize that he came to save mankind from Death!

THE CURSE OF DEATH

Remember Jesus' statement in John 5:

> **John 5:21** For just as the Father raises the dead and **makes them alive**, thus also the Son **makes alive** whomever he wishes. (LEB)

Ever since Adam and Eve were cast from the Garden of Eden and thus prevented from having access to the tree of life, mankind has faced the certainty of death. The fruit of the tree of life would have enabled Adam and Eve to live forever. God warned Adam that if he were to eat of the tree of knowledge of good and evil, that he would surely die.

Indeed, Adam did die. His access to the tree of life was taken away from him. Adam exchanged immortality for mortality. We will see this as a powerful teaching not only from Jesus. The apostle Paul hammers on this as a core issue of Christianity. We will look at his writings on this shortly.

If man were to ever have hope of immortality again and restore that level of intimate fellowship with God the Father, we would need intervention on our behalf. God indeed had a plan of intervention. His plan was his son Jesus, and the restoration of *zoe*. But there was a problem.

The problem was that the penalty for Adam's sin had remained imposed on all mankind since that day. We have all been born under that curse. We are destined to be born and die. Our *psuche* has no hope of immortality. The penalty of death has been decreed and cannot be revoked. We have no hope of removing this curse ourselves. Our death is certain unless someone intervenes.

Someone has…

THE CURSE OF DEATH WILL BE REMOVED

John shows us in Revelation that the curse of death will ultimately be removed. Notice that as the river of the water of zoe flows from the throne of God and the lamb, as well as from the tree of zoe, the curse of death will be done away with forever. It is the water of life (symbolic reference to the zoe-giving Holy Spirit) that replaces the curse of death with eternal zoe.

> **Revelation 22:1-3** And he showed me the river of the water of life (zoe), clear as crystal, coming out from the throne of God and of the Lamb in the middle of its street, and on both sides of the river is the **tree of life (zoe)**, producing twelve fruits—yielding its fruit according to every month—and the leaves of the tree are for the healing of the nations. And **there will not be any curse any longer**, and the throne of God and of the Lamb will be in it. (LEB)

> **Revelation 21:3-8** And I heard a loud voice from the throne saying, "Behold, the dwelling of God is with humanity, and he will take up residence with them, and they will be his people and God himself will be with them. 4 And he will wipe away every tear from their eyes, and **death will not exist any longer**, and mourning or wailing or pain will not exist any longer. The former things have passed away."5 And the one seated on the throne said, "Behold, I am making all things new!" And he said, "Write, because these words are faithful and true." 6 And he said to me, "It is done! I am the Alpha and the Omega, the beginning and the end. **To the one who is thirsty I will give water from the spring of the water of life freely**. 7 The one who conquers will inherit these things, and I will be his God and he will be my son. 8 But as for the cowards and unbelievers and detestable persons and murderers and sexually immoral people and sorcerers and idolaters and all liars, their share is in the lake that burns with fire and sulphur, **which is the second death**. (LEB)

13

Eating Jesus, and Drinking His Blood - What It Means

It is when we believe in Jesus and consciously depend on the sacrifice of his death on the cross for us that we *metaphorically* eat his flesh and drink his blood.

EATING JESUS' FLESH

When Jesus said that we must eat his "flesh", he was referring to his "body" that was crucified on the cross. Earlier, we learned that we consume Jesus (the bread of *zoe*) by believing in him and depending on him as the giver of *zoe*. It is by our active *dependence* on the sacrifice of his body (his death on the cross) that we metaphorically eat his flesh.

DRINKING JESUS' BLOOD

His blood is referring to his actual blood that he bled out during his crucifixion. However, the phrase "drinking his blood" is also metaphorical, in the sense that we drink his blood by actively *counting* on his blood to cover (or forgive) our sins.

Remember, Jesus had just answered the question that the crowd asked him, "what must we do to be doing the work that God requires?" Jesus answered, "Believe in the one he has sent".

SUMMARY: EATING JESUS' FLESH AND DRINKING HIS BLOOD

In summary, when we do the following things, we are *figuratively feeding* on Jesus.

- ➢ Wholeheartedly believe Jesus is the Son of God.
- ➢ Lay hold of his sacrifice on the cross by counting on his death as payment for our own death sentence.
- ➢ Count on his blood for the forgiveness of our sins.

Believing in him, trusting him, and depending on him

for what he has done for us on the cross **is**

the metaphorical eating and drinking of Jesus.

There is nothing literal about what he is saying here. Don't get hung up on literally eating and drinking Jesus. These verses have no direct connection with partaking (eating) of the Lord's Supper or believing that a cracker miraculously turns into his body (the notion of transubstantiation), etc.

Note: Jesus does later institute the memorial known as the Lord's Supper in the gospels (Matthew 26:26-29, Luke 22:14-20, Mark 14:22-25) the night before he is crucified. But even in these instances, it is not commanded or portrayed as a literal eating of Jesus' flesh and blood. Jesus says to do this "in remembrance of me." It is a memorial, just as the Passover was a memorial.

Partaking of the bread and wine is a symbolic remembrance (memorial) of what Jesus has done for us. In 1 Corinthians 11:23-26, the apostle Paul says we not only do this to commemorate Jesus' death and resurrection, but also to proclaim his death and resurrection until he returns.

IMPORTANCE OF RESURRECTION

Had Jesus not died and then resurrected, his teachings on eternal zoe and our assurance of resurrection from the dead would be meaningless. It is indeed his resurrection that punctuates the entire problem that mankind that has faced since Eden, specifically... death. Jesus came to give us eternal zoe, in lieu of eternal death.

After his apostles understood these things, spreading this truth would become their lifelong purpose. They themselves would be transformed by the truth of Jesus' teachings, but only after Jesus was resurrected from the dead and the Holy Spirit was bequeathed to them by Jesus.

The Spirit then helped them to recall his teachings and understand them. These transformed men then went into the world, taking the message with them. They gave the rest of their lives to spreading this gospel ("gospel" means "good news") throughout the nations. In fact, all but two of the apostles died as martyrs for preaching about Jesus. Would you like to take a guess as to which one of them died in their old age? I will share this answer at the end of this chapter.

EAT THIS BREAD AND LIVE FOREVER

> **John 6:58** "This is the bread that came down from heaven, not as the fathers ate and died. The one who eats this bread will **live forever**." (LEB)

Jesus once again contrasts the difference between the manna that their ancestors ate with the bread from heaven (himself). The difference is that those ancestors died, while those who feed on the "true bread" from heaven will live forever.

John 6:60 Thus many of his disciples, when they heard it, said, "This saying is hard! Who can understand it?" (LEB)

It is not only the crowd that struggles with this metaphor. His disciples who have accompanied him for much of his ministry (including the twelve apostles) struggle with understanding and accepting this metaphor as well.

John 6:61-63 But Jesus, because he knew within himself that his disciples were grumbling about this, said to them, "Does this cause you to be offended? Then what if you see the Son of Man ascending where he was before? The Spirit is the one who gives **life (zoe)**; the flesh profits nothing. The words that I have spoken to you are spirit and are **life (zoe)**. (LEB)

Jesus gives another important clarification here. He explains that it is the Spirit that gives life (*zoe*).

The Spirit is the one who gives life (zoe); the flesh profits nothing

The flesh is of no help when it comes to getting *zoe*. Some English versions translate this as "the flesh counts for nothing." The flesh is just part of the bodily experience and can do nothing to help a person gain eternal life (*zoe*).

Jesus reiterates the importance of the Holy Spirit in the next verse.

The words that I have spoken to you are spirit and are life (zoe).

He explains, "The words I am speaking to you, they are spirit and life". In other words, don't get hung up on the flesh and blood stuff. I am speaking to you using Passover metaphors with fleshly terms that are illustrating a spiritual truth. It is as if Jesus is saying, "Everything I have been saying to you is about what the Spirit will do in the believer. It will impart *zoe* into the believer, so that ultimately the believer will not die at the second death, but will instead be resurrected from the dead to live forever.

HOLDING ON TO WHAT YOU KNOW AND BELIEVE

John 6:66-69 For this reason many of his disciples drew back and were not walking with him any longer. So Jesus said to the twelve, "You do not want to go away also, do you?" Simon Peter answered him, "Lord, to whom would we go? You have the words of **eternal life (zoe)**. And we have believed, and have come to know, that you are the Holy One of God." (LEB)

Jesus knew that many in the crowd were going to leave. Now he challenges his disciples testing their tenacity. At some point in our human lifetimes, we are going to run into confusion or difficult times that may be very hard for us to cope with or to understand. These difficulties can sometimes last for a season of life and can be very dark and confusing.

But we can choose to be like Peter and say, "Where else can we go? You have the words of eternal *zoe*. We have come to believe and to know that you are the Holy One of God."

Peter may not have understood all the metaphors that Jesus was using on this day. But he did know one thing for certain, Jesus had the "words of eternal zoe". No amount of doubt or confusion was going to detract Peter from holding onto that belief.

What a great example: hold on to what we know, even if everything else is confusing. Hold on to Jesus. He has the words of eternal *zoe*. There is no other way to *zoe*.

KEY CONCEPTS DEFINED IN JOHN 6

There are several major definitions from Jesus in John 6. He introduced these concepts in previous chapters of John, but now he gives us deeper insight.

- ➢ Death is the problem.
- ➢ There is a solution that will keep a person from dying. It is the bread of life *(zoe),* which a person can consume figuratively (by believing in Jesus and counting on his death on the cross as payment for their own penalty of death).
- ➢ It is the Spirit of God that gives (imparts) *zoe*.

WHAT IS LEFT TO DEFINE?

Jesus has introduced what he identifies as the problem of mankind and God's solution. The problem is death due to sin. His solution is *eternal zoe* for those who will put their trust in him.

But, at this point we do not have Jesus' complete definition of death. What does it mean to be in a state of death, and what does that look like for our *psuche* after we die on earth?

Jesus will unfold this over the next five chapters of John. When we finally understand just what Jesus is saving us from, his mission will be totally apparent to us.

Without a clear understanding of death we are left with a blurry interpretation of the message of salvation, resulting in inaccurate doctrine.

Now, for the answer to the earlier question about which apostle died in their old age: the apostle John, who wrote the gospel according to John, died around AD 102. In addition to the gospel according to John, he also wrote 1st, 2nd, and 3rd John and the Book of Revelation. While John did not die as a martyr, he was persecuted for his teaching and was exiled to the island of Patmos until he was very old. It was on the island of Patmos that he received the vision of Revelation. It is believed he was eventually released from Patmos due to old age, then moved to Ephesus where he later died of natural causes.

14

John 8 - I Am the Light of the World

As we move into John 8, we come to a flash point between Jesus and the Jews—even many of the Jews who have believed in him thus far. Jesus is trying to break through paradigms and traditions that the Jews have strongly adhered to for millennia. However, he is not willing to patronize them just to maintain their loyalty.

He knows he is only with them for short time. Jesus must challenge them to see the truth, to come to his light and to come to him for *zoe*, even at the risk of offending them. This is not a debate for the curious observer. Jesus pushes everyone to the limit of their beliefs and understanding. He offers them the opportunity **to be set free**. Those who choose to be offended will be left in **slavery**.

John 8 is literally a do-or-die chapter. This chapter is a clash between eternal truth and long-held assumptions, between life (*zoe*) and death. Those with the fortitude to hold on to Jesus' teaching through this struggle for clarity shall become children of God.

I Am the Light of the World.

"I Am" Statement 2

Jesus begins this conversation in 8:12 with another "I Am" statement.

> **John 8:12** Then Jesus spoke to them again, saying, "I am the light of the world! The one who follows me will never walk in darkness, but will have the **light of life (zoe)**." (LEB)

LIGHT OF THE WORLD ILLUMINATES PATH TO *ZOE*

Jesus is the light of the world, because he reveals the path to eternal life. Those who follow him will not continue to walk in darkness of this world, but will see the path to eternal life.

THERE ARE TWO ASPECTS TO THIS LIGHT

First Aspect – Zoe saves us from the darkness of death. All mankind is currently living in the darkness of sin and death. Jesus brings the light of *zoe* into this dark realm, thus bringing the certainty of *zoe* to all who otherwise face certain death. Remember, believers cross over from death to *zoe*.

Isaiah prophesies of the birth of Jesus into this land of darkness:

Isaiah 9:2 The people who walked in darkness have seen a great light, light has shined on those who lived in a land of darkness … (LEB)

Isaiah 9:6 The For a child has been born for us; a son has been given to us. And the dominion will be on his shoulder, and his name is called Wonderful Counselor, Mighty God, Everlasting Father, Prince of Peace (LEB)

John the Baptist was born about 6 months prior to Jesus' birth. His father Zechariah (who had been mute during his wife's pregnancy), begins speaking the following prophetic words about his son John after his birth. Zechariah is quoting from Isaiah as he makes this prophecy. He is prophesying about his son John ("you will go before the Lord to prepare his ways"), and then prophecies about Jesus. When he speaks of the sunrise and light he is referring to Jesus. Notice the connection between darkness and the "shadow of death".

Luke 1:76-79 And so you, child, will be called the prophet of the Most High, for you will go on before the Lord to prepare his ways, to give knowledge of salvation to his people by the forgiveness of their sins, because of the merciful compassion of our God by which the dawn will visit to help us from on high, **to give light to those who sit in darkness and in the shadow of death**, to direct our feet into the way of peace (LEB)

In Matthew's gospel, he points out that Jesus's ministry begins as a fulfillment of these same verses from Isaiah:

Matthew 4:13-16 And leaving Nazareth, he went and lived in Capernaum by the sea, in the region of Zebulun and Naphtali, in order that what was spoken by the prophet Isaiah would be fulfilled, who said, "Land of Zebulun and land of Naphtali, toward the sea, on the other side of the Jordan, Galilee of the Gentiles the people who sit in darkness **have seen a great light, and the ones who sit in the land and shadow of death**, a light has dawned on them. (LEB)

David also speaks of darkness and death in the 23rd Psalm. There are two snippets from Psalm 23 where it appears David's confidence in the Lord is directly tied to his assurance that God will deliver him when he goes through the valley of shadow of death, and his ultimate confidence of his resurrection to be with the Lord forever.

Psalm 23:4,6 Even though I walk through the valley of the **shadow of death**, I will fear no evil… and I shall dwell in the house of the Lord forever.

Note: Mankind lives in the shadow of death. The certainty and permanence of death that looms over all men casts a dark shadow. The traditional view does not understand this significance, and underplays the role of death in the destiny of man. In fact, the traditional view practically ignores the significance of death, due to its fastidious preoccupation with its notion of "hell", and its assumption that all men are immortal.

It should be noted that neither John nor Paul, ever used the Greek word Gehenna (most often translated as hell) in any of their 18 books of the New Testament. If hell was the issue, they would have mentioned it. The true issue from Genesis to Revelation is "death".

Second Aspect – Walking in the light means that believers will have the Spirit of Christ to help them navigate through their journey in this first lifetime with wisdom and insight. Believers have the *zoe* of Jesus within them via the indwelling Holy Spirit.

This insight is not available from human wisdom or any philosophy of man. It is not a matter of having a high IQ, a good education or life experiences. This is not merely a statement where Jesus suggests that his wisdom is better than that which the world gives.

Jesus is categorically stating that he is truly the only light of the world. He is using the metaphor of light to illustrate a vital reality. Without his light your world is dark. You don't have the tools to identify and navigate the realities that exist all around you because you can't see them. The only way to have this light, this discernment, is via the indwelling Holy Spirit.

15

John 8 — Dying in Sin

DYING IN SIN

In 8:21, Jesus sternly warns those who are listening about the consequences of failing to believe that he is the Messiah. The consequences: **they will die in their sin.**

> **John 8:21-24** So he said to them again, "I am going away, and you will seek me and will die in your sin. Where I am going you cannot come!" Then the Jews began to say, "Perhaps he will kill himself, because he is saying, 'Where I am going you cannot come.'" And he said to them, "You are from below; I am from above. You are from this world; I am not from this world. Thus I said to you that **you will die in your sins**. For if you do not believe that I am he, **you will die in your sins**. (LEB)

Jesus just told them three times in this text that it is possible they will die in their sins.

WHAT DOES JESUS MEAN BY, "YOU WILL DIE IN YOUR SINS?"

Admittedly, this concept of dying in our sins is very significant. Even if we may not completely understand what Jesus means, it is certain that no one would want to die in their sin.

So, just exactly what does Jesus mean by the term "die in our sins?" At this point in our study, which of the following choices do you think best describes what Jesus is saying **here**?

- When we die, we won't go to heaven.
- When we die, we will end up in hell.
- My sins will end up killing me because they are bad for my health.
- My sins have such a grip on me that I cannot seem to get away from them, and I will end up dying in this condition.
- I am already under a status (or sentence) of death according to Jesus (due to sin). Therefore, if I don't believe in him my destiny of death will remain unchanged. I need a savior to save me from my current fate.

Let's see if we can zero in on what Jesus is saying. Earlier, in John 5:24, Jesus said that those who have believed have crossed over from a status of death . . . to a status of life (*zoe*). Here in John 8, Jesus merely restates the exact same precept but points out the negative consequence instead of just focusing on eternal *zoe*. He is using the carrot and the stick approach. Up until now in his teachings, Jesus has primarily focused on the positive aspect of receiving *eternal zoe* if we believe. Now he is hitting the self-righteous, judgmental Pharisees with the stick, that they will die in their sin.

A MODERN DAY METAPHOR OF A SAVIOR: A FIREMAN

By not believing Jesus a person stays stuck in the condemned sentence (of death) that they have been living under due to the consequences of sin. This would be like refusing to accept the hand of a fireman who can pull you out of a burning building. You would be in effect destined to die since you are already in the burning building. You face certain death unless you take the hand of the fireman. Your status doesn't change if you refuse to take the fireman's hand, because you were going to die anyway before the fireman showed up. However, if you take the fireman's hand your status changes from one of certain death to one of being saved. You have received your life back so to speak.

If a person chooses to believe in Jesus, they cross over from death to life. The status of death is due to sin. So, if a person chooses not to believe, they merely remain in a status of death. If they never believe, then they will ultimately die in their sin.

If a person chooses to believe in Jesus, they cross over from death to life. If a person never believes, they merely remain in a status of death and will ultimately die in their sin.

APPLICATION

The following is essentially what happens when we believe. Our *psuche* is essentially preserved (saved from death) by the gift of eternal *zoe* (assurance of living forever). Although this gift is offered to all mankind for no more than believing with all their heart (it is free), it came with the ultimate price. *Jesus paid for this by laying down his own psuche, thus taking our death penalty in our stead.*

Jesus clearly predicts his death (of his *psuche*) in John 10. Jesus will allow himself to be tortured nearly to the point of death and then subsequently be killed by crucifixion. There is no question about this; Jesus' *psuche* is going to be killed. He is going to die.

Why would Jesus willingly do this? Because he knew that the penalty of sin (since the fall of Adam) was the impending death of **our** *psuche*. The Father's plan was to redeem all mankind who would believe by sending his Son to die in our place. Jesus took our death penalty upon himself. If we but accept the crucifixion of his body for us, accept the spilling of his blood in lieu of ours, and follow him with all our heart, we not only get our status of death removed, but we <u>also</u> receive eternal zoe, enabling us to become children of God and live forever.

There are also immediate blessings that come with this gift that we begin receiving at the moment of belief. We do not have to wait until our physical death to reap the benefits of participating in the divine nature. This gift of *zoe* not only allows us to live forever; it allows us to enjoy sweet fellowship with the Father and the Son in the here and now. The Spirit will flow from within us today to give us the opportunity of understanding, insight, and greater faith, resulting in the bearing of the fruit of the Spirit (see Galatians 5:22-23).

Spoiler Alert: It's possible you may be a bit confused at this point with all this talk about the penalty of death, dying in sin, having an initial status of death, crossing over to life (zoe), and so forth. I'm just giving you a heads up. It is going to continue to be a bit confusing until we get through a few more chapters.

Some of this confusion is due to the incorrect paradigm about death that so strongly influences current Christian thought.

What I can tell you at this point which may help some with the confusion, is that Jesus primary mission is not concerned with saving you from your earthly death. He is very intent however, in saving you from the second death. It is the second death that is at the core of what Jesus has been talking about this whole time in the gospel according to John.

Jesus will thoroughly define this issue in the next few chapters.

However, this does not mean that our psuche (in this lifetime) is beneath his concern. That is hardly the case. But as we will see when Jesus is speaking of not dying or never dying, he is referring to the second death, not someone's earthly death (first death).

Remember, Jesus frequently talks about zoe proleptically, referring to the absolute assurance that the believer has of their psuche being raised from the dead to eternal zoe. (The state of being alive forever).

Resurrection has *always* been the end game of Jesus message.

Resurrection has always been the end game of Jesus message

16

John 8 - Jesus Indicts Satan

JESUS INDICTS SATAN FOR THE DEATH OF ADAM AND EVE

John 8:31-42 Then Jesus said to those Jews who had believed him, "If you continue in my word you are truly my disciples, and you will know the truth, and the truth will set you free." They replied to him, "We are descendants of Abraham and have not been enslaved to anyone at any time. How do you say, 'You will become free'?" Jesus replied to them, "Truly, truly I say to you, that everyone who commits sin is a slave of sin. And the slave does not remain in the household forever; the son remains forever. So if the son sets you free, you will be truly free. I know that you are descendants of Abraham. But you are seeking to kill me, because my word makes no progress among you. I speak the things that I have seen with the Father; so also you do the things that you have heard from the Father." They answered and said to him, "Abraham is our father!" Jesus said to them, "If you are children of Abraham, do the deeds of Abraham! But now you are seeking to kill me, a man who spoke to you the truth which I heard from God. This Abraham did not do. You are doing the deeds of your father!" They said to him, "We were not born from sexual immorality! We have one father, God!" Jesus said to them, "If God were your father, you would love me, for I have come forth from God and have come. For I have not come from myself, but that one sent me. (LEB

As we continue in John 8, the crowd insults Jesus by accusing him of being an illegitimate child.

The crowd makes this angry accusation about Jesus right after he challenges their claim that they are free. Their claim was based solely on being physical descendants of Abraham.

Jesus takes this discussion a step further by saying Abraham is not their Father, but rather Satan is.

John 8:43-47 "Why do you not understand my way of speaking? Because you are not able to listen to my message. You are of your father the **devil**, and you want to do the desires of your father! **That one was a murderer from the beginning**, and does not stand firm in the truth, because truth is not in him. Whenever he speaks the lie, he speaks from his own nature, because **he is a liar and the father of lies**. But because I am telling the truth, you do not believe me. Who among you convicts me concerning sin? If I am telling the truth, why do you not believe me? The one who is from God listens to the words of God. Because of this you do not listen—because you are not of God." (LEB)

There are a lot of points that could be made here. Jesus doesn't say that their father is the devil just to retaliate to their insult. He points out that they cannot understand what he is saying because they belong to the devil, who fathers their deception. In addition, within a year's time there are those in the crowd who will want to murder Jesus, following in the steps of their father (Satan), who was a murderer from the beginning.

But for our purpose, we are going to focus on what Jesus says about Satan (the devil).

JESUS EXPLAINS SEVERAL FACTS ABOUT SATAN

➢ He was a murderer from the beginning.
➢ He does not hold to the truth.
➢ There is no truth in him.
➢ Lies are his native language.
➢ He is the father of lies.

GENESIS 3:1-6

When Jesus says Satan was a "murderer from the beginning," he is referring to the account of Adam and Eve in the book of Genesis (the Hebrew word *genesis* means "beginning").

> **Gen. 3:1-6** Now the serpent was more crafty than any other wild animal which Yahweh God had made. He said to the woman, "Did God indeed say, 'You shall not eat from any tree in the garden'?" The woman said to the serpent, "From the fruit of the trees of the garden we may eat, but from the tree that is in the midst of the garden, God said, 'You shall not eat from it, nor shall you touch it, lest you die'." **But the serpent said to the woman, "You shall not surely die**. For God knows that on the day you both eat from it, then your eyes will be opened and you both shall be like gods, knowing good and evil." When the woman saw that the tree was good for food and that it was a delight to the eyes, and the tree was desirable to make one wise, then she took from its fruit and she ate. And she gave it also to her husband with her, and he ate. (LEB)

Satan lied to Eve in the garden of Eden leading her to stray from the truth. In turn Eve convinced Adam to follow her in this deception, and they sinned. The result was death. Jesus is indicting Satan for the death (murder) of Adam and Eve at the beginning. On the day that Adam and Eve disobeyed God and ate of the forbidden tree, they were cast out of the Garden of Eden and lost access to the "tree of zoe".

They were now under a sentence of death since they no longer had access to the tree of zoe (zoe means being alive), which provided them immortality. This resulting banishment from the tree of life in the Garden of Eden left Adam and Eve with the certain impending death of their *psuche*. This action has resulted in all mankind living in a state of certain death to this day.

Satan continues to attempt to deceive you and me every day, trying to prevent us from understanding the truth, in hopes that he can keep us in a state of death. He was a murderer from the beginning, and he continues to be. He is intent on murdering you! In fact, he has basically already accomplished this. You are trapped in your mortality unless you accept Jesus' gift of eternal *zoe*.

The resulting banishment from the Tree of Life in the Garden of Eden
left Adam and Eve with the certain impending death of their psuche.
This action has resulted in all mankind living under this
state of impending death. We need a Savior.

SATAN IS STILL AT WORK IN THE *PSUCHE* OF UNBELIEVERS

In the verses below, the apostle Paul lays out 4 important points:

➢ Prior to believing in Jesus, his readers were dead in their sins.
➢ Satan is still at work in unbelievers who are unwittingly doing his will in their flesh and mind.
➢ Prior to believing, Paul's readers were children of wrath, as all mankind has been since Adam.
➢ Even though we were "dead" in our trespasses (sin), God made us alive together with Christ.

Eph. 2:1-5 And you, although you were **dead in your trespasses and sins**, in which you formerly walked according to the course of this world, according to the ruler of the authority of the air, the spirit now working in the sons of disobedience, among whom also we all formerly lived in the desires of our flesh, doing the will of the flesh and of the mind, and we were children of wrath by nature, as also the rest of them were. But God, being rich in mercy, because of his great love with which he loved us, and **we being dead in trespasses, he made us alive together with Christ** (by grace you are saved) (LEB)

Paul says we were (past tense) dead in our trespasses and sins. And that even though we were dead in trespasses, God has made us alive (in verse 5, the word alive has zoe at it's root) with Christ. This is much like the statement that Jesus himself made in John chapter 5, where he describes this process as crossing over from a status of "death" to a status of "*zoe*".

This takes place when the believer is born again (this second birth is not of the flesh, but of the Holy Spirit). The Holy Spirit comes to live within the psuche of the believer, upon their belief. The believer then becomes a child of God.

We will take a look at Paul's clear teaching on this concept of life and death in the next chapter.

PAUL'S TEACHINGS ON DEATH FROM 1 CORINTHIANS

The apostle Paul addresses this issue of death in two of his letters to the early churches. Paul wrote the first letter to the church at Corinth about two decades after Jesus' resurrection. He wrote the letter to the church at Rome a few years later.

In these letters, Paul points out a stark contrast between Adam and Jesus.

We will look first at Paul's explanation in 1 Corinthians 15.

1 Cor. 15:21-22 For since through a man came death, also through a man came the resurrection of the dead. For just as in Adam **all die**, so also in Christ **all will be made alive**. (LEB)

Paul begins this section on the *resurrection* by introducing the fact that death came to all mankind through Adam. By contrast, the resurrection of the dead comes through Jesus. Notice the emphasis on the fact that in Christ all *will be made "alive"*.

There are three points to see here:

1- "Being made alive" is speaking of the future resurrection.
2- "Being made alive" is the opposite of being *physically dead*.
3- "Being made alive" is not the opposite of being tormented forever in hell.

Paul's conversation focuses on physical life and physical death. There is no narrative going on here that is based on spiritual life and spiritual death. The traditional view insists in many cases that when you see a narrative about life, death and/or perishing, it is referring to spiritual life and death.

---

1 Cor. 15:45 Thus also it is written, "The first man, Adam, became a living soul" (zosan-psuche) the last Adam became a life-giving (zoe is the root word) spirit. (LEB)

1 Corinthians 15:45 gives us one of the clearest insights from the New Testament into the connection between psuche and zoe, and the respective roles of these two words throughout the Bible.[2]

This connection between these two words is first seen in Genesis at the beginning of creation, and this connection is repeated in the New Testament. In fact, this connection will last unto eternity. The phrase "living soul" is originally seen in Genesis 2:7 when God breathes into Adam and he becomes a "living soul", or as it is translated in some versions: "living creature" or "living being". (Note: The exact equivalent Hebrew words to the Greek words psuche and zoe are the Hebrew words Chaya and nephesh, which are used in Genesis 2:7)

Genesis 2:7 when Yahweh God formed the man of dust from the ground, and he blew into his nostrils the breath of life, and the man became a **living creature**. (LEB)

Notice that in Genesis 1:20-24 the same phrase "living creatures" is used for the animals that God created, including sea creatures, birds, and land animals.

Gen 1:20-24 And God said, "Let the waters swarm with swarms of **living creatures**, and let birds fly over the earth across the face of the vaulted dome of heaven. 21 So God created the great sea creatures and every **living creature** that moves, with which the waters swarm,

---

[2] Chris Date "Rethinking Hell Live 026: What the Bible Really Says About What 'Life' Means." Podcast video, YouTube.com. https://www.youtube.com/watch?v=HgtG2XGkULI&t=7s

according to their kind, and every bird with wings according to its kind 24 And God said, "Let the earth bring forth **living creatures** according to their kind: cattle and moving things, and wild animals according to their kind." And it was so.

One important take away from the above verses is the clarification that we get on the word "soul". Most Christians believe the word "soul" represents some immortal spirit-like component of themselves that lives on forever, that is unique to humans. This definition of "soul" is not supported anywhere in the Bible, period! In fact, there is not a unique word for "soul" in the Bible. The word that soul is translated from, just means "a being or creature". If you are a human, then you are a human being.

That being said, you are a unique being (psuche). Your psuche consists of your life, your personality, (comprising everything that is unique about you), your thoughts, memories, relationships, emotions, and so on. But there is nothing inherently immortal or "spirit-like" about your psuche. Your psuche can indeed live on forever, if you receive God's gift of eternal zoe, but there is nothing about psuche that inherently suggests that it will live on forever on it's own. The notion of an immortal soul came from man. One of the earliest sources of this incorrect idea came from Plato and Socrates. This belief was a strong paradigm throughout Greek culture in the days of the early church. This incorrect paradigm began to influence and infiltrate church doctrine by the beginning of the third century AD and remains a strong paradigm today.

For a scholarly analysis of these words in Genesis and in Paul's writings, I would recommend an excellent video done by Chris Date (from Rethinking Hell).[3] Chris is one of the most scholarly (and needed) voices of clarity in our time on the subject of immortality in the Bible.

Let's review the fundamental meaning of "zoe". Zoe is a noun, and is based on the verb zao, which means "to live, be among the living, be alive (not lifeless, not dead)".

See zao definition: https://biblehub.com/greek/2198.htm

Zoe (noun) means "the state of being alive."

So, back to our verse in 1 Cor 15:45. Here we see the word zao, used in an adjective form "zosan", interpreting as "living". It is used in combination with the word psuche to give us the two-word phrase "living soul". This describes Adam after God breathed life into his body, he then became a living soul or living creature just like the animals that God also breathed into, making them alive.

Do you see the significance of these two words? Adam's psuche became living when God created Adam from dust and breathed into him. The word zosan indicates that Adam's psuche became alive.

Adam was created as a living soul (zosan psuche). He was also given access to the tree of life which would sustain his psuche forever, but immortality was not part of Adam's basic nature. He would live forever only as long as he continued to have access to the tree of life. But, when he and Eve

---

[3] Chris Date "Rethinking Hell Live 026: What the Bible Really Says About What 'Life' Means." Podcast video, YouTube.com. https://www.youtube.com/watch?v=HgtG2XGkULI&t=7s

were driven from the Garden of Eden, they lost all access to the tree of zoe. The emphasis of the contrast here between Adam and Jesus is that Adam was merely a living psuche.

Adam was created as a soul or being (psuche).

He had been granted access to the "tree of zoe",

but immortality was not part of his intrinsic nature.

On the other hand, Jesus has *zoe* within himself. In other words, immortality is inherently a part of Jesus' divine nature. The Godhead is not dependent upon anyone else or anything else for their capacity of zoe "being alive". Jesus has been sent by God the Father to provide "eternal zoe" to all mankind that believes in him. Thus, Jesus is the *"zoe-giving spirit"*. In other words, it is this inherent zoe within Jesus that he gives to believers via the gift of the indwelling Holy Spirit. It is the Holy Spirit imparted unto the believer's psuche that conveys the zoe of Jesus into that person.

Jesus, on the other hand has Zoe (the state of being alive)

within himself intrinsically, he is immortal. The Spirit of Christ

(aka Holy Spirit) gives zoe (eternal zoe) to believers.

In fact, if you look at the Greek-English Interlinear for this verse, it clearly describes Jesus as the "spirit making live" (*zoe* is the root).

https://www.scripture4all.org/OnlineInterlinear/NTpdf/1co15.pdf

O	ECXATOC	ΑΔΑΜ	ЄIC	ΠΝЄΥΜΑ	ΖѠΟΠΟΙΟΥΝ
ho	eschatos	adam	eis	pneuma	zOopoioun
G3588	G2078	G76	G1519	G4151	G2227
t_ Nom Sg m	a_ Nom Sg m	ni proper	Prep	n_ Acc Sg n	vp Pres Act Acc Sg n
THE	LAST	ADAM	INTO	spirit	makING-LIVE vivifying

It is the Spirit of Christ (the Holy Spirit) that conveys *zoe* into the believer, giving the believer zoe. At this point the believer is now participating in God's divine nature due to the indwelling Holy Spirit.

1 Cor. 15:47-49 The first man is from the earth, made of earth; the second man is from heaven. As the one who is made of earth, so also are those who are made of earth, and as the heavenly, so also are those who are heavenly. And just as we have borne the image of the one who is made of earth, we will also bear the image of the heavenly. (LEB)

Notice that as humans, we initially bear the image of the first man (Adam). We have human DNA and as such we are a human psuche. Unless and until we are born again, we remain a mortal psuche.

If we believe, we are then born again of the Spirit of God. At that point we become children of God. We then bear the image (spiritual DNA so to speak) of Jesus because the Spirit of God indwells us. One way this image is manifested in the believer is via the fruit of the Holy Spirit that may be displayed in their life.

There will be a final stage of this image that will be revealed when we have our new resurrected bodies, which will be imperishable. At that point, the believer will fully bear the image of Christ, in that they will have an imperishable body in like nature to that of Jesus.

While we are still living in our mortal bodies during our present life on earth in this age, we experience the zoe of the Trinity living within us. As mentioned earlier in this book, there are many benefits to this indwelling of the Holy Spirit during our present life, but the ultimate fulfillment of this comes at the resurrection when the Spirit will raise us from the dead (resurrection) to eternal life. It is the Spirit of God that gives zoe.

1 CORINTHIANS 15 (SELECTED VERSES)

25 For it is necessary for him to reign until he has put all his enemies under his feet. 26 **The last enemy to be abolished is death**.

32 **If the dead are not raised, let us eat and drink, for tomorrow we die**.

50 But I say this, brothers, that flesh and blood is not able to inherit the kingdom of God, nor can corruption inherit incorruptibility. 51 Behold, I tell you a mystery: we will not all fall asleep, but we will all be changed, 52 in a moment, in the blink of an eye, at the last trumpet. For the trumpet will sound, **and the dead will be raised imperishable**, and we will be changed. 53 For it is necessary for this perishable body to put on incorruptibility, and **this mortal body to put on immortality**. 54 But whenever this perishable body puts on incorruptibility and this mortal body puts on immortality, then the saying that is written will take place:

"Death is swallowed up in victory.

55 Where, O death, is your victory?

Where, O death, is your sting?

56 Now the sting of death is sin, and the power of sin is the law. 57 But thanks be to God, who gives us the victory through our Lord Jesus Christ! (LEB)

Let's examine some key points in the above passage.

The last enemy for Jesus to destroy is death. Why is this significant?

If you hold to the traditional view, how do you explain the emphasis that Paul makes here? For instance, Paul says "where o death is your victory?" This statement is the pinnacle of Paul's argument at this point. Yet the traditional view struggles to provide a cogent explanation of this verse, without twisting it to mean something other than what it is visibly saying.

In the gospel of John, we see Jesus telling his followers that those who believe in him will not die and will never die. In the verses from the previous page, Paul's emphasis is clearly on physical death, (not the idea of "hell" or "spiritual death" as defined by the traditional view).

Other points in this passage:

> Jesus vanquishes death by his own resurrection from the dead. If Jesus had not risen from the dead, then we would have no hope of resurrection. (In part 3 of this book, we will see where Jesus finally destroys death in the book of Revelation).

> Flesh and blood cannot inherit the kingdom of God. If you remember in John 3:5-6 that Jesus used a similar expression of being born again to explain to Nicodemus that a man must be born again of the Spirit (thus receiving zoe) in order to enter the kingdom of God.

> The believer will be resurrected imperishable and immortal. We will exchange mortality for immortality.

> Death will be vanquished for the believer.

> The sting that results in death, is sin.

THE STING OF DEATH IS SIN! BUT THAT'S NOT THE END OF THE STORY

In other words, sin's sting is a lethal venom that has resulted in death for all men since the time of Adam.

The good news of Jesus's salvation is that this deadly sting is overcome by the Spirit of God which gives eternal *zoe* to the believer.

There are a few steps involved in this process. First, Jesus willingly sacrificed his own psuche upon the cross, as a substitute for the death sentence of our own psuche. His psuche was then resurrected from the dead, becoming victorious over death, and victorious over Satan. Then, in addition to removing our death sentence, Jesus proceeds to give us zoe (being alive) forever.

PAUL'S TEACHINGS ON DEATH FROM THE BOOK OF ROMANS

Rom. 5:9 Therefore, by much more, because we have been declared righteous now by his blood, we will be saved through him from the wrath. (LEB)

There are two interesting points Paul makes here.

- First, we have been declared righteous by Jesus' blood. Remember in John 6:53, Jesus said, "Very truly I tell you, unless you eat the flesh of the Son of Man and drink his blood, you have no zoe in you." That was a metaphor for depending upon the righteous blood of Jesus that paid for our sins to justify us before God the Father. We are dependent upon Jesus' righteousness which is freely given to us as believers. We have no righteousness of our own merit. Our unrighteousness merit deserves death.

- Secondly, Paul mentions God's wrath and how much more we shall be saved from this wrath. If you remember, in John 3:36, John the Baptist mentioned the wrath of God. "Whoever believes in the Son has eternal zoe, but whoever rejects the Son will not see zoe, for God's wrath remains on them."

Rom. 5:10 For if, while we were enemies, we were reconciled to God **through the death of his Son**, by much more, having been reconciled, **we will be saved by his life (zoe)**. (LEB)

Don't miss the key point that Paul makes here. Before we can talk about *zoe*, we have to deal with the sin issue! Sin makes us enemies of God and the sentence of sin against God is death. We have to reconcile this issue, before we can discuss life.

It is only by the death of Jesus on behalf of the believer that our death has been paid for, reconciling us with God the Father. This is the first aspect of our salvation... redeeming the believer from death.

After being reconciled with God through the death of his Son, we can then lay hold of the fact that the final aspect of our salvation is that we have been given eternal zoe, which comes from Jesus via the Holy Spirit. It is only by this infusion of Jesus' *zoe* into the psuche of the believer, that the believer will themselves be resurrected from death.

Note: The key is to not just merely believe (Jesus said that even the demons believe, and they tremble at the thought of him), but to believe by entrusting our *psuche* to Him.

To *truly believe* means to place trusting faith in Jesus. This includes a complete trust in his sacrifice on the cross for us and dependence on his spirit for life (*zoe*) and the light that comes with it, so that we may walk in the fullness of this *zoe*. With this trust comes obedience to his leading us as Lord of our lives. This is a lifelong endeavor, as Jesus strips away our pride, sin, fears, selfishness, and self-reliance step by step—one precept, one stronghold at a time.

Rom. 5:12-15 Because of this, just as sin entered into the world through one man, and death through sin, so also death spread to all people because all sinned. For until the law, sin was in the world, but sin is not charged to one's account when there is no law. But death reigned from Adam until Moses even over those who did not sin in the likeness of the transgression of Adam, who is a type of the one who is to come. But the gift is not like the trespass, for if by the trespass of the one, the many died, by much more did the grace of God and the gift by the grace of the one man, Jesus Christ, multiply to the many. (LEB)

Sin and death came to all mankind, since the sin of Adam. It was through Adam that this consequence of sin came upon all men. It is through Jesus that life (*zoe*) becomes available to all men who will believe.

> **Rom. 5:17-21** For if by the trespass of the one man, **death** reigned through the one man, much more will those who receive the abundance of grace and of the gift of righteousness reign in **life (zoe)** through the one, Jesus Christ. Consequently therefore, as through one trespass came **condemnation** to all people, so also through one righteous deed came **justification of life (zoe)** to all people. For just as through the disobedience of the one man, the many were made sinners, so also through the obedience of the one, the many will be made righteous. Now the law came in as a side issue, in order that the trespass could increase, but where sin increased, grace was present in greater abundance, so that just as **sin reigned in death**, so also **grace would reign through righteousness to eternal life (zoe)** through Jesus Christ our Lord. (LEB)

Before Jesus came, sin reigned in death. That is, the certainty of death due to sin was unquestionable. Sin has held a powerful iron grip over the fate of the psuche of all men. However, since the resurrection of Jesus, grace now reigns via the righteousness of Jesus that is imputed to believers (rather than believers having to rely on their own worthless righteousness). This new reign results in eternal zoe (saving our psuche from death) for all mankind that will believe and accept this gift.

Just as sin has reigned in death since Adam's fall,

grace now reigns through righteousness

to bring Eternal Life (Zoe) through

Jesus to those with trusting faith

THE WAGES OF SIN

> **Rom. 6:23** For the compensation due sin is **death**, but the gift of God is **eternal life (zoe)** in Christ Jesus our Lord. (LEB)

This verse summarizes what Paul has just said in Romans chapters 5 and 6.

Could this message be any clearer?

Could it be said more simply?

The wage of sin is death!

Can you see why it is so vital that we understand what Jesus and Paul were saying when they spoke of life and death?

If we redefine "life and death" by twisting both words to make them fit the traditional doctrine of eternal torment in hell, or the traditional notion of "spiritual life and death," then we end up changing what Jesus originally said, as well as distorting Paul's clear teaching.

So, we may be preaching that Jesus saves, which is entirely true. But we end up conveying an incorrect interpretation of the gospel as to the message of what we are being saved "from" and what we are being saved "to."

Is this really what we want? Do you see the gravity of this issue?

If you hold to the traditional view... then how do you explain Romans 6:23? The traditional view explains this verse as being foundational to all Christianity yet cannot cogently explain just why it is so foundational. The traditional view resorts to fancy footwork to explain its way "around" the simple but profound truth that this verse is plainly speaking about physical death. Physical death is the narrative that Paul's audience would have understood. They would not have made some strange connection that this was referring to spiritual death. Nor would they have interpreted this statement as a symbolic reference to separation from God (spiritual death) for eternity.

NOTE REGARDING THE TREE OF LIFE (ZOE)

The tree of life within the garden of Eden imparted immortality unto man. It allowed him to live forever. Access to the tree of life was cut off intentionally when Adam and Eve were driven from the garden. Being banned from the garden was in fact, their sentence of death.

The Bible says little about the tree of life again, until the very end in the book of Revelation. In Revelation 20, John speaks about the day of judgment. On the day of judgment, those whose names are found in the book of *zoe* will be given *eternal zoe*.

Then in Revelation 21, John speaks of a new heaven and a new earth. There will be a holy city of God that comes down out of heaven unto the new earth, and God will dwell there with mankind.

Also, there will be no more death since the old order of things will have passed away!

Finally in Revelation 22, John speaks of a river of zoe that will flow through this new kingdom. Straddling the river there will be a tree, whose leaves are for the healing of nations. It is the tree of *zoe*. The tree of zoe marks the beginning and the end of God's word.

Can you imagine what that scene will be like? I recognize much of Revelation uses symbolic representations, and it is possible the Tree of Life may be metaphorical for the "life-giving spirit of Christ". But this source of life will surely be evident to those of us whose names are written in the "book of zoe". Whatever that glorious moment of resurrection might be like, it is my heart's desire to be there. Won't you accept this gift from God, and join me there on that wonderful day?

The Bible speaks little about the Tree of Life again, until the book of

Revelation. In Revelation 22, John speaks of a river of zoe that will

flow through the new kingdom. Straddling the river, there

will be a tree, whose leaves are for the healing of nations.

It is the **Tree of Zoe** (the state of being alive).

This **Tree of Zoe** marks the beginning and the end of God's word.

THE POWER OF A PARADIGM

A paradigm is an established perspective by which each of us interprets those things we experience. Our paradigm develops and changes over time through our experiences, by what we have seen and learned. Some have compared a paradigm to the color of glasses you wear. Your paradigm colors how you see things and how you interpret what you see and hear. Our paradigms strongly influence the way we think and react to what is going on around us.

While a paradigm can be very strong, at the same time it can have a great weakness. In fact, the stronger a paradigm is, the greater its weakness may be. If the paradigm encounters something that is outside of its perspective or experience, it will seek to shape the encounter to make it conform to its understanding. A paradigm's weakness can be due to the paradigm being so strong and so rigid that it prevents a person from correctly interpreting reality.

As we have progressed through this study, we have seen where Jesus' teachings challenged the paradigms of those he was speaking to. In many cases, the people ended up walking away disillusioned or angry with Jesus. Some dismissed him as being demon possessed because they either could not accept or understand the things he was teaching.

Jesus once used a metaphor to describe this "paradigm conflict" as pouring new wine into an old wineskin (Luke 5:36-39). He said you must pour new wine into a new wine skin, otherwise the old wine skin will burst losing the wine. He was using this metaphor to refer to people's hearts, their attitudes, and their inability to flex enough to embrace his teaching.

Paradigms can also be dangerous. The Pharisees and scribes ended up killing Jesus because his claims were totally outside of their paradigm. Their hearts had become hardened like an old wineskin. There was no room for Jesus' teaching in their paradigm.

As we have progressed through this book, it may be possible that your own paradigm has been challenged. Let's look at some of the common paradigms that can shape interpretations of the Bible today.

The following statements represent paradigms that have been firmly entrenched for over fifteen hundred years. These powerful paradigms are very influential:

- ➤ Every person is born with an immortal soul.
- ➤ If a person has a saving faith in Jesus, that person's soul will go to heaven for eternity.
- ➤ If a person is not a believer, that person's soul will spend eternity in hell.
- ➤ The penalty for sin is death. This "death" is defined as a "spiritual death", identified as a permanent separation from God. This "death" includes staying "alive" in hell while continuously being burned by fire and eaten by worms for eternity.

As you move ahead in this book, examine how your own paradigms may be limiting how you interpret what Jesus is saying. Just because we are separated from his original listeners by millennia, the issue of how we listen remains the same. The quest here is for clarification and truth.

For instance, how do you define "eternal zoe"? If you define it as being in heaven forever, then what is the significance of the word "zoe". You see, the traditional view really believes that all men already have eternal life (i.e., they have immortal souls). The traditional view explains that the venue of eternal living will be in either in heaven or hell. So, the traditional view believes this is merely a just matter of the quality of eternal life, that differs between those going to heaven vs hell.

The traditional also explains that the word "life" focuses on "spiritual life", not physical life. So, while the saved enjoy spiritual "life" by direct fellowship with God, the damned are separated from God forever, so they are in some respect "spiritually dead".

The truth is that the consistent use of zoe (the state of being alive) throughout the Bible focuses on the physical existence and life of a person.

Paul's emphasis on life and death that we have just seen in 1 Corinthians and Romans focuses on physical death, and the believer's resurrection from the dead to physical life, this time to live forever.

On the other hand, the wicked will be resurrected to judgment, which will result in their being cast into the lake of fire, which John defines in Revelation as the second death. This second death will be final, there is no coming back from this destruction. The unsaved will perish forever. They will be permanently, totally, physically dead.

Jesus depicts a "paradigm conflict" as pouring new wine into an old

wineskin. He said you must pour new wine into a new wine skin,

otherwise the old wine skin will burst losing the wine.

He uses this metaphor to refer to people's rigid paradigms and

their inability to flex enough to embrace his teaching.

TRADITIONAL PROBLEMS

One of the problems that the traditional view has with permanent death, is that they cannot fathom this as being everlasting punishment. In their mind everlasting punishment must mean some ongoing punishment that never stops inflicting some sort of pain or anguish upon the unsaved. Let me ask you. Do the verses we have been reading portray death as punishment? Is permanent death everlasting?

Many of the verses that the traditional view insists portray eternal torment in hell are verses that speak of eternal destruction. I prefer to take these verses for what they say. Eternal destruction is eternal destruction, being destroyed forever. Some choose to call this annihilation. The Bible never uses this word. However, it does repeatedly refer to destruction and the second death. Destruction is simply being put to death forever, with no possibility of resurrection.

The traditional view also insists eternal torment is the only way there can be infliction of degrees of punishment. But there is no imperative that this can only be accomplished by eternal torment. There is nothing to prevent God from inflicting whatever manner and time of punishment that he may see fit to inflict upon an individual before that person is ultimately put to death.

THE SPIRIT'S ROLE IN OVERCOMING DEATH

The Holy Spirit, Spirit of God, Spirit of Christ, and the Spirit of the Son are names used for the Holy Spirit throughout the New Testament. These are all referring to the same Holy Spirit. For an example see the following verse. As you read these verses, notice that it is this Spirit that conveys *zoe* to humans. Eternal *Zoe* comes from the indwelling spirit of Christ Jesus.

> **Rom. 8:9-11** But you are not in the flesh but in the Spirit, if indeed the Spirit of God lives in you. But if anyone does not have the Spirit of Christ, this person does not belong to him. But if Christ is in you, the body is dead because of sin, but the **spirit is life (zoe)** because of righteousness. And if the Spirit of the one who raised Jesus from the dead lives in you, the one who raised Christ Jesus from the dead **will also make alive your mortal bodies** through his Spirit who lives in you. (LEB)

OUR GUARANTEE OF WHAT IS TO COME

Even though "eternal" zoe is yet to be manifested, we are guaranteed of this by the indwelling of God's Holy Spirit. See the following verses in Ephesians and 2 Corinthians. Some translations use the phrase "the Holy Spirit who is the *guarantee* of our inheritance". The idea is that the Holy Spirit's indwelling of the believer is their assurance or seal (guarantee) of their redemption.

> **Eph. 1:13-14** In whom also you, when you heard the word of truth, the gospel of your salvation, in whom also when you believed you were **sealed with the promised Holy Spirit,** who is the **down payment of our inheritance,** until the redemption of the possession, to the praise of his glory. (LEB)

> **2 Cor. 1:21-22** Now the one who establishes us together with you in Christ and who anoints us is God, **who also sealed us and gave the down payment** of the Spirit in our hearts. (LEB)

As believers we participate in God's divine nature in the here-and-now. We have not yet been resurrected unto eternal life (*zoe unto the ages)*, but we do now have the *zoe of Christ* living within us, via the indwelling Holy Spirit. The Holy Spirit conveys the immortal life of Jesus unto the believer, making us alive with Christ, and giving us the assurance of being resurrected from the dead to live again, this time unto the age (eternal zoe).

We don't actually enter "eternal life" until the day of resurrection. But, we must not miss the fact that believers already possess *zoe* and participate in *zoe* now. (Again, I hate to be redundant, but I just want to be sure that we understand. We enter zoe now, due to the zoe of the Godhead indwelling us now.) Thus we have complete assurance (hope) of future "eternal zoe" now, in addition to having all the blessings of the Spirit of God living within us, now.

We just have not been resurrected yet into our new imperishable bodies, which will ultimately occur on the resurrection day, when the dead in Christ will be resurrected to live forever.

THE SPIRIT OF GOD CONVEYS ZOE

It is the Holy Spirit that gives or conveys zoe. Zoe is used implicitly in the following verses to refer to eternal life.

> **John 6:61-63** But Jesus, because he knew within himself that his disciples were grumbling about this, said to them, "Does this cause you to be offended? Then what if you see the Son of Man ascending where he was before? The Spirit is the one who gives **life (zoe)**; the flesh profits nothing. The words that I have spoken to you are spirit and are **life (zoe)**. (LEB)

> **2 Corinthians 3:5-6** Not that we are adequate in ourselves to consider anything as from ourselves, but our adequacy is from God, 6 who also makes us adequate as servants of a new covenant, not of the letter, but of the Spirit, for the letter kills, **but the Spirit gives life (zoe)**. (LEB)

I hate to be redundant, but I am showing Romans 8:11 again, just to re-emphasize that it is the Spirit of God that will give life to the believer, by raising the believer from the dead.

> **Romans 8:11** And if the Spirit of the one who raised Jesus from the dead lives in you, the one who raised Christ Jesus from the dead **will also make alive your mortal bodies through his Spirit who lives in you**. (LEB)

17

Jesus Says Death Can Be Avoided

If you recall from John 6, Jesus identified death as the problem that all mankind faces. He began a stark contrast by pointing out that the Jew's ancestors ate the manna (bread) but eventually died.

> **John 6:47-49** "Truly, truly I say to you, the one who believes has **eternal life (zoe)**. I am the bread of **life (zoe)**. Your fathers ate the manna in the wilderness and they **died**." (LEB)

He was specifically referring to the Israelites who ate the manna during the forty-year period of wandering in the desert. Jesus makes a contrast between the manna that they ate (and yet died) with the true bread that comes down from heaven (himself).

Jesus said that if a person eats of this living bread (referring to himself) that person will not die, in fact that person will live forever.

> **John 6:50-51** "This is the bread that comes down from heaven so that someone may eat from it and **not die**. I am the living bread that came down from heaven. If anyone eats from this bread, **he will live forever**. And the bread that I will give for the **life (zoe)** of the world is my flesh." (LEB)

NEVER SEE DEATH?

As we now return to John 8, Jesus continues with teaching about death. He now tells the Jewish crowd that if they obey his word, they will never see death.

> **John 8:51** "Truly, truly, I say to you, if anyone keeps my word, **he will never see death**." (ESV)

This claim escalates an already tense confrontation, as it is way outside of the Jews' paradigm. They resort to calling him demon-possessed because they see his statement as extremely outrageous.

Let me ask you... Is there any way this could possibly be true?

Could it be true that a person who obeys Jesus' word will **never** see death? Does this line up with what Jesus has already taught thus far in the gospel according to John?

As we progress through John, we will see Jesus continuing to press this topic of death. We will come to understand that it is one of the primary components of his message. This should not surprise us, as it is tied directly to his message of *zoe*.

Let's keep moving in John 8.

> **John 8:48-53** The Jews answered him, "Are we not right in saying that you are a Samaritan and have a demon?" Jesus answered, "I do not have a demon, but I honor my Father, and you dishonor me. Yet I do not seek my own glory; there is One who seeks it, and he is the judge. Truly, truly, I say to you, if anyone keeps my word, **he will never see death**." The Jews said to him, "Now, we know that you have a demon! Abraham died, as did the prophets, yet you say, 'If anyone keeps my word, he will never taste death.' Are you greater than our father Abraham, who died? And the prophets died! Who do you make yourself out to be?" (ESV)

Let's take a closer look at the following snippet (8:51) from the verses above. I believe there is a crucial component in this verse that has been missed, that is fundamental to understanding Jesus' message.

> **John 8:51** "Truly, truly, I say to you, if anyone keeps my word, **he will never see death**." (ESV)

Pause with me for just a second. Would you agree this statement was way outside the crowd's paradigm? I dare say this is way outside my paradigm, and probably yours as well. I have never personally known someone who has never died, (except for everyone that is currently alive, but you know what I mean) so this statement would be very hard for me to accept. Why would Jesus make such an outlandish claim?

As you consider this verse, remember that just a few seconds earlier in this conversation (8:24), Jesus told the crowd that if anyone did not believe in him, they would die in their sins.

> **John 8:24** I told you that you would die in your sins, for, unless you believe that I am he **you will die in your sins**. (ESV)

These two verses are part of a continuous conversation that took place in one encounter. The crowd is still pondering what Jesus said only a minute earlier in 8:24 when he makes the statement in 8:51. Only by keeping this in mind can we even begin to understand what Jesus is saying now in 8:51.

It's as if Jesus is saying, "I told you that if you do not believe in me, you will indeed die in your sins. But, I want to tell you what will happen if you do believe in me and hold to my teachings! Not only will you not die in your sins, but you will also never see death!"

Ok, let's think about these statements for a minute. Let's assume that only Jesus' closest followers believed in him, so maybe 11 guys? (I am just saying this for argument's sake). Within a few decades most of these apostles were killed for their faith. The last one to die was the writer of the gospel of John, about 70 years after Jesus' resurrection.

So, it's safe to assume they are all dead. So, does it make sense that Jesus actually meant "if you believe you will never see death"?

This is a huge question. This statement by Jesus is foundational to his teaching.

In my opinion there are two possible ways to interpret what Jesus' intent was with this statement.

1 - JESUS IS SPEAKING PROLEPTICALLY ABOUT DEATH

Jesus was speaking proleptically about death just like he speaks about zoe. So, Jesus is again focusing on the end game. He is focused on the day of resurrection, and what is at stake for all mankind. The believer will be resurrected from the dead, to live forever. This would also be known as "never dying". However, if we prefer to stick with the translation as "never see death", then we would take this phrase as a reference to the second death. Regardless of how we decide to interpret this, Jesus is not referring to a person's first death in this verse.

On the other hand, there is another possibility here. There may be a clearer translation available.

2 - IN NO CASE SHALL YOU BE BEHOLDING DEATH IN THE EON

Obviously, the Jews that heard Jesus' statement were offended by what he said because it was so preposterous to them. But is it possible that our English translation has missed a key part of his statement that would have been just as outlandish and offensive but more clearly tied to what Jesus has been teaching?

In the LEB translation, notice the different rendering of this verse.

> **John 8:51** Truly, truly I say to you, if anyone keeps my word, he will never experience death forever." (LEB)

I like how this reads much better. I believe it is very close to being correct. To have a better understanding of what Jesus is saying, let's look at the original Greek text.

INTERLINEAR GREEK-ENGLISH NEW TESTAMENT

Greek-English Interlinear New Testaments have been used as reference material for generations by biblical scholars. The online access to this resource is a wonderful study tool. What you are going to see does not require you to be a linguistics expert or Greek scholar.

Look at the original Greek verse (John 8:51) on the following page. It is from a Greek-English Interlinear New Testament, which can be found online at the following link:

http://www.scripture4all.org/OnlineInterlinear/NTpdf/joh8.pdf

The benefit of an Interlinear translation is that it shows the original Greek word with an appropriate English word below. You do not have to be a Greek scholar to see that a key aspect of this original Greek text has been omitted from the English translation. As you can see, the Greek text here does not "exactly" say that "whoever obeys my word shall **never** see death".

See the screen shot below:

| 8:51 | AMHN amEn G281 Hebrew AMEN verily | AMHN amEn G281 Hebrew AMEN verily | ΛΕΓω legO G3004 vi Pres Act 1 Sg I-AM-sayING | YMIN humin G5213 pp 2 Dat Pl to-YOU⁽ᵖ⁾ to-ye | EAN ean G1437 Cond IF-EVER | TIC tis G5100 px Nom Sg m ANY anyone | TON ton G3588 t_ Acc Sg m THE | ΛΟΓΟΝ logon G3056 n_ Acc Sg m saying word | TON ton G3588 t_ Acc Sg m THE | EMON emon G1699 ps 1 Acc Sg MY |

| THPHCH tErEsE G5083 vs Aor Act 3 Sg SHOULD-BE-KEEPING | ΘΑΝΑΤΟΝ thanaton G2288 n_ Acc Sg m DEATH | OY ou G3756 Part Neg NOT | MH mE G3361 Part Neg NO | ΘΕωΡΗCΗ theOrEsE G2334 vs Aor Act 3 Sg he-SHOULD-BE-beholdING | EIC eis G1519 Prep INTO | TON ton G3588 t_ Acc Sg m THE | ΑΙωΝΑ aiOna G165 n_ Acc Sg m eon |

Copyright 2010 Scripture4all Foundation – www.scripture4all.org

Look carefully at the last 3 words in this verse. The last 3 words are "eis ton aiOna", meaning "into the eon".

Do you see this phrase "into the eon" (or anything resembling this) in the English translation shown in the right-hand margin adjacent to the Greek text? Did you see this expression in the text of John 8:48-53 that was previously displayed a few pages earlier?

51 . Verily, verily, I say unto you, If a man keep my saying, he shall never see death.

110

This idea of "eternity" or "forever" projected by the phrase "into the eon" is missing entirely in most English translations. So, my question for, is if it were included, could it possibly change the meaning of this text?

From the screen-snippet above, you can see the Greek roughly reads something like this:

> "Amen, Amen, I am saying to you, if ever anyone my word should be keeping, death not no should he be beholding into the eon." (my paraphrase)

Jesus' use of the phrase "into the eon" expresses the same concept he has been using for "eternal life" throughout John and the other gospels. Jesus is speaking about death "into the eon".

Another notable omission in my opinion in the English translation is the use of two negatives—"not no"—that occur in the Greek immediately prior to the phrase "he should be beholding into the eon." This is the combination of the two Greek words *ou mE*.

According to *Strong's Greek Dictionary* (see website link below), the double negative *ou mE* should be read as an extra emphatic "not even a possibility" or "in no case" or "never." So, the word "never" that we see in the English translation could be deemed appropriate, but may fail to emphasize the gist that Jesus was making of "not even a possibility". Jesus is emphatically stating that there is absolutely no way that believers are going to be experiencing death into the eon.

http://Biblehub.com/greek/3364.htm

INTO THE EON

Let's take a look at some different possible outcomes of this translation.

First, let's look at the English translation as it is often seen.

> "Very truly I tell you, whoever obeys my word will never see death." (ESV)

Next, let's look at using the double negative interpreted as "in no case" and include the phrase "into the eon" (following the Interlinear translation).

> "Very truly, I am saying to you, if ever anyone my word should be keeping, death in no case should he be beholding into the eon." (my paraphrase)

Lastly, let us use the word "experience" in lieu of "should be beholding" but still include the phrase "into the eon."

> "Very truly I am saying to you, if anyone my word should be keeping, in no case (not even a possibility) shall he be experiencing death into the eon." (my paraphrase)

Can you see the significant difference between the first translation and the last two?

Does "never see death" mean the same thing as "in no case (not even a possibility) shall he be experiencing death into the eon?"

I liked the word "experiencing" that the LEB translation used.

I believe the true gist of this verse is:

> "Very truly, I am saying to you, if anyone keeps my word, then in no case shall that person experience death into the eon." (my paraphrase)

This could be understood as either:

1- Those who keep Jesus' word will not <u>continue</u> to experience death forever. In other words, that person will not remain dead forever. Instead, at some point they will be resurrected back to life. That is, they will be resurrected from the dead to eternal zoe.

2- Or it could be directly referring the second death, in which case it is simply saying that believers will not experience death into the eon. (On the other hand, non-believers will die at the second death, and will be dead into the eons. They will be permanently dead).

Either way you want to translate this verse (and similar verses coming up), we absolutely have to get a clear understanding of what Jesus is saying about avoiding death.

Jesus is not referring to someone the first death that we will all experience in this world. This first death has happened to everyone that has ever lived (believers or not) in the millennia since his teaching. So, he must be talking about something else.

Remember in John 6, Jesus told the crowd that a person could eat of this bread (himself) and not die. That was very straightforward. There were no extra words to include or omit there. So, what did Jesus mean when he said that? Again, everyone that was present on that day has died since then. So, this first death cannot be what he was talking about.

Rather, Jesus had to be using the phrase "not die" proleptically.

THE STRAW-MAN ARGUMENT

I often hear a traditional argument that goes something like this: If people do not hear the message of eternal torment in hell, then what is there to motivate them to repent and accept Jesus's message of salvation? The traditionalist doesn't see death as a deterrent to sin, or the idea of avoiding eternal death as sufficient motivation to draw people to Christ. In their view, they seem to think most people would say "if I am merely going to die forever due to me rejecting Christ, then that's no big deal, I will go on my merry way until I die".

There are at least two responses to this argument:

First, everyone will either be resurrected to eternal zoe, or they will be resurrected to judgment. At the judgment everyone whose names are not written in the book of zoe (being alive), will be thrown into the lake of fire, which is identified as the second death. Jesus's talks about there being weeping and gnashing of teeth at this judgment. Weeping indicates immense sorrow and regret. Gnashing of teeth represents a person's intense anger, probably angry at God's judgment and their sense that God's judgment is unfair, or maybe angry at what they recognize as their own stubbornness.[4] Either way it is not a pretty picture. The Bible talks about degrees of punishment. God is quite capable of inflicting whatever judgment and punishment on a person that he determines, including suffering and pain if he deems that to be just, before that person is destroyed (killed) in the lake of fire.

Second, and more importantly, we must put ourselves in the shoes of those that Jesus was talking to. The Jews in the crowd had no concept that Jesus's reference to Gehenna, was pointing to "eternal torment". Eternal torment is the straw-man view, that most traditional Christians believe in. This view never existed in Jesus's mind nor in the minds of the crowds listening to him.

The Jews knew what the real issue was. The issue was death. The death sentence that Adam and sin had wrought on mankind was THE REAL issue. Gehenna was an infamous valley just outside of Jerusalem. The Jews would have understood Jesus's reference to Gehenna to refer to an apocalyptic prophecy of judgment and massive slaughter of the wicked. (Death, not long-term suffering). This apocalyptic judgment of Gehenna (from the prophet Jeremiah) is covered in the chapter on Gehenna in part 3 of this book.

We must remember that the gospel was good news. Jesus's teaching brought relief to mankind, because it saved them from what they already knew was the judgment for sin, which is death. This WAS the motivation.

This was the basis of the disagreement that existed between the Sadducees and the Pharisees. Both groups knew that death was the issue. But the Sadducees believed that death was final. Death as far as they could see in the scriptures was a done deal, there was no solution for it. The Pharisees on the other hand, believed the scriptures (Old Testament) did indeed speak of coming back to life, but they just could not connect the dots as to how this would take place. Look at John 5:40.

> **John 5:40** You search the scriptures because you think that you have **eternal life (zoe)** in them, and it is these that testify about me. And you are not willing to come to me so that you may have **life (zoe)**. (LEB)

Jesus is speaking to directly to this issue, that the Pharisees were looking to the scriptures thinking that somehow the scriptures would bring them eternal zoe (being resurrected to be alive forever). Yet Jesus chides them for not being willing to see that the scriptures were pointing to him, as the source for this zoe.

---

[4] Edward Fudge, "gnashing of teeth," EdwardFudge.com, Accessed 5/3/22, https://edwardfudge.com/2014/01/gnashing-of-teeth/

THE SECOND DEATH

John speaks of the second death several times in the book of Revelation. (Revelation 2:11, 20:6, 20:14, and 21:8). This concept is in total agreement with everything Jesus says in the gospel according to John. For example, when someone dies, it is their *psuche* that dies. If they are a believer, their *psuche* is saved (preserved) for eternal zoe.

In other words, a believer's *psuche* will not remain dead unto the eon. If a person is not a believer, they do not have this hope.

Think about this. Even Jesus died. In John 10, Jesus explains that he will lay down his *psuche* for his sheep (not his *zoe* but his *psuche*!). Jesus' *psuche* will be killed when he is crucified, but he will be able to take it up again.

Peter reviews this death and resurrection of Jesus's psuche in his sermon in Acts 2 (See chapter: Hell No – the Book of Acts).

When someone dies, it is their psuche that dies.

If they are a believer, their psuche is saved for eternal zoe.

That is, their psuche will be resurrected from the dead to live forever.

FINAL ANALYSIS OF JOHN 8

Why is it important that we have a clear understanding of Jesus' use of these words?

Well, it's important if we want to have clarity as to what Jesus focused on.

Or is it okay that we confuse what the issues really are? How will that affect our lives? How will that affect our message and our emphasis?

The question boils down to this: what is Jesus identifying as mankind's problem? What does he say the real issue is? What is man's predicament and status prior to believing in Him? What is the result of sin?

If we believe in him in order that we might be saved . . . then just what are we being saved *from*?

WHAT'S THE REAL PROBLEM?

What is the *real* problem that Jesus has identified in the gospel according to John?

Is it hell? Did you know that Jesus is never recorded using the word *Gehenna* in the gospel according to John? In fact, John never uses the word *Gehenna* in any of his writings (John wrote the gospel according to John, 1 John, 2 John, 3 John, and the Book of Revelations). The apostle Paul never used the word *Gehenna* in any of his writings either.

However, John does use the word *Hades* four times in the book of Revelation. But *Hades* should never be translated as "hell" or confused with *Gehenna*. Jesus and the New Testament authors had a unique definition of *Hades* that sets it totally apart from *Gehenna*.

For that matter, *Gehenna* should not be translated as "hell" either. Hell is a pagan word that was used to replace the word *Gehenna* centuries after Jesus used the word *Gehenna*. *Gehenna* was the proper name of a location just outside of Jerusalem that in Jesus' day, had an infamous history associated with apocalyptic judgment and destruction.

Note: Traditional teaching will sometimes conflate the words Gehenna and Hades, using the English word "hell" to refer to both of these Greek words. This is a huge distortion of the New Testament and Jesus's teaching. Neither Jesus nor the New Testament authors would have ever used these two words interchangeably. These two words represent different events or venues that occur in the future after a person dies. Hades occurs after the first death for everyone. Gehenna occurs after the resurrection to judgment only for those whose names are not written in the book of zoe. Gehenna is used by Jesus to refer to the judgment of the lake of fire that John describes in Revelation as the second death. Hades and Gehenna are covered in part 3 of this book.

18

John 10 – The Good Shepherd

In John 10, Jesus begins a metaphor involving sheep, the gate to the sheep's pen, and the good shepherd. This extensive metaphor contains two of his famous "I Am" statements.

I am the Gate for the Sheep – Jesus says, "If anyone enters by me, he will be saved and will go in and out and find pasture" (ESV). Jesus is the only "way" to being saved. He defines the result of this salvation twice in John 10, as being eternal zoe.

I am the Good Shepherd –Jesus is focused on what the good shepherd (himself) is going to do. He is going to lay down his psuche so that his sheep might have eternal zoe.

The use of Zoe in John 10

Zoe only appears twice in John 10. But each time, it's use is very powerful. The first time zoe appears (John 10:10) it is being used implicitly to refer to future eternal zoe. "I came that they may have zoe and have it beyond measure."

Zoe is used explicitly the second time it appears as "eternal zoe". Jesus says, "I give them eternal zoe, and they will never perish."

Remember, zoe at its core means 'being alive'. When used to refer to humans, zoe is speaking of being physically alive, or the expectation of resurrection from death to being physically alive a second time, this time forever. The use of zoe is not referring to spiritual life or some higher level of blessed life.

The use of Psuche in John 10

Jesus uses the word psuche three times to refer to himself. In fact, he says that as the Good Shepherd he will lay down his psuche. He is predicting that he is going to die. He then uses the word "it" several times to refer back to his dead psuche and says that he has the authority to take possession of it again (speaking of his own psuche resurrecting from the dead).

The Tale of Two Contrasts

There are two important contrasts that Jesus makes throughout this shepherd metaphor in John 10. One is the same contrast that he has made repeatedly in the gospel of John, the contrast between zoe and death. The other contrast is between what the thief (Satan) intends to do to the sheep (kill and destroy), and what the Good Shepherd has come to do (give them eternal zoe). Again, do not get confused about what is going on here. John 10 is frequently misconstrued to say that it is talking about spiritual life, and/or some level of higher blessed life. This not only misrepresents what Jesus is teaching, it misses the whole point of the chapter. This chapter is about physical life vs physical death and resurrection to eternal zoe.

The Sheep and Shepherd metaphor

First, a little background will be helpful. Shepherds out in the countryside often brought their sheep together into a communal sheep pen during the night in order to keep the sheep safe while the shepherds slept. One shepherd would be on watch as the gatekeeper. Thus, the sheep pen provided protection for the sheep during the night. The gate was the only way in or out of the pen.

Anyone who attempted to remove the sheep other than through the gate would be regarded as a thief. The only one who could enter by the gate was the shepherd of the sheep. When the gatekeeper opened the gate for the shepherd, the shepherd would then call out to his sheep. His sheep would recognize the voice of their shepherd and quickly find their way out of the large group of sheep in order to follow their shepherd.

It is using this scenario that Jesus makes the first "I Am" statement that takes place in this metaphor.

I Am the Gate for the Sheep.

"I Am" Statement 3

This is Jesus speaking in John 10:

> **John 10:1-9** "Truly, truly, I say to you, he who does not enter the sheepfold by the door but climbs in by another way, that man is a thief and a robber. But he who enters by the door is the shepherd of the sheep. To him the gatekeeper opens. The sheep hear his voice, and he calls his own sheep by name and leads them out. When he has brought out all his own, he goes before them, and the sheep follow him, for they know his voice. A stranger they will not follow, but they will flee from him, for they do not know the voice of strangers."
>
> This figure of speech Jesus used with them, but they did not understand what he was saying to them. So, Jesus again said to them, "Truly, truly, I say to you, I am the door of the sheep. All who came before me are thieves and robbers, but the sheep did not listen to them. I am the door. If anyone enters by me, he will be saved and will go in and out and find pasture." (ESV)

Using the metaphor of being the door (or gate) for the sheep, Jesus emphasizes that whoever enters the sheep pen through him will be saved. This is the primary point Jesus is making in John 10:1-9. It is only through Jesus that anyone can be saved. There is no other way (or door/gate) that leads to salvation.

Also, his sheep will be able to come and go from the sheep pen and will find pasture. This is an indirect reference to Psalm 23, when King David says, "The Lord is my shepherd. He leads me to green pastures." Many of the Jews would have picked up on this reference and the fact that Jesus is referring to himself as this shepherd. Some of the Jews may have seen Jesus as flirting with blasphemy here, making himself equal with the shepherd in the 23rd Psalm. Jesus connection with the 23rd Psalm is no accident, and he will delve even deeper into this parallel with his next "I Am" statement.

JESUS STATES HIS PURPOSE

Next comes 10:10, when Jesus states his purpose for coming into the world.

> **John 10:10** The thief comes only to steal and kill and destroy. I came that they may have **life (zoe)** and have it abundantly. (ESV)

Analyzing the First Sentence

> The thief comes only to steal and kill and destroy

Jesus says the thief comes only to steal, kill, and destroy. This is a direct reference to Satan and his objective to distort the truth, thereby stealing the hearts and minds of man. By luring the sheep away with his voice of lies, Satan steals the sheep in order to keep them from being saved. Satan's intent is the death and destruction of the sheep. Jesus will bring up Satan's intent to kill and destroy the sheep again a few verses later in John 10:28.

Keep in mind that Jesus has been contrasting *zoe* with death and destruction (perishing) throughout John. It is Jesus' purpose (mission) to save the sheep by giving them life (*zoe*), in lieu of the death and destruction intended by Satan.

If you recall the contrast Jesus made in John 5, where he said there will be a resurrection to zoe, and there will be a resurrection to judgment (judgment refers to destruction, aka the second death).

> **John 5:24, 28-29** Truly, truly I say to you that the one who hears my word and who believes the one who sent me has **eternal life (zoe)**, and does not come into judgment, but has passed from **death into life (zoe)**.
>
> "Do not be astonished at this, because an hour is coming in which all those in the tombs will hear his voice 29 and they will come out—those who have done good things to a **resurrection of life (zoe)**, but those who have practiced evil things to a **resurrection of judgment**. (LEB)

The contrast portrayed is zoe versus death, and zoe versus judgment. Judgment is equated with death in verse 24, "does not come into judgment, but has passed from death into life (zoe)." Thus, the judgment being spoken of is death. Ultimately this equates to the second death that the unsaved will experience after they are resurrected to judgment.

Analyzing the Second Sentence

The *good news* comes in the second sentence in John 10:10. Jesus clarifies his entire purpose for coming to earth in the form of a man.

119

I came that they may **have life (*zoe*) and have it abundantly**.

Let's break this verse down. First, Jesus says that he has come that his sheep (those people who will believe in him) might have zoe.

Zoe, at its root means, "the state of being alive" (the opposite of being dead). It is just that basic, it is simple. Jesus is not using zoe here to refer to some level of higher quality life or blessed life that he is promising to the believer such as great health, prosperity, or fulfilling some destiny or higher potential.

Consider what Jesus is contrasting here! The thief (Satan) comes to steal the sheep, then kill them. Jesus is making a direct statement of his purpose (why he has come) that is in direct opposition to death and destruction.

Jesus has come to give the sheep zoe (eternal zoe) in lieu of the death and destruction that the thief intends. Jesus has come to rescue the sheep from the state of death (the sentence of death) that Satan was directly responsible for, when he lied to Eve and misled her and Adam to disobey God.

Let's look at the words kill and destroy. The word for kill here means to slay, or kill. This is pretty clear. But what about destroy? Why would Jesus use a word very similar to kill, to follow the word kill? When I still held to the traditional view, this verse was a bit fuzzy to me in several ways, but I just figured the kill and destroy was sort of a redundant statement emphasizing the death and destruction of a person's future, their potential, their marriage, their happiness, etc. Just fill in the blank, if you listen to Satan he is going to kill and destroy whatever is precious to you. But I was way off on my understanding at that time. Jesus does mean kill, as in put to death. But as for destroy, is this just a redundant mention of death, or is there more to this?

Compare what Jesus said in Matthew 10:28:

> And do not be afraid of those who kill the body but are not able to kill the soul (psuche),
> but instead be afraid of the one who is able to destroy both soul (psuche) and body in hell.
> (LEB)

Jesus uses the word "kill" twice, but then says to fear the one who can "destroy" both soul and body in Gehenna. Kill means kill here. But the word destroy comes from the Greek word apollumi which means utterly destroy.

Note: Jesus uses apollumi three times in John to refer to the final destruction (the second death) of the unsaved. (John 3:16, 10:10,28). Apollumi generally means utterly destroyed, perish or totally lost, with no chance of recovery. In 3:16 and 10:28 it is translated as perish. When speaking of humans, it can refer to a person being killed (their first death), or it can refer to their second death (permanent death). For more information on the use of the words, "perish, destroy, and lost" see the chapter dedicated to this in Part 3 of this book.

Why do I bring this up? Because I believe Jesus' use of these two words is very intentional. He has already used both words in the Gospel of John, but now he uses them in the same sentence. It is quite possible that Jesus is delineating 2 distinctly different results by using these two different words. Satan has already been successful in getting all of us killed. This is called the first death. This came about when man was driven from the Garden of Eden and no longer had access to the tree of life. At that point man was destined to die. So, we all die the first death, and if it were not for the gift of eternal zoe that Jesus brought to light, our first death would be our final end. We would all stay dead. But God has a plan for resurrection that Jesus tells us about in John 5 and is explained in many places throughout the New Testament. Those whose names are in the book of zoe (the book of life), will be resurrected to eternal zoe. Those whose names are not in the book of life will be thrown into the lake of fire, called the second death. The unsaved will be destroyed at this point, they will no longer exist.

ABUNDANT LIFE: WHAT IT MEANS

Next, let's look at the word "abundant". The phrase "abundant life" has frequently been used out of context. However, for now I want to focus on what Jesus is really saying and intending with this statement.

The Greek word "perisson" in this verse has been translated most frequently in English translations as "abundantly". I want to share other meanings that this word can have. There is no biblical imperative that forces us to use the word "abundant". Although if you understand what Jesus is saying here, there is nothing wrong with using the word "abundant", I just think there are some clearer options.

Again, think about what Jesus is trying to say here. Jesus is making a stark contrast with what the thief is attempting to do to the sheep, versus what Jesus has come to do. The thief has come to steal, kill and destroy. As just mentioned, the word destroy is likely referring to the second, permanent death (eternal death).

In contrast, Jesus has come to give the sheep eternal zoe. Here in John 10:10 Jesus is merely using a unique (different) phrase that is just another way of describing eternal life. Most frequently Jesus uses the phrase "zoe unto the ages", which is translated into English as eternal life.

In this instance, in direct opposition to the death and destruction that Satan intends, Jesus has come to give the sheep "zoe" (the state of being alive), and that they might have this zoe "beyond measure".

This is just another way of saying "zoe unto the ages".

If you are interested in looking at the definition for "perisson" go the link below:

https://biblehub.com/str/greek/4053.htm

From this link you can see many similar definitions of the word that could be used. Look at some of these options below:

> Exceedingly; beyond what is anticipated; exceeding expectation; more abundant; going past the expected limit; exceeding some number or measure or rank or need; beyond measure.

Summary of John 10:10

In opposition to the death and destruction that Satan intends for the sheep, Jesus has come to give the sheep zoe that will last indefinitely, without measure. In other words, Jesus has come to give the sheep eternal life. Just as he has been doing for the last several chapters of John, Jesus is contrasting eternal zoe versus eternal death.

Think this over

To be honest with you, I initially thought about soft pedaling John 10:10 and not cutting to the chase. Since this verse has had a huge influence on all sectors of Christian teaching, I was reluctant to say what I believe this verse is truly teaching. I was concerned that many readers would be so put off by my interpretation that they would lay this book down and dismiss everything I have said. (Basically, throwing the baby out with the bath water). If you feel offended or put off, I will just ask you to keep reading until we are done with Jesus' teachings up through John chapter 11.

John 10:10 has been huge not only in the prosperity gospel (Word of Faith movement), but in traditional Christian teaching as well. Both have focused on "abundant life" as some level or "quality of blessed life" that is beyond what the Christian might experience otherwise. The prosperity gospel through its name-it-and-claim-it emphasis has twisted the meaning of this verse. More traditional Christian teaching misses the original context as well due to the fact they look at the word "life" as someone might look at this word in a typical English setting, as opposed to understanding what zoe means in the original Greek.

Does Perisson focus on Quality or Quantity?

When you combine the English word "abundant" with the English word "life", it seems to make sense to say that Jesus is talking about some higher level of spiritual walk, a blessed life or better *quality* of life.

But zoe is not used in the New Testament to refer to "life" in that sense. Zoe at its core means "the state of being alive". It is the opposite of being dead. Zoe is used 135 times in the New Testament. It is never used anywhere else in the New Testament to refer to a quality of existence. Why would Jesus change course here in John 10:10? This idea would be completely out of context with the whole narrative seen in John chapter 10. Or for that matter anywhere else in the Gospel of John or John's other writings where he uses zoe heavily, such as 1 John and the Book of Revelation.

So, when Jesus says he has come to give his sheep "zoe" he is specifically speaking of "making them physically alive", as opposed to the thief making them dead. Jesus is making a powerful and straightforward contrast. Jesus is contrasting Satan's purpose of death and destruction with Jesus's solution to this death sentence, which is resurrection to eternal zoe. Jesus's whole narrative is focusing on resurrection from the dead to eternal zoe (being physically alive forever). John is building this narrative step by step beginning in John 1:4 until he completes building this narrative in John chapter 11. After John 11, he begins to focus on Jesus final teachings, his final days with his disciples, building up to the crucifixion and then resurrection. If we follow this building of zoe that John reveals to us chapter by chapter, we will graduate in John chapter 11 with a full understanding of eternal zoe, death and resurrection. (The bullseye)

Again, when the Greek word "perisson" is used to describe the zoe that Jesus is giving to his sheep he is not referring to a "quality of life" as the traditional view has typically regarded the phrase, rather he is specifically referring to the time period (duration) of being alive after the resurrection to eternal zoe. So, instead of quality, perisson is referring to <u>quantity</u>.

Zoe is like a light switch

Zoe is a simple word. As you know by now, it means "being alive" as opposed to not being alive. As a simile, think of zoe being as simple to understand as a light switch. A light switch is either on or it is off. There is no in-between, the light is either on or it is off. There is also no quality associated with this status of on or off. You can't say, "oh if you do this or that, your light will be on so much better". No, the switch is only on, or it is off. If you want to get very bright or beautiful lights that is an entirely different matter and has nothing to do with the switch. In like manner, if you have zoe that means you are alive. Your quality of life is another matter entirely and is not addressed in John 10:10. On the other hand, Jesus' mention earlier in John 10 where he talks of the sheep finding good pasture could be seen as referring to blessings associated with Jesus being our Good Shepherd, but the statements regarding zoe are focused on resurrection to eternal life.

Don't get me wrong, there are many fruits and blessings associated with having the Spirit of Christ (aka Holy Spirit) living within you. I speak about this several times in this book. But John 10:10 is not talking about these blessings. In 10:10, Jesus is focused like a laser beam on life and death.

John 10:10 is a purpose statement! Jesus specifically says, "I have come to give my sheep zoe (being alive)". This verse is huge, we cannot afford to misunderstand what Jesus is saying here.

Jesus will hammer this point again a few verses later when we get to John 10:28.

THE GOOD SHEPHERD WILL LAY DOWN HIS PSUCHE

I Am the Good Shepherd.

"I Am" Statement # 4

So far, we have been focusing on Jesus' teaching about zoe in John 10. But John 10 is a HUGE chapter on psuche as well! In fact, if you understand the connections Jesus is making between zoe and psuche in this chapter, you will understand the thrust of the entire Bible. (On the contrary, if you do not understand the use of zoe and psuche here, you will miss what Jesus is really saying in John 10).

Jesus is about to explain what the "Good Shepherd" is willing to do, as opposed to the hired hand. Jesus is using the term "Good Shepherd" to refer to himself. The Good Shepherd is going to die for the sheep.

Jesus says he is going to lay down his psuche 3 times in John 10 (verses 11,15,17). He then elaborates on this by referring to his psuche by using the pronoun "it" 5 more times in John 10!

John 10:11 "I am the good shepherd. The good shepherd lays down his **life (psuche)** for the sheep. (LEB)

10:14-15 "**I am the good shepherd**, and I know my own, and my own know me, just as the Father knows me and I know the Father, and I lay down my **life (psuche)** for the sheep. (LEB)

10:17-18 Because of this the Father loves me, because I lay down my **life (psuche)** so that I may take possession of **it** again. 18 No one takes **it** from me, but I lay **it** down voluntarily. I have authority to lay **it** down, and I have authority to take possession of **it** again. This commandment I received from my Father." (LEB)

Jesus is telling the crowd he is going to willingly die. That is what "laying down his psuche" is referring to. Jesus' psuche is going to die when he is crucified.

John 10 gives us great insight into God's purpose for sending Jesus to the earth as a human. Jesus came to take the "death sentence" of mankind upon himself. Jesus died. His psuche was killed! But he had the authority to take his psuche up again. In other words, Jesus either resurrected due to zoe being a part of his nature, or due to zoe being restored to his psuche via the Holy Spirit. The exact mechanics of the process are not explained but are not necessary in order to understand that this was the plan of the Godhead. Jesus would die in the place of man and his psuche would be raised from the dead.

To summarize, in addition to taking our death sentence for us, Jesus came to give us zoe (being alive) forever. There are two parts to this salvation. Taking away our death sentence by dying for us and then giving us eternal zoe (resurrection from our first death to live forever).

Note: If you jumped into this book halfway and are not sure you understand the different roles that zoe and psuche are playing in John 10, then I would recommend going back and reading Part 1 of this book.

Satan has come to kill and destroy the sheep.

Jesus has come to give them zoe.

There is no mention of eternal suffering.

The ultimate fate of the sheep is clearly

depicted as either Life or Death

Summary: The simple contrast in John 10 is this:

> ➢ Satan has come to kill and destroy the sheep
> ➢ Jesus has come to save the sheep by laying down his psuche (dying) in lieu of the sheep's psuche being destroyed.
> ➢ However, this is not the end. Jesus will resurrect from the dead. He will also give the sheep this hope of resurrecting from the dead to eternal zoe.

There is no mention of eternal suffering or everlasting torment.

The ultimate fate of the sheep is clearly contrasted: Life or Death.

Be sure you realize this point: Jesus did not come to give us *psuche*; we already have psuche (that is, we are psuche).

Jesus came to lay down his psuche, taking our death sentence for us, so that ultimately he could give us zoe. He came to give us *eternal zoe*, in order to save our *psuche* forever.

Jesus did not come to give us psuche. We already exist as psuche.

Jesus came to give us eternal zoe, in order to save our psuche forever.

PURPOSE STATEMENTS

One more note: Jesus makes purpose statements in the other gospels as well. But they all boil down to the same thing, Jesus has come to save the lost (lost also comes from the word perisson). Jesus has come to give eternal zoe to those who will trust and believe in him as the Son of God, and Savior of the world. The lost are in a state of death. John's purpose statement in John 10:10 only varies from the other gospels' purpose statements because John focuses on man's state of death.

For example, see Jesus' statement in Mark 10:45. A first glance it may seem to indicate a different purpose, but upon closer inspection, it is saying the exact same thing as John 10. Jesus came to give his psuche as a ransom for the many who will believe.

> Mark 10:45 "For even the Son of Man did not come to be served but to serve, and to give his life (psuche) as a ransom for many" (ESV)

Notice that there is no way in current English Bibles to see the clear differentiation that Jesus makes in this verse. Jesus came to give his psuche as a ransom for many. (Not his zoe). Without understanding the difference in how Jesus and the New Testament authors consistently use psuche and zoe, it is very difficult if not impossible to have clarity about Jesus' purpose.

ABUNDANT LIFE: CLARIFYING WHAT IT IS <u>NOT</u>

We have just identified what Jesus meant when he spoke of "having *zoe* beyond measure." Unfortunately, we must now clarify what Jesus did *not* mean by this expression. This verse has tragically been misunderstood and misrepresented perhaps more than any other verse in the Bible.

The "Prosperity Gospel" or "Word of Faith " message promising health and wealth does not come from Jesus, period!

Just imagine the believing woman who watched her children being tortured and killed at the hands of the Roman emperors in the second and third centuries AD. Also consider the believing women who watched the exact same thing occur in 2015 and 2016, when ISIS invaded the cities of Iraq. Those women had just as much *zoe within them* and as abundantly, as any believer living on Wall Street or driving an expensive car in Beverly Hills!

In fact, those women likely had a greater measure of God's *zoe*, as the only way they could persevere through something like that (long enough to be killed themselves) was to hold on to Jesus' promises very tightly.

A person who is suffering with terminal cancer, or has a physical disability, or a person living in poverty can absolutely have certainty of eternal *zoe*. Abundant *zoe* has nothing to do with a person's financial status, social status, health, or physical life expectancy. Instead, it has to do with the absolute certainty of eternal zoe, that comes from the indwelling zoe of God (via his indwelling Holy Spirit), that guarantees that believer that they will rise from death to live forever.

Thank God for that! Let's quit beating ourselves up for not keeping up with the financial, physical, or social success of others and then blaming ourselves for not being good enough or having enough faith.

That is not to say that God does not care about the believer that is going through intense suffering and possibly even death. He promises to be with that person, through an intimate personal relationship as our heavenly father. This is a personal, caring relationship that is so close that we can call the God of the universe, "abba" father. He cares deeply about his children and is with us no matter what. But he does not guarantee that we won't see sadness, hardship, suffering or premature death.

See how David expressed his faith in the midst of suffering, unknown future and even facing the prospect of death, in the 23rd Psalm.

> **Psalm 23:4** Even though I walk through the valley of the shadow of death, I will fear no evil, for you are with me; your rod and your staff, they comfort me. (ESV)

When David said he walked through the valley of the shadow of death, he did not say he was confident that he would not die. Rather, he said he would not fear evil, for he was confident that God would be with him, comforting him.

> **Psalm 23:6** Surely goodness and mercy shall follow me all the days of my life, and I shall dwell in the house of the Lord forever.

David was confident in God's goodness and mercy during his life on earth, (no matter his circumstances), as we see in Psalm 23:6. However, his confident statement "and I shall dwell in the house of the Lord forever" turns his focus from his present life to his confidence of resurrection to eternal life. This is not the only place David makes such a statement. We will see David make this confident statement again when we get to Peter's sermon in Acts 2.

"Abundant Zoe" has nothing to do with a person's financial status,

social status, health, or physical life expectancy.

Let's get rid of the self-blame that is put on Christians who have a terminal disease and are not only dealing with the increasing pain and struggle of the disease itself but also the isolation and guilt that their church culture (in some cases) casts upon them due to the prevailing notion that their failure to be healed is due to their own lack of faith.

Shame on those who preach this lie! Shame on those who add to the pain and isolation of these dear believers!

Let's get rid of the horrid lie of "abundant *life*"! This does not come from Christ. If it doesn't come from Jesus, then take a wild guess where it comes from, based on what Jesus says in John 8 and 10.

CONTINUING CONTRAST BETWEEN ZOE AND DESTRUCTION

Sometime later in John 10, Jesus is at the Festival of Dedication in Jerusalem. He is confronted there by several Jews who question him about his identity.

Jesus resumes his conversation, continuing to use the metaphor of the shepherd and the sheep. In 10:28, Jesus makes a defining statement about eternal *zoe* and its polar opposite.

Remember, earlier in John 10:10, Jesus contrasted the fact that he came to give the sheep life (*zoe*), whereas the thief comes to kill and destroy.

John 10:10 "The thief comes only to steal and kill and destroy. I came that they may have life (*zoe*) and have it abundantly." (ESV)

Now, in 10:28, Jesus contrasts *zoe* again using essentially the same wording he used in 10:10. Perish is the English word translated from the Greek word "appoluntai". This is the same root of the word for "destruction" in 10:10.

John 10:27-30 "My sheep hear my voice, and I know them, and they follow me. I give them eternal life (zoe), and they will never perish, and no one will snatch them out of my hand. My Father, who has given them to me, is greater than all, and no one is able to snatch them out of the Father's hand. I and the Father are one. " (ESV)

127

Jesus reiterates that he will give eternal *zoe* to his sheep and that they will never perish. "Perish" and eternal zoe are exact opposites! It is implicit that by giving his followers eternal zoe, they are saved from perishing (eternal death).

TAKING A CLOSER LOOK AT "PERISH"

John 10:28 I give them eternal life (zoe), and they will **never perish**, and no one will snatch them out of my hand. (ESV)

John 10:28 And I give them eternal life (zoe), and they will **never perish <u>forever</u>,** and no one will seize them out of my hand. (LEB)

Jesus says his sheep will never perish. If you recall from John chapter 8, these "never" verses don't exactly say "never." Notice that the LEB version above includes the word forever. This is more accurate in my opinion, but still a bit hard to understand.

In verse 28 the Greek word *apolontai* comes from *apollumi* and means "utterly destroy." It is frequently translated into English as "perish" or "destroy."

Look at the Interlinear Greek-English verse on the next page.

Read the English word for word translation below the Greek (John 10:28). Does it say "**never perish?**"

| 10:28 | KArω
kagO
G2504
pp 1 Nom Sg Con
AND-I | ZωHN
zOEn
G2222
n_Acc Sg f
LIFE | AIωNION
aiOnion
G166
a_Acc Sg f
eonian | ΔIΔωMI
didOmi
G1325
vi Pres Act 1 Sg
AM-GIVING | AYTOIC
autois
G846
pp Dat Pl m
to-them
them | KAI
kai
G2532
Conj
AND |

| ΑΠΟΛωΝΤΑΙ
apolOntai
G622
vs 2Aor Mid 3 Pl
THEY-SHOULD-BE-beING-destroyED | EIC
eis
G1519
Prep
INTO | TON
ton
G3588
t_Acc Sg m
THE | AIωNA
aiOna
G165
n_Acc Sg m
eon | KAI
kai
G2532
Conj
AND |

| OY
ou
G3756
Part Neg
NOT | MH
mE
G3361
Part Neg
NO |

| AYTA
auta
G846
pp Acc Pl n
them | EK
ek
G1537
Prep
OUT | THC
tEs
G3588
t_Gen Sg f
OF-THE | XEIPOC
cheiros
G5495
n_Gen Sg f
HAND | MOY
mou
G3450
pp 1 Gen Sg
OF-ME |

| OYX
ouch
G3756
Part Neg
NOT | APΠΑCEI
harpasei
G726
vi Fut Act 3 Sg
SHALL-BE-SNATCHING | TIC
tis
G5100
px Nom Sg m
ANY
anyone |

28 And I give unto them eternal life; and they shall never perish, neither shall any [man] pluck them out of my hand.

If you combine the English words below the Greek, the verse will read something like this: "Not No they should be being destroyed into the eon." The double negative leading phrase "not no" should be read as an emphatic expression such as "in no case."

This results in the verse reading as:

"in no case should they be being destroyed into the eon"

ANOTHER LOOK

The LEB translated this as "they will never perish forever".

This can be understood in one of 2 ways. In either case Jesus is emphatically stating, "there is absolutely no way this will happen":

1- Jesus is either saying his sheep will not remain dead forever, rather Jesus intends to resurrect his sheep from their first death to eternal zoe.

2- Or Jesus is saying that his sheep will not suffer the second death. That is, they will be raised to eternal zoe, as opposed to those who are resurrected to judgment. Those resurrected to judgment will *perish* in the lake of fire (the second death), where they will be destroyed into the eon (dead forever).

Either statement would be saying the same thing. Depending on how you arrange the focus of the sentence it is just worded slightly different.

WHAT DOES "PERISH" OR "DESTROY" MEAN?

If 10:28 doesn't mean death into the eon, then how do you explain it without going into some long detour?

In most cases where you see the word perish in the New Testament, and it is referring to a person (as opposed to an object), it is referring to a person's death. Why then, would we choose to explain it differently when Jesus contrasts eternal zoe with perishing?

The traditional view frequently chooses to define perishing as "permanent separation from God while undergoing eternal torture in hell." Seriously? How does one reach this conclusion other than by ignoring the plain meaning of perish, and then resorting to some lengthy, bewildering explanation? This obfuscation cannot be supported from any of Jesus' teachings in the gospel according to John or from any of John's other books (1, 2 or 3 John or the book of Revelation) nor can it be supported from any of the apostle Paul's writings.

We will take a detailed look at the New Testament's use of this word in Part 3 of this book.

The definition for *apollumi* can be found at http://Biblehub.com/greek/622.htm

Zoe's implicit and explicit use in 10:10 and 10:28

Notice that 10:10 and 10:28 are both referring to eternal life. There is no reasonable way to explain that 10:10 is focusing on some level of blessed life, and then just a few verses later 10:28 is speaking of something entirely different. Rather, both verses are speaking of eternal life. 10:10 is using a nuance that implicitly refers to eternal zoe. 10:28 is explicitly speaking of eternal zoe.

John 10:10 The thief comes only so that he can steal and kill and destroy; I have come so that they may have life (zoe), and have it abundantly. (LEB)

John 10:28 And I give them eternal life (zoe), and they will never perish forever (LEB)

Finally, compare Jesus use of apollumi in John 3:16 below to verses 10:10,28 above. Notice the contrast in each verse, that depicts zoe versus perish and destroy.

John 3:16 For in this way God loved the world, so that he gave his one and only Son, in order that everyone who believes in him will not perish, but will have eternal life (zoe).

19

John 11

THIS WILL NOT END IN DEATH

John 11 starts out with Jesus receiving an urgent message from a family that is very dear to him. The brother Lazarus is deathly ill. Lazarus' two sisters, Mary and Martha, are caring for him and they have sent an urgent message to Jesus notifying him that Lazarus is dangerously ill.

This family is devoted to Jesus, and they are faithful believers. The sisters have seen Jesus heal many types of disease and illness and are confident that Jesus can save their brother. But this occasion is extremely urgent as Lazarus is deathly ill. When Jesus hears of Lazarus' illness, he makes a very strange statement. He states that this sickness will not *end in death*, when in fact he knows, Lazarus is going to die!

Indeed, Jesus intentionally stays where he is for two more days to make certain that Lazarus will die. He does not want to rush to Bethany at the request of the sisters in time to save Lazarus.

After remaining where he is for two more days, Jesus tells his disciples, "Let's back go Judea." He explains to his disciples that their friend Lazarus is ill and has fallen asleep. Jesus says that he is going back to Bethany (Lazarus' hometown) to wake him.

The disciples reply to Jesus that if Lazarus is sick, sleeping will help him to get better. Jesus used the term "asleep" to describe the state of Lazarus' death, but the disciples still think of it as literal sleep at this point.

So then, Jesus tells them plainly that Lazarus is dead.

Jesus has been complicit (sovereignly) in orchestrating Lazarus' death in order to demonstrate that he (Jesus) has power over death. John 11 is the pinnacle of everything that Jesus has taught up until this point. Up until now, it has been just that... talk. But now, Jesus is going to powerfully demonstrate both who he is and his purpose.

> **John 11:1-16** Now, a certain man was ill, Lazarus of Bethany, the village of Mary and her sister Martha. It was Mary who anointed the Lord with ointment and wiped his feet with her hair, whose brother Lazarus was ill. So the sisters sent to him, saying, "Lord, he whom you love is ill." But when Jesus heard it, he said, "This illness does not lead to death. It is for the glory of God, so that the Son of God may be glorified through it." Now, Jesus loved Martha and her sister and Lazarus. So when he heard that Lazarus was ill, he stayed two days longer in the place where he was. Then, after this, he said to the disciples, "Let us go to Judea again." The disciples said to him, "Rabbi, the Jews were just now seeking to stone you, and are you going there again?"

Jesus answered, "Are there not twelve hours in the day? If anyone walks in the day, he does not stumble, because he sees the light of this world. But, if anyone walks in the night, he stumbles, because the light is not in him." After saying these things, he said to them, "Our friend Lazarus has fallen asleep, but I go to awaken him." The disciples said to him, "Lord, if he has fallen asleep, he will recover." Now Jesus had spoken of his death, but they thought that he meant taking rest in sleep. Then Jesus told them plainly, "Lazarus has died, and for your sake I am glad that I was not there, so that you may believe. But let us go to him." So Thomas, called the Twin, said to his fellow disciples, "Let us also go, that we may die with him." (ESV)

TAKING A CLOSER LOOK

John 11:4 But, when Jesus heard it, he said, "**This illness does not lead to death**. It is for the glory of God, so that the Son of God may be glorified through it." (ESV)

Jesus knew that Lazarus was about to die. Jesus was not lying or intentionally misleading his disciples. Jesus' intent can be understood in the phrase "does not lead to death."

Ultimately, this will not end in death as Jesus will demonstrate when he gets to Lazarus' hometown of Bethany. There is something to be aware of at this point in Jesus' ministry. Jesus is either partially or totally sovereign. His close relationship with God his Father enables him to either foresee or even possibly orchestrate this event. But to be sure the events in this chapter are totally orchestrated by God to bring clarity as to Jesus' purpose and who he is.

Everything in John's gospel thus far has been preparing us for the clarifying moment that will occur in the next few verses.

Just as we have seen throughout the Gospel of John, Jesus has been focusing on the "End Game". His focus is on saving man from eternal death by giving them eternal life. He has been consistently speaking of the assurance of resurrecting from the dead to eternal zoe, never to die again. So, in 11:4 when Jesus said that Lazarus illness does not lead to death, he was not speaking of the death that Lazarus just experienced. Rather he is referring to Lazarus not remaining dead forever. Jesus will spell this out in the next few verses.

YOUR BROTHER WILL RISE AGAIN

Jesus and his disciples arrive in Bethany four days after Lazarus has died. As they approach Lazarus' home, Martha (Lazarus' sister) runs out to meet Jesus. Martha is broken hearted, and she pours out her heart to Jesus about her beloved brother, Lazarus. She is confident that if Jesus had been there, he could have cured Lazarus and prevented him from dying. She cannot understand why Jesus did not come to his rescue.

After all, they had sent word to Jesus that Lazarus was sick. Yet, even during her current disappointment and confusion, she still reaches out to Jesus for some type of hope, even though she is not sure what to hope for. She does not understand why Lazarus had to die. Despite her despair and confusion, she lets Jesus know that she still believes in him.

In this very intimate conversation between Jesus and Martha, John provides the final clarification on *zoe*. If you blink you will miss the whole thing. But it is the skilled and inspired hand of the author (John) who places this clarifying statement not amid a large group of half-hearted believers, curious onlookers or murderous critics . . .

Rather, it is a soft-spoken statement made by Jesus as he tenderly lifts the fallen face of one who has wholeheartedly believed in him, followed him and served him. Looking directly into the eyes of this dear, broken-hearted sister, he whispers truth and hope to her.

Truth and hope that now resonate throughout the world and have done so for two millennia.

That is how life and death works though, isn't it? It is indeed a very personal thing. You may fear losing a dearly loved one or maybe even fear death for yourself. It is not the message that is spoken to crowds that will bring you comfort in the end. At the end, it is knowing that Jesus is looking into your eyes and speaks truth, hope, and love, that he will take you home to where you belong, in God's family.

> **John 11:17-32** Now, when Jesus came, he found that Lazarus had already been in the tomb four days. Bethany was near Jerusalem, about two miles off, and many of the Jews had come to Martha and Mary to console them concerning their brother. So when Martha heard that Jesus was coming, she went and met him, but Mary remained seated in the house. Martha said to Jesus, "Lord, if you had been here, my brother would not have died. But, even now, I know that whatever you ask from God, God will give you."
>
> Jesus said to her, "Your brother will rise again." Martha said to him, "I know that he will rise again in the resurrection on the last day." Jesus said to her, "I am the resurrection and the life. Whoever believes in me, though he dies, yet shall he live, and everyone who lives and believes in me shall never die. Do you believe this?" She said to him, "Yes, Lord; I believe that you are the Christ, the Son of God, who is coming into the world." When she had said this, she went and called her sister Mary, saying in private, "The Teacher is here and is calling for you." And when she heard it, she rose quickly and went to him. Now, Jesus had not yet come into the village, but was still in the place where Martha had met him.
>
> When the Jews, who were with her in the house consoling her, saw Mary rise quickly and go out, they followed her, supposing that she was going to the tomb to weep there. Now, when Mary came to where Jesus was and saw him, she fell at his feet, saying to him, "Lord, if you had been here, my brother would not have died." (ESV)

MARTHA'S PLEA

> **John 11:21-22** Martha said to Jesus, "Lord, if you had been here, my brother would not have died. But, even now, I know that whatever you ask from God, God will give you." (ESV)

Martha holds on to what she knows from the things she has seen Jesus do, as well as what she has heard him teach. She has no doubt that he is the Messiah, the son of God and that God will do whatever he asks. While she is confessing her unwavering faith in Jesus, she appears at the same time to hint that she knows that Jesus can raise her brother from the dead.

John 11:23-24 Jesus said to her, "Your brother will rise again." Martha said to him, "I know that he will rise again in the resurrection on the last day." (ESV)

Jesus assures her that her brother will rise again. Martha expresses that she understands Jesus' teachings about eternal zoe. She also knows her brother was a believer, which explains her confidence of his resurrection at the last day. Martha has clearly been following Jesus' teachings for a long time and has an understanding of his teachings on *zoe*, including the resurrection.

THE DEFINING MOMENT

Dear friend. Let me be transparent with you as to how I feel about John 11:25-26. From time to time I have mentioned verses that I have said are key to understanding Jesus's message. And when I've said that I truly meant it with all my heart. But in John 11:25-26, we come to the culmination of Jesus's teaching on zoe in the Gospel of John. Everything we have seen thus far in John has prepared us for this exact moment. From this point forward, John will turn his focus to Jesus final teachings, his last moments with his disciples, his crucifixion and his resurrection. In 11:25-26 John provides us with the final clarity as to the role of Jesus's zoe.

Even Jesus's own sovereignty (as he has shown by orchestrating Lazarus death), has brought us to this defining moment. Please don't miss this, this is *indeed the defining moment*. Jesus is about to define both verbally and by action what zoe and the resurrection are all about. We are about to get clarity as to Jesus's powerful role in the assurance that should be the focus of every believer.

As we proceed into John 11:25,26 please remember the nuances of zoe. Jesus is going to state that he is "the zoe". What does he mean by this? If you recall from chapter 4 (Nuances of Zoe), there can be more than one nuance being used here. I believe Jesus is saying two things here, which are basically pointing to the same thing, but that's the deal with nuances, they are subtly tied together. When Jesus says "I am the zoe" he is saying:

- I am the source of zoe (the source of being alive). More specifically he is referring to being the source of being alive again, upon the resurrection from the dead.
- I am the zoe. That is, it is Jesus's own zoe indwelling the psuche of the believer that accomplishes two very powerful things. First while the believer is still alive in this present world, Jesus's zoe living within the believer gives them the absolute assurance that they will be resurrected from the dead to live again. Second, it is this same zoe of Jesus, through the same indwelling Holy Spirit that will raise the believer from the dead, to zoe again, this time to live forever. This is known as zoe unto the ages, or eternal zoe. This is translated in English bibles as 'eternal life'.

JESUS' REPLY TO MARTHA

Jesus now responds to Martha's statement, where she says that she knows that her brother will rise again in the resurrection at the last day.

Jesus' response to Martha incorporates another of his "I Am" statements. This statement summarizes Jesus primary purpose and God's solution to the problem of death.

This the most purposeful verse in the gospel according to John.

Indeed, this statement is the fulfillment of the whole Bible.

I Am the Resurrection and the Zoe

"I Am" Statement 5

John 11:25-26 Jesus said to her, "**I am the resurrection and the life (zoe)**. Whoever believes in me, though he dies, yet shall he live, and everyone who lives and believes in me shall never die. Do you believe this?" (ESV)

Jesus is making a factual statement to reassure Martha, clarifying who he is and helping her understand what is about to take place in the next few minutes. There are two verses here with the second verse building upon the first. Let's look at this construct beginning with the first verse.

I AM THE RESURRECTION AND THE *ZOE*

John 11:25 Jesus said to her, "I am the resurrection and the life (zoe). (ESV)

Jesus replies to Martha's statement that she knows Lazarus will rise again in the resurrection on the last day. It is like Jesus is holding her gaze, looking into her eyes, and gently speaking the following:

'Martha, do you realize who you are talking to? I am the resurrection you speak of. I am the *zoe*, which makes resurrection possible. You are talking to the one individual in the universe who is the source of zoe that will make resurrection possible'.

Jesus gives believers *zoe* via the impartation of the indwelling Holy Spirit into the psuche of the believer in order that they might be resurrected to eternal *zoe*.

So, when Jesus says, "I am the resurrection and the *zoe*," he is being profoundly accurate.

There are two more critical sentences to look at in these two verses, let's continue.

WHOEVER BELIEVES, THOUGH HE DIES, YET SHALL HE LIVE

John 11:25-26 Jesus said to her, "I am the resurrection and the life (zoe). Whoever believes in me, though he dies, yet shall he live . . ." (ESV)

While Jesus comforts and encourages Martha, he is also clarifying her understanding. Since Lazarus was a believer, Martha can have confidence that even though Lazarus has died, he shall live again.

To Summarize: The one who believes in Jesus as the Messiah, the Son of God, can confidently be assured that even if they die, they will live again. That is, they will resurrect from the dead.

Anyone who believes in Jesus as the Messiah, the Son of God,

can confidently know that even though they

die a bodily death, they will live again.

That is, they will rise from the dead.

What better way to drive this point home than to raise Lazarus from the dead? We are about to witness Jesus finally demonstrate who he is and his authority to make the claims he has been making about zoe all through the gospel according to John up to this point.

Note: We are about to look at the third and final statement that Jesus makes in these two verses. However, this statement will be the most difficult that we have encountered in our study. In most English translations, the next verse appears to contradict what Jesus just said in the previous sentence.

Yet, it is this last statement that culminates everything John has been preparing us for: the ultimate purpose of Jesus and the zoe that he gives.

WHOEVER LIVES AND BELIEVES IN ME SHALL NEVER DIE

This last sentence of Jesus' reply to Martha is the final clarification that John provides for us into the purpose of *zoe*.

> **John 11:26** . . . and everyone who lives [root word of zoe] and believes in me shall never die. (ESV)

Jesus begins by reiterating what he just said in the previous sentence. He does this for emphasis. In other words, Jesus is now clarifying the person from the previous sentence as "that person who lives and believes".

Then Jesus makes a profound statement about the assurance that "this person who lives and believes" can confidently hold onto. Don't miss this. This is the apex of everything we have learned so far about zoe in the gospel of John.

According to the ESV translation, Jesus says this person **shall never die**. That sounds awesome, right? But does this accurately portray what Jesus said?

Jesus just said in verse 25 that this person will indeed die. Does it make sense to say in the very next sentence that this person will never die? Maybe it does, maybe not, let's dig into this statement.

A PERSPECTIVE FROM THE LEB

Let's take another look at John 11:25-26, this time from the Lexham English Bible.

> **John 11:25-26** Jesus said to her, "I am the resurrection and the life. The one who believes in me, even if he dies, will live, 26 and everyone who lives and believes in me will never die forever. (LEB)

I like this English translation better. I think it does a better job of conveying what Jesus said here. But just exactly what does it mean to never die forever? Or could it be worded even more clearly?

From the Greek text on the following page, we can see that the first verse might be read as:

> **John 11:25** I am the resurrection and the zoe. The one believing into me, even if ever he may be dying, he shall be living.

Jesus says this as a prelude to what he is about to demonstrate. Remember, Lazarus is dead and lying in the tomb. Jesus is going to prove his authority to make this statement (if ever he may be dying) by raising Lazarus from the dead (he shall be living).

Now, to verse 26. If you remember from John 8, whenever the English translation reads "shall never die," it doesn't exactly state that in the original Greek. The Greek words that Jesus uses here are almost identical to the wording he used in John 8.

Carefully read the word-for-word translation that is shown below the Greek words for John 11:25-26 in the screen capture on the following page.

You can also see this by going to the following link:

https://www.scripture4all.org/OnlineInterlinear/NTpdf/joh11.pdf

11:25

EITTEN	H	AYTH	O	IHCOYC	ErW	EIMI	H	ANACTACIC
eipen	hE	autE	ho	iEsous	egO	eimi	hE	anastasis
G2036	G3588	G846	G3588	G2424	G1473	G1510	G3588	G386
vi 2Aor Act 3 Sg	t_ Nom Sg f	pp Dat Sg f	t_ Nom Sg m	n_ Nom Sg m	pp 1 Nom Sg	vi Pres vxx 1 Sg	t_ Nom Sg f	n_ Nom Sg f
said	THE	to-her	THE	JESUS	I	AM	THE	UP-STANDing resurrection

KAI	H	ZWH	O	PICTEYWN	EIC	EME	KAN
kai	hE	zOE	ho	pisteuOn	eis	eme	kan
G2532	G3588	G2222	G3588	G4100	G1519	G1691	G2579
Conj	t_ Nom Sg f	n_ Nom Sg f	t_ Nom Sg m	vp Pres Act Nom Sg m	Prep	pp 1 Acc Sg	Cond Con
AND	THE	LIFE	THE	one-BELIEVING one-believing	INTO	ME	AND-[IF]-EVER even-if-ever

ATTOOANH	ZHCETAI
apothanE	zEsetai
G599	G2198
vs 2Aor Act 3 Sg	vi Fut midD 3 Sg
he-MAY-BE-FROM-DYING he-may-be-dying	SHALL-BE-LIVING

11:26

KAI	TTAC	O	ZWN	KAI	PICTEYWN	EIC
kai	pas	ho	zOn	kai	pisteuOn	eis
G2532	G3956	G3588	G2198	G2532	G4100	G1519
Conj	a_ Nom Sg m	t_ Nom Sg m	vp Pres Act Nom Sg m	Conj	vp Pres Act Nom Sg m	Prep
AND	EVERY	THE	one-LIVING one-living	AND	BELIEVING	INTO

EME					
eme					
G1691					
pp 1 Acc Sg					
ME					

MH	ATTOOANH	EIC	TON	AIWNA	OY
mE	apothanE	eis	ton	aiOna	ou
G3361	G599	G1519	G3588	G165	G3756
Part Neg	vs 2Aor Act 3 Sg	Prep	t_ Acc Sg m	n_ Acc Sg m	Part Neg
NO	MAY-BE-FROM-DYING may-be-dying	INTO	THE	eon	NOT

PICTEYEIC	TOYTO
pisteueis	touto
G4100	G5124
vi Pres Act 2 Sg	pd Acc Sg n
YOU-ARE-BELIEVING	this

25 Jesus said unto her, I am the resurrection, and the life: he that believeth in me, though he were dead, yet shall he live:

26 And whosoever liveth and believeth in me shall never die. Believest thou this?

THREE POSSIBLE INTERPRETATIONS

If you assemble the words in 11:26, it will easily read as follows:

And every one living and believing into me, in no case may be dying into the eon.

I believe Jesus is building upon his statement in 11:25 by further clarifying it in verse 26. He is stating one of three things, which are all essentially the same result. He is either saying:

1. He may indeed be saying this person <u>will never die forever</u>. If this is the best translation, then Jesus is referring to the *resurrected* believer. (The term *living and believing* is referring to the believer after they have been resurrected from the dead). In this case, Jesus is saying that the resurrected believer will not die again. This would not be the case with the unsaved. They will be resurrected unto judgment, where they will be put to death forever (at the second death). This second death is indeed permanent. They do die forever.
2. The second scenario is similar to the one above. With the main difference being that the believer who is still alive (living and believing unto me) in their present life in this present world, has the absolute assurance of not dying the second death. They do not have to fear the second death.
3. That the believer who is still alive (living and believing unto me) in their present life in this present world, has the absolute assurance of not remaining dead into the eon. In other words, they can have absolute confidence that Jesus (the source of zoe) will raise them from the dead. This is my preferred interpretation, but all three of these interpretations end up with the same result, that is, the believer will be resurrected from the dead, to never die again.

All 3 of these scenarios are clear statements about resurrection. John 11:25-26 is 100% focused on resurrection from death to eternal life. Jesus is the resurrection, and it is his zoe (the power of an indestructible life) that will raise all believers from the dead.

JESUS RAISES LAZARUS FROM THE DEAD

John 11:33-44 When Jesus saw her weeping, and the Jews who had come with her also weeping, he was deeply moved in his spirit and greatly troubled. And he said, "Where have you laid him?" They said to him, "Lord, come and see." Jesus wept. So the Jews said, "See how he loved him!" But some of them said, "Could not he who opened the eyes of the blind man also have kept this man from dying?" Then Jesus, deeply moved again, came to the tomb. It was a cave, and a stone lay against it. Jesus said, "Take away the stone." Martha, the sister of the dead man, said to him, "Lord, by this time there will be an odor, for he has been dead four days." Jesus said to her, "Did I not tell you that if you believed you would see the glory of God?"

So they took away the stone. And Jesus lifted up his eyes and said, "Father, I thank you that you have heard me. I knew that you always hear me, but I said this on account of the people standing around, that they may believe that you sent me." When he had said these things, he cried out with a loud voice, "Lazarus, come out." The man who had died came out, his hands

141

and feet bound with linen strips, and his face wrapped with a cloth. Jesus said to them, "Unbind him, and let him go." (ESV)

TAKING A CLOSER LOOK

John 11:38-39 Then Jesus, deeply moved again, came to the tomb. It was a cave, and a stone lay against it. Jesus said, "Take away the stone." Martha, the sister of the dead man, said to him, "Lord, by this time there will be an odor, for he has been dead four days." (ESV)

What better way to prove that you are indeed the source of resurrection and zoe (the state of being alive) than to raise someone from the dead in the midst of a large group of people who knew this dead person, have been there several days mourning for him and supporting the family? This validates all that Jesus has taught throughout the gospel according to John. Raising Lazarus from the dead confirms Jesus' authority as God's son to give *zoe* to those who believe and to resurrect them from death.

Raising Lazarus from the dead was a sign of Jesus' power over death, and the ultimate resurrection he makes available for all who will believe. Lazarus will indeed die again later. Lazarus' ultimate resurrection will come on the final resurrection day.

You see, it is not the first death that Jesus intends to save us from. It is the second death. We are resurrected to eternal life (*zoe unto the ages*). Remember that Jesus told his disciples earlier in this chapter that this would not "end" in Lazarus' death, even though Jesus knew Lazarus was already dead.

It is this **end** that we must all comes to grips with. Jesus does not intend to let any of us "end" in death. But the ultimate choice is ours. We can receive his life (*zoe*) and preserve our *psuche* by believing in the truth about who he is, and what he has done for us . . .

Or we can face the certainty of the perishing of our *psuche*.

HOLDING ON TO WHAT YOU BELIEVE

Notice Martha's reply when Jesus asks if she believes his statement about death and the resurrection and the life (*zoe*).

John 11:25-27 Jesus said to her, "I am the resurrection and the life (zoe). Whoever believes in me, though he die, yet shall he live, and everyone who lives and believes in me shall never die. Do you believe this?" She said to him, "Yes, Lord; I believe that you are the Christ, the Son of God, who is coming into the world." (ESV)

In the midst of Lazarus' death and Jesus' delay in coming, Martha is distressed, confused, disappointed, and hurt. As she looks to Jesus, her heart is filled with pain and a deep question: "Why did Lazarus have to die?" She believed in Jesus deeply. She trusted him. Now she questions in her heart… Can she still trust him?

Her answer to Jesus's question "Do you believe this?", is profound.

John 11:27 She said to him, "Yes, Lord; I believe that you are the Christ, the Son of God, who is coming into the world." (ESV)

Her belief held fast, even though she did not understand all that was going on. Her statement was one of conviction. "No matter what, I am holding on to my belief that you are the Messiah, the one who is promised to come into the world. I don't understand what you are doing right now, but I believe you are in control. I don't understand why things are going the way they are, but I will hold onto you."

Jesus says that if we believe, we will see the glory of God. Faith often comes before complete understanding. In fact, sometimes we may never get the full understanding that we seek in this lifetime. Faith comes first. Holding on to the dear truth that we believe, even in spite of those things that cause us to doubt and question, is genuine faith. We will see Jesus' glory, sometimes dimly, but just enough to keep us going. Then some day, we will see him in all his glory.

THE RESURRECTION OF LAZARUS

John 11:41-42 So they took away the stone. And Jesus lifted up his eyes and said, "Father, I thank you that you have heard me. I knew that you always hear me, but I said this on account of the people standing around, that they may believe that you sent me." (ESV)

This death and resurrection of Lazarus was orchestrated by God the Father and Jesus his son. The purpose of the resurrection of Lazarus was to punctuate Jesus' teaching about life (*zoe*) and death by demonstrating his authority and power over death. It was done for the benefit of the people who were there, so that any doubts as to Jesus' credibility were removed. In fact, the word of Lazarus' resurrection spread like wildfire and caused many to believe in Jesus.

For this reason, the Pharisees sought not only to kill Jesus but Lazarus as well. See the verses below from John 12:

John 12:9-11 When the large crowd of the Jews learned that Jesus was there, they came, not only on account of him but also to see Lazarus, whom he had raised from the dead. So the chief priests made plans to put Lazarus to death as well, because on account of him many of the Jews were going away and believing in Jesus. (ESV)

20

Elaborating on *Zoe*

The crux of Jesus's teaching on zoe culminated in John chapter 11.

But there are still some interesting conversations about zoe remaining to be seen in the gospel of John.

JOHN 12

Let's look at some excerpts from the last few chapters of John, where Jesus continues his teaching using *zoe*.

> **John 12:23-25** And Jesus answered them, "The hour has come for the Son of Man to be glorified. Truly, truly, I say to you, unless a grain of wheat falls into the earth and dies, it remains alone; but if it dies, it bears much fruit. Whoever loves his **life (psuche)** loses it, and whoever hates his **life (psuche)** in this world will keep it for **eternal life (zoe)**." (ESV)

Can you understand what Jesus is saying in the first part of the paragraph above? Can you see how this makes sense with respect to *zoe*? Jesus is explaining the need for his death.

The seed that Jesus speaks of is himself. Jesus was using this metaphor to describe the process of him dying, literally dying, and then coming back to life (zoe) upon his resurrection. His seed (The spirit of Jesus aka the Holy Spirit) then bears fruit by indwelling believers, imparting zoe unto them. This seed (the zoe of Jesus) assures believers of resurrection from the dead to live forever.

In the second paragraph (verse 25), Jesus emphasizes that the person who hates their *psuche* in this world will keep it for eternal *zoe*. Hating your own *psuche* is a way of saying that you are not seeking your own selfish, worldly desires and that you are not afraid of sacrificing your *psuche* if you are persecuted unto death.

Your psuche will be preserved for eternal zoe (your psuche will resurrect from the dead to live again, this time forever) due to the fact that zoe indwells you. Jesus' zoe (the metaphorical seed in these verses) will bear fruit by resurrecting you to live forever.

This "bearing fruit" may also be a reference to the fruit of the spirit in the life of the Christian during their lifetime on earth, in this present age. But the connection of the fruit (based upon the context of the whole paragraph) appears to be connecting Jesus death and resurrection, to the keeping or preserving the psuche of the believer unto eternal zoe.

> **John 12:47-50** "If anyone hears my words and does not keep them, I do not judge him; for I did not come to judge the world but to save the world. The one who rejects me and does not

receive my words has a judge; the word that I have spoken will judge him on the last day. For I have not spoken on my own authority, but the Father who sent me has himself given me a commandment—what to say and what to speak. And I know that his commandment is **eternal life (zoe).**" (ESV)

Jesus states his purpose here again but uses slightly different words. He did not come to judge the world. He came to save the world by giving believers eternal *zoe*. Whoever rejects Jesus' words of salvation will be judged by the very words they disdained, because they refused to come to Jesus, the only source of zoe.

Jesus explains that he follows his Father's commands in all that he says. Jesus understood the mission that the Father had sent him on. Jesus' obedience to his Father's commands has resulted in a path for mankind to eternal zoe. Coming to earth as a mortal man, to die for all mankind's sin, and to provide eternal zoe to those who will believe, was the fulfillment of the commands from the Father. Jesus was sent on a mission; he had a purpose which he faithfully accomplished.

JOHN 14

I Am the Way, the Truth, and the Zoe.

"I Am" Statement 6

In John 14:6 we see another of Jesus' famous "I Am" statements. Jesus is spending his last evening with his disciples before he is crucified. The disciples are unaware what is about to happen, as Jesus will not be betrayed until later in the evening. Jesus delivers his final teaching to his disciples in his last hours with them. He gives them words of direction and comfort that they will need in the coming days, weeks, and years.

> **John 14:1-6** "Let not your hearts be troubled. Believe in God; believe also in me. In my Father's house are many rooms. If it were not so, would I have told you that I go to prepare a place for you? And if I go and prepare a place for you, I will come again and will take you to myself, that where I am you may be also. And you know the way to where I am going."
>
> Thomas said to him, "Lord, we do not know where you are going. How can we know the way?"
>
> Jesus said to him, "I am the way, and the truth, and the **life (zoe)**. No one comes to the Father except through me." (ESV)

Breaking This Down - John 14:6

➤ **Jesus is the only way** (the only path) that God has provided for man to be saved from death and to be rejoined in fellowship with God for eternity.

➤ **Jesus is the truth.** Jesus is specifically referring to the truth about *who he is and his purpose*, that a person embraces in order to be saved.

➤ **Finally, Jesus is the *zoe*.** When someone believes in Jesus they cross over from death to *zoe*. The *zoe* of Jesus is deposited within the believer via the indwelling Holy Spirit, bringing the assurance of eternal *zoe* to that person's *psuche*. The believer is thus born again, a second time, this time by the Holy Spirit. Jesus's statement about being *the zoe* is technically right on point. Jesus is our zoe. It is his indwelling zoe that will resurrect us to eternal zoe.

➤ **Important Note:** Jesus's statment about being *the zoe* is not some broad philosophical statement about a type or quality of life. In our modern day-to-day English terminology, we might say something like, "being a successful business person or engineer is a good life". This figure of speech denotes a *quality* of lifestyle. But this is not anything like what Jesus is saying. Zoe means "being alive". Jesus is speaking specifically about being our source for "being alive" when we are resurrected from the dead to live forever.

As Jesus continues encouraging his disciples during his last evening with them, he tells them about the Holy Spirit, which the Father will give to the disciples to indwell them. The terms Holy Spirit, Spirit of Truth and Spirit of Christ (Jesus) are used interchangeably in the New Testament, and all refer to the Spirit of God.

> **John 14:15-17** "If you love me, you will keep my commandments. And I will ask the Father, and he will give you another Helper, to be with you forever, even the Spirit of truth, whom the world cannot receive, because it neither sees him nor knows him. You know him, for **he dwells with you** and **will be in you**." (ESV)

Notice that Jesus says the Spirit currently lives <u>with</u> them (due to Jesus' current physical presence with them) and will soon be <u>in</u> them (when Jesus bestows the Spirit upon them to indwell them). Jesus will bestow the Spirit upon them after he is resurrected from the dead (this event is recorded in John 20:22).

Jesus assures them that he will not leave them as orphans. Again, this is due to the indwelling presence that they will receive from him when he bestows the Holy Spirit into them, which will remain within them even after Jesus ascends back to Heaven.

BECAUSE I LIVE, YOU ALSO WILL LIVE

Lastly, Jesus remarks to them that because he lives, they also will live. This is huge, please don't miss this powerful verse!

> **John 14:17-19** "You know him, for he dwells with you and will be in you. I will not leave you as orphans; I will come to you. Yet a little while and the world will see me no more, but you will see me. **Because I live, you also will live.**" (ESV)

There are three points here that are critical to understand.

1. Jesus lives, for two reasons. First, he has zoe (the inherent capacity for being alive) within himself and is not dependent on anyone or anything else for his being alive and remaining alive. Now, that all changed when he became human. Hebrews 2 tells us that he became lower than the angels, by becoming a human... for the purpose of suffering death.

2. Jesus was crucified. He did indeed die. He lost his psuche, his psuche was killed, he was as dead as a doornail. But God raised him back to life via the Holy Spirit. We aren't given enough information to totally understand the mechanics of this process, but that's ok. We understand that the source of zoe (being alive) comes from the trinitarian Godhead, and that the design and purpose of Jesus' death and resurrection was to bring Jesus back to zoe (becoming alive again).

3. So, Jesus is telling his disciples that just as he will live (after he is resurrected) that they can also expect to live. This is a clear promise from Jesus to his disciples that they will be resurrected from the dead.

Remember what Jesus previously said about the seed dying and bearing much fruit in John 12:24? The seed that Jesus spoke of was himself. Jesus was using this metaphor to describe the process of him dying, (literally dying), and then coming back to life (zoe) and his seed (eternal zoe) bearing fruit by bringing all believers back to zoe, to live forever. This seed (the zoe of Jesus) began to indwell all believers, assuring them of living forever. The zoe of Jesus is immortal and imparts immortality to the psuche of believers.

JOHN 15

I Am the True Vine.
"I Am" Statement 7

In the following verses Jesus uses the metaphor of himself as the vine, whereas believers are the branches attached to the vine. The point he makes here is that the branches must "remain" in the vine. The branch is dependent upon the life flowing from the vine to keep it alive, help it grow, and ultimately bear fruit. Without this sustenance flowing from the vine, the branch has no hope of growing or bearing fruit.

> **John 15:1-8** "I am the true vine, and my Father is the vinedresser. Every branch in me that does not bear fruit, he takes away, and every branch that does bear fruit, he prunes, that it may bear more fruit. Already, you are clean because of the word that I have spoken to you. Abide in me and I in you. As the branch cannot bear fruit by itself unless it abides in the vine, neither can you unless you abide in me. I am the vine; you are the branches. Whoever abides in me and I in him, he it is that bears much fruit, for, apart from me, you can do nothing. If anyone does not abide in me, he is thrown away like a branch and withers; and the branches are gathered, thrown into the fire, and burned. If you abide in me, and my words abide in you, ask whatever you wish, and it will be done for you. By this, my Father is glorified, that you bear much fruit and so prove to be my disciples." (ESV)

The Greek word for "remain" is *meno*. This word means "abide, dwell within, or remain." It denotes one person dwelling or living within a home.

Jesus is instructing them to remain in his word, allowing his word to dwell in them. This metaphor is a perfect illustration of the life-giving sustenance of *zoe* within the believer.

The believer's assurance of eternal zoe is due to Jesus indwelling them through the Holy Spirit. The ultimate end game of Jesus's zoe indwelling the believer will be revealed at the resurrection when the believer is raised from dead with a new imperishable body that will live forever.

However, in the interim while the believer is still alive in this world, Jesus desires for them to be fruitful. In order for the believer to grow and be fruitful they must abide in Jesus' teachings, daily meditating on the truth and seeking application of God's word in their lives.

This also entails prayer, watchful waiting, and dependence upon God. As we depend in this manner upon the "vine," Jesus' Spirit (Holy Spirit) flows into and through the believer, providing growth and fruit.

The final caveat that Jesus makes is that apart from him... we can do nothing. In other words, the branch cannot expect to survive, grow, and bear fruit unless it remains in the vine. We cannot consistently and effectively resist sin or bear the fruit of the Spirit without continually abiding in Jesus.

Paul lists the fruit of the Spirit in Galatians 5:22-23.

Gal. 5:22-23 But, the fruit of the Spirit is love, joy, peace, patience, kindness, goodness, faithfulness, gentleness, self-control. (ESV)

All believers will continue to deal with their sinfulness to one degree or another. To the extent in which we abide in Jesus (keeping in step with the Spirit), we will be more like him. But even so, when we sin it is this conscious abiding in his love despite our sin that still provides comfort and assurance that we are still his, bathed in his forgiveness and never-ending love.

This is a love that pursues us based on his faithfulness, not ours. It is a love that always draws us back to him. Never, ever consider yourself too far gone, too unworthy to draw back to him. There is no such thing as being too unworthy. There is only one who was worthy, and he died for you, in order to draw you unto himself.

Gal. 5:25 If we live by the Spirit, let us also keep in step with the Spirit. (ESV)

Gal. 5:25 Since we live by the Spirit, let us walk in step with the Spirit (BSB)

Paul makes an important point here in 5:25, that *since* it is by the Holy Spirit that we now live then it *behooves* us to keep in step with this life-giving Holy Spirit.

Please don't miss this connection. It is only because of the indwelling Holy Spirit, that we live (in the sense that we have the spirit of Christ living within us enabling us to live forever, in essence already possessing eternal zoe). Remember, it is the Holy Spirit that imparts zoe (immortality… the assurance of living forever) into the psuche of the believer.

Paul is calling us therefore to keep in step with the Holy Spirit.

Have you ever tried dancing with a partner? Generally, one partner will lead, and the other must keep in step with the one that is leading. That's what we do when we remain in Jesus. We are essentially keeping in step with the Spirit, allowing Jesus to lead us and staying in cadence with him. We fumble, stumble, step on his toes, but his loving, patient hand ever encourages us, never letting us go, never tiring of our poor dance. Just hold on to his hands, look in his eyes, and never give up seeking to keep in step with Jesus' Holy Spirit.

It is never us leading, although we have a strong tendency to try to lead, usually to poor avail. Instead, let us always seek to keep in step (cadence) with Jesus' gentle guidance through prayer and meditation on his word, seeking his guidance on how to apply his word to our lives.

To the extent that we do this, we will bear his fruit. If we do not, then at best, we will be a branch that survives but bears little or no fruit.

> **Since** it is by the Holy Spirit that **we now live**, then it **behooves**
>
> us **to keep in step** with this **life-giving Holy Spirit**

JOHN 17

Jesus further defines "eternal *zoe*" as personally knowing the Father and the Son.

> **John 17:1-3** Jesus said these things, and lifting up his eyes to heaven he said, "Father, the hour has come! Glorify your Son, in order that your Son may glorify you— just as you have given him authority over all flesh, in order that he would give **eternal life (zoe)** to them—everyone whom you have given him. Now this is **eternal life (zoe)**: that they know you, the only true God, and Jesus Christ, whom you have sent. (LEB)

When Jesus says that "this is eternal zoe", he is referring to this relationship with the Father and the Son that is the very source of eternal zoe for the believer. Jesus uses the idea of *knowing* as another expression of this *abiding* relationship of the believer with the Father and the Son.

In Jesus' prayer above, we can also see that an intrinsic aspect of eternal *zoe* is knowing God on a personal basis.

It is through the indwelling Spirit that we are brought into the family of fellowship with the Father, Son, and Spirit. This is the restoration of Eden. Man had a personal knowledge of God while in the Garden of Eden. When Adam and Eve were driven out of the garden, they lost access to the tree of zoe which would have allowed them to live forever. In addition, they lost access to their direct personal relationship with God. It was God's intent to bring man back into this close relationship.

In John 17:26, Jesus clarifies this process a bit more during his prayer to God the Father. He has made the Father known to his apostles and will "continue" to make the Father known to them. This "continuing" process will come through the indwelling Spirit which is yet to come. Jesus makes it clear to the apostles that he is not leaving them as orphans but that he will come back to them via the indwelling spirit. This personal revelation of God has been emphasized by Jesus in the preceding chapters as well, (as seen in John 14:15-21 and John 16:7-14).

> **John 17:26** "I made known to them your name, and I will continue to make it known, that the love with which you have loved me may be in them, and I in them." (ESV)

Getting to know God on this personal level is lifelong process for the Christian. As we imperfectly listen and abide in Jesus, our intimate knowledge will wane and ebb. But God is mercifully patient and loving and constantly woos us to be ever closer to him if we but take the time to be still, abide, listen, and rest in Jesus. God is faithful even when we are not. Never give up on yourself!

JOHN 20

Near the end of his gospel, John summarizes his intent for writing this narrative about Jesus. His heart's desire was that his readers might believe that Jesus is the Messiah, the Son of God, and that by believing that they might have the absolute assurance of living forever. When John uses zoe in this manner, he is speaking proleptically about the believer's assurance of being raised from the dead to eternal zoe.

There is no other way to receive eternal zoe except through Jesus.

> **John 20:30-31** Now, Jesus did many other signs in the presence of the disciples, which are not written in this book; but these are written so that you may believe that Jesus is the Christ, the Son of God, and that by believing you may have **life (zoe)** in his name. (ESV)

21

The Three Stages of *Zoe*

The concept of stages is not specifically delineated in the Bible. I am merely using the idea of stages, to help describe the process of *zoe* within the believer.

STAGE ONE – ENTERING ZOE

A believer's *psuche* enters zoe at the moment of their belief. One major aspect of the gift of zoe is its immortal (eternal) nature. The believer's *psuche* has been born again of the "*zoe*-giving" Holy Spirit and has become a child of God. They have crossed over from death to the assurance of living forever. They become partakers of the divine nature in the here and now (i.e., they have the gift of *zoe* dwelling within them in this temporal life.)

> **Matt. 18:8-9** And if your hand or your foot causes you to sin, cut it off and throw it from you! It is better for you to enter into **life (zoe)** crippled or lame than, having two hands or two feet, to be thrown into the eternal fire! And if your eye causes you to sin, tear it out and throw it from you! It is better for you to enter into **life (zoe)** one-eyed than, having two eyes, to be thrown into fiery hell! (LEB)

When Jesus is speaking of entering zoe, it is in this present age. This takes place at the instant a person wholeheartedly believes. Think of this as the first of three stages of *zoe*.

> **Eph. 2:1-5** And you, although you were dead in your trespasses and sins, in which you formerly walked according to the course of this world, according to the ruler of the authority of the air, the spirit now working in the sons of disobedience, among whom also we all formerly lived in the desires of our flesh, doing the will of the flesh and of the mind, and we were children of wrath by nature, as also the rest of them were. But God, being rich in mercy, because of his great love with which he loved us, and **we being dead in trespasses, he made us alive together with Christ** (by grace you are saved). (LEB)

In Stage One, God makes the believer alive with Christ. The believer (even though they were dead in their trespasses) crosses over from death to *zoe*.

The believer has entered life (*zoe*) because the source of zoe begins to indwell them at the time of their belief. The *zoe of Jesus* indwells the believer's *psuche* via the indwelling Holy Spirit.

Note 1: Just to get rid of any confusion, a person's psuche before belief and their psuche after belief is the same psuche. The only difference is that upon believing, their psuche is indwelt by the Spirit of God, conveying zoe into their psuche. Their psuche has passed from the certainty of death, into assurance of eternal zoe. The believer's psuche now has a dual nature: one that is human and one that has become a child of God, participating in God's divine nature.

Note 2: Please pardon this random note, but there may be some readers wondering why I do not make mention of baptism in this book. My lack of dealing with baptism, is not to say that baptism does not play a role in the conversion of the believer. Baptism is just a separate topic that is not part of the zoe-focus of this book. Other than Jesus baptism, John has little to say about baptism in his gospel, or his other books in the New Testament. It just never comes up in any of John's statements surrounding zoe. I do not deal with baptism, or really any other topics that are not directly related to zoe's use in the New Testament.

STAGE TWO - BEARING THE FRUIT OF THE ZOE GIVING SPIRIT

During a believer's first life they are still stuck in this world so to speak, with their mortal bodies, their fleshly desires, and the constant daily tug of war with sin. But they have already entered life (zoe).

The believer's ability to bear the fruit of the Spirit during this time is dependent upon the believer keeping in step with the Spirit (this also known as abiding in Christ). It is living within the context of depending upon the zoe that is within them, which nurtures, sustains, comforts, bears fruit within the believer's psuche. The Spirit can reassure and encourage the believer in whatever circumstances they find themselves in.

This fruit is not automatic for the believer. It is the result of a daily choice and responsibility for the believer to abide in Jesus and keep in step with the Holy Spirit. To the extent that a believer does this, they will bear this fruit. But as humans we tend to walk in our flesh. This walk is a daily struggle for our affections that never ends during this temporal lifetime.

STAGE THREE - FULFILLMENT OF ETERNAL ZOE

> **Mark 10:29-30** Jesus said, "Truly, I say to you, there is no one who has left house or brothers or sisters or mother or father or children or lands, for my sake and for the gospel, who will not receive a hundredfold now in this time houses and brothers and sisters and mothers and children and lands, with persecutions, and in the age to come **eternal life (zoe)**." (ESV)

In the age to come, the believer will be resurrected with an eternal, imperishable body. Think of this as the third and final stage. This is the ultimate purpose of zoe. We won't see this final stage of zoe until we put on immortality with an imperishable body (at the time of the resurrection).

Resurrection to eternal zoe, is the hope of the believer. Without confidence in the resurrection, there is no hope at all.

SUMMARY OF STAGES

As humans, we are composed of body and *psuche*. We will lose our *psuche* (our *psuche* will die forever) if we have not been given eternal zoe. The believer's *psuche* is preserved (saved) by the gift of zoe. This effect begins while we are still living in our mortal bodies (Stage One).

Once we are born again of the Holy Spirit, and the zoe of Jesus lives within our psuche, we live the remainder of our temporal psuche upon earth, walking with the Spirit dependent upon it to bear fruit in our lives (Stage Two).

On the day of the future resurrection, our mortal flesh-and-blood bodies (of those believers who may still be alive at the time) must be changed to imperishable in order to dwell in the eternal kingdom of God. (Stage Three). However, most believers will have already died, and will be resurrected with imperishable bodies to live forever (also Stage Three).

GUARANTEE OF STAGE THREE

> **Eph. 1:13-14** In him you also, when you heard the word of truth, the gospel according to your salvation, and believed in him, were sealed with **the promised Holy Spirit, who is the guarantee of our inheritance until we acquire possession of it**, to the praise of his glory. (ESV)

Even though this imperishable state of our bodies is yet to be manifested, we are guaranteed of this future event by the current indwelling of God's Holy Spirit.

The Holy Spirit is the guarantee of our inheritance until we acquire possession of it.

> **2 Cor. 1:21-22** And it is God who establishes us with you in Christ, and has anointed us, and who has also put his seal on us and **given us his Spirit in our hearts as a guarantee**. (ESV)

So, what do we possess in this age (now)?

We have the indwelling of *zoe* (which is immortal) at the time of our belief, making us children of God. We have crossed over from death to life (*zoe*) at the point of belief. We now participate in the divine nature. We then live in a dual nature simultaneously, living in the mortal flesh while also having the Spirit of God living within us, providing us with assurance of resurrection to eternal life.

We do not acquire possession of our imperishable, immortal bodies (our inheritance in the age to come) until we are resurrected. But we have assurance that this will indeed happen because we know we have been sealed with the promised Holy Spirit, that imparts zoe.

22

Zoe & the Kingdom of God

The kingdom of God may be the most important theme permeating both the Old and New Testaments. As we see Jesus and the New Testament authors zeroing in on eternal zoe, can we see a connection to the Kingdom of God?

Let's look at the conversation that Jesus had with Nicodemus in John chapter 3.

John 3:1-19 Now there was a man of the Pharisees whose name was Nicodemus, a ruler of the Jews. 2 This man came to him at night and said to him, "Rabbi, we know that you are a teacher who has come from God, for no one is able to perform these signs that you are performing unless God were with him." 3 Jesus answered and said to him, "Truly, truly I say to you, **unless someone is born from above, he is not able to see the kingdom of God.**" 4 Nicodemus said to him, "How can a man be born when he is an old man? He is not able to enter into his mother's womb for the second time and be born, can he?"

5 Jesus answered, "Truly, truly I say to you, **unless someone is born of water and spirit, he is not able to enter into the kingdom of God.** 6 What is born of the flesh is flesh, and what is born of the Spirit is spirit. 7 Do not be astonished that I said to you, 'It is necessary for you to be born from above.' 8 The wind blows wherever it wishes, and you hear the sound of it, but you do not know where it comes from and where it is going. **So is everyone who is born of the Spirit.**"

9 Nicodemus answered and said to him, "How can these things be?" 10 Jesus answered and said to him, "Are you the teacher of Israel, and you do not understand these things? 11 Truly, truly I say to you, we speak what we know, and we testify about what we have seen, and you do not accept our testimony! 12 If I tell you earthly things and you do not believe, how will you believe if I tell you heavenly things? 13 And no one has ascended into heaven except the one who descended from heaven—the Son of Man. 14 And just as Moses lifted up the snake in the wilderness, thus it is necessary that the Son of Man be lifted up, 15 **so that everyone who believes in him will have eternal life.**"

16 For in this way God loved the world, so that he gave his one and only Son, in order that **everyone who believes in him will not perish, but will have eternal life.** 17 For God did not send his Son into the world in order that he should judge the world, but in order that the world should be saved through him. 18 The one who believes in him is not judged, but the one who does not believe has already been judged, because he has not believed in the name of the one and only Son of God. 19 And this is the judgment: that the light has come into the world, and people loved the darkness rather than the light, because their deeds were evil.

Jesus gets right to the point with Nicodemus. He tells Nicodemus that unless someone is born from above, they cannot enter the kingdom of God. The conversation is a bit confusing to Nicodemus, but Jesus explains that a person must be born again, not of the flesh, but this time being born of the Spirit. Throughout the gospel of John we see that it is the spirit of God that conveys eternal zoe unto a person. Without this indwelling spirit, a person has no hope whatsoever of resurrection from the dead. The coming kingdom will consist of those whose names are written in the book of zoe, who will be resurrected from the dead (by the holy spirit) to live forever (eternal zoe), in the kingdom of God.

Anyone whose name is not written in the book of life, (who has not been born again of the indwelling Spirit), will be judged on the judgement day and will ultimately *perish*. Thus the contrast that Jesus makes in John 3:16 between eternal zoe and perishing. Those who are to perish will be cast into the lake of fire, which John identifies in Revelation as the "second death".

Matthew also equates eternal life with the kingdom:

> **Matthew 19:16-30** And behold, someone came up to him and[s] said, "Teacher, what good thing must I do so that I will have **eternal life (zoe)**?" 17 And he said to him, "Why are you asking me about what is good? There is one who is good. But if you want to enter into **life (zoe),** keep the commandments!" 18 He said to him, "Which ones?" And Jesus said, "Do not commit murder, do not commit adultery, do not steal, do not give false testimony, 19 honor your father and your mother, and love your neighbor as yourself." 20 The young man said to him, "All these I have observed. What do I still lack?" 21 Jesus said to him, "If you want to be perfect, go, sell your possessions and give the proceeds to the poor—and **you will have treasure in heaven**—and come, follow me." 22 But when the young man heard the statement, he went away sorrowful, because he was one who had many possessions.
>
> 23 And Jesus said to his disciples, "Truly I say to you that with difficulty a rich person will enter into the **kingdom of heaven**! 24 And again I say to you, it is easier for a camel to go through the eye of a needle than a rich person **into the kingdom of God**." 25 So when the disciples heard this, they were extremely amazed, saying, "Then who can be saved?" 26 But Jesus looked at them and said to them, "With human beings this is impossible, but with God all things are possible." 27 Then Peter answered and said to him, "Behold, we have left everything and followed you. What then will there be for us?" 28 And Jesus said to them, "Truly I say to you that **in the renewal of the world**, when the Son of Man sits on his glorious throne, you who have followed me—you also will sit on twelve thrones judging the twelve tribes of Israel. 29 And everyone who has left houses or brothers or sisters or father or mother or wife or children or fields on account of my name will receive a hundred times as much, and will inherit **eternal life (zoe)**. 30 But many who are first will be last, and the last first.

Notice Jesus's reply to the question, "what good thing must I do so that I will have eternal zoe?" In v23 Jesus equates entering eternal zoe with entering into the kingdom of heaven. Thus, entering the kingdom of heaven (or kingdom of God in v24) is in some way equivalent to entering eternal zoe. Jesus finalizes this discussion about entering the kingdom of God in v29 by equating it with inheriting eternal zoe.

The equivalence of entering the kingdom with entering zoe, has to do with the requirements as set forth by the previous passage from John 3. A person has to be born again, not of the flesh again, but this time of the spirit of God. It is the spirit that conveys eternal zoe unto the believer, assuring them of resurrection from the dead to eternal zoe. If you are not alive after the judgement day, you certainly won't be able to enter the kingdom of God. It is those who are resurrected from the dead to eternal zoe, that will physically be in the kingdom on that day.

Notice in v28 that Jesus says, that it is at the "renewal of the world," that those who have followed him will inherit eternal life. I don't want to deviate from the focus of this book into a debate on heaven, but I just want to point out that it is quite possible that eternal life will not be in "heaven" as traditional Christianity has depicted, but rather in the new earth.

Consider the first 3 beatitudes in Mathew 5:

Matt. 5:3-5 "Blessed are the poor in spirit, because **theirs is the kingdom of heaven**. 4 Blessed are the ones who mourn, because they will be comforted. 5 **Blessed are the meek, because they will inherit the earth**.

What are the meek inheriting? Does this not sound a lot like Matthew 19:28?

The kingdom of God and the kingdom of heaven are the same. Of the synoptic gospels, Matthew is the only gospel author that uses the phrase kingdom of Heaven. Mark and Luke use kingdom of God instead of kingdom of Heaven, where they record the same instances of Jesus' teaching. Therefore, these two phrases represent the same thing.[5]

God's kingdom of heaven is everywhere that believers are currently alive in this age. The kingdom of heaven is not just in heaven. Believers live as subjects of the kingdom, with Jesus as our Lord. His Holy Spirit indwells the psuche of believers in the *here and now*, making them children of God, subjects of the kingdom, and possessors of the zoe of Jesus.

Luke 17:20-21 Now when he was asked by the Pharisees **when the kingdom of God would come**, he answered them and said, "The **kingdom of God** does not come with things that can be observed, 21 nor will they say, 'Behold, here it is!' or 'There!' For behold, the **kingdom of God is in your midst**." (LEB)

Notice Jesus said that the kingdom of God was in the midst of the people. This occurs in two ways, first of all the king was standing right there. Secondly, anyone who becomes a believer becomes a citizen of the kingdom. Today the kingdom of God (heaven) is in our midst whenever a believer is in our midst.[6] The king lives within that person via the indwelling holy spirit.

A person enters zoe when they are born again, with the sure expectation that this will ultimately result in that person being resurrected from the dead to eternal zoe. In like manner, a person enters the kingdom when they are born again. When a person is born again, the indwelling holy spirit makes that

---

[5] Steve Gregg "The Kingdom of God" {Video} YouTube.
https://www.youtube.com/watch?app=desktop&v=SZinsde-vEE

[6] Steve Gregg "The Kingdom of God" {Video} YouTube.
https://www.youtube.com/watch?app=desktop&v=SZinsde-vEE

person a child of God, simultaneously making that person a citizen of the kingdom. The ultimate realization of the kingdom of God will occur when that person is resurrected from the dead to physically live forever in the kingdom of God. (Wherever that may be, in whatever form God decrees, as He establishes his forever kingdom).

Part Three

Clarifying Hell

Important Note:

Parts 1 and 2 lay the foundation for understanding Part 3.

Please do not read Part 3, without reading Parts 1 and 2.

Thank You

23

Obvious Questions That Arise

There has been a good deal of debate regarding "hell" over the centuries. However, there are some Christians who are reluctant to discuss this topic, and others who might even consider those who question the concept of "eternal torment in hell" as heretics. This is unfortunate, as most believers on both sides of this issue are genuinely seeking to understand the truth in God's word. As such, we should extend grace to one another. One's understanding of "hell" is not a "salvation" issue.

I believe a vital (and undeniable) aspect of Jesus' teaching on *zoe* is its direct connection and contrast to death, *Gehenna* and *Hades*. It is difficult to have a clear understanding of Jesus' teaching on Hades and Gehenna, without understanding Jesus' teaching on psuche, zoe, and death. They are fundamentally and inextricably linked.

Understanding this connection is essential to understanding the purpose of Jesus and the end state of man. Yet, in some English Bibles there is little to no distinction made between Hades and Gehenna. In addition, these two words are often conflated in mainstream Christian teaching and preaching. While Hades and Gehenna are both strongly contrasted against zoe, and both occur after death, they are completely different and have dramatically different roles. They occur at different times and do not overlap in any way. Hades is currently in existence, but it won't be after the resurrection. After the resurrection to judgment, Gehenna will come into play.

Failing to understand these connections and differences will seriously handicap your ability to understand the importance and clarity of Jesus' message.

A vital aspect of Jesus' and the New Testament's teaching

on zoe is the consistent contrast that is portrayed of:

Zoe versus Death

& Zoe versus Hades and Gehenna.

The study that we have been doing on *psuche* and *zoe* generates obvious questions about the afterlife.

As we have seen, Jesus often contrasts *zoe* against death. In fact, Jesus has shown us that it is indeed death that is the problem that all mankind faces. It is only by the gift of eternal *zoe* that a person may escape death-into-the-ages. Eternal zoe was central to Jesus' focus throughout his ministry.

It is death's association with *Hades* and *Gehenna* (though in completely different ways) that makes this discussion about Hades and Gehenna so necessary.

To clarify, zoe is always contrasted in scripture as an opposite to death, Hades and Gehenna. (The contrast with Gehenna occurs only in the New Testament). Furthermore, death is closely associated with both Hades and Gehenna, but its association with these two venues is completely different. When a person dies, they enter Hades (in the Old Testament this is known as sheol). Hades is temporary and only lasts until the resurrection from the dead. The second death (of the unsaved) takes place in Gehenna after the resurrection. This second death in Gehenna is permanent.

By the way, zoe is also contrasted against perishing and destruction. Perish and destroy/destruction come from the Greek root word apollumi. In many cases the use of these words refers to death. Frequently perish, destroy, and destruction are referring specifically to the second (eternal) death. One of the most notable examples of this use is John 3:16. (Note: Perish, destroy, destruction never refer to everlasting torment in hell, despite the traditional view's attempt to twist and portray these words to fit their paradigm.)

It is very important to understand the difference between *Hades* and *Gehenna* and the role that these two venues/events hold for the destiny of mankind. Failing to understand these differences will likely leave you with misconceptions as to what Jesus really taught. But, before we can discuss these ideas, we need to have a better understanding of the Bible's teaching on immortality.

> It is very important to understand the difference
>
> between Hades and Gehenna and the role that these two
>
> venues/events hold for the destiny of mankind.

THE SECOND DEATH

In Revelation 20:14, John speaks of the *second death* that occurs when those whose names are not written in the *book-of-zoe* are thrown into the lake of fire. The traditional belief tends to portray the *second death* as eternal torment in hell. This stance by its very nature is dependent upon the belief that every person has an *immortal soul.*

But Jesus clearly indicates that an unbeliever's *psuche* will be *destroyed* in *Gehenna.*

> **Matt. 10:28** And do not fear those who kill the body but cannot kill the **soul (psuche)**. Rather fear him who can destroy both **soul (psuche)** and body in hell (Gehenna). (ESV)

If a person's *psuche* is immortal, then how can it be destroyed?

And if one's *psuche* is destroyed, then how can it remain to be eternally tormented?

Psuche is merely mortal. Immortality does not come into play until the resurrection when only those people whose names are written in the *book of zoe* will be given *eternal zoe.*

> Those whose names are in the Book of Zoe will be given Eternal Zoe.
>
> Eternal Zoe (by definition) "is" immortality.
>
> Believers are not immortal prior to their resurrection.
>
> At the resurrection they will be resurrected to receive Eternal Zoe.

GOD ALONE IS IMMORTAL

1 Tim. 6:15-16 . . . he who is the blessed and only Sovereign, the King of kings and Lord of lords, **who alone has immortality**, who dwells in unapproachable light, whom no one has ever seen or can see. To him be honor and eternal dominion, Amen. (ESV)

1 Timothy 6:16 teaches that God alone is immortal. Man on the other hand, is not. Immortality is a gift bestowed upon the believer when they receive eternal zoe. (Again, just to clarify... immortality and eternal zoe mean the same thing, i.e., being alive forever).

Rom. 2:4-8 Or do you presume on the riches of his kindness and forbearance and patience, not knowing that God's kindness is meant to lead you to repentance? But because of your hard and impenitent heart you are storing up wrath for yourself on the day of wrath when God's righteous judgment will be revealed. He will render to each one according to his works: **to those who by patience in well-doing seek for glory and honor and immortality, he will give eternal life (zoe)**; but for those who are self-seeking and do not obey the truth, but obey unrighteousness, there will be wrath and fury. (ESV)

In Romans 2:4-8, Paul preaches that God's patience and kindness is meant to lead man to repentance. To those who by perseverance in well-doing seek for glory and honor and immortality, he will give eternal *zoe*.

If humans already have immortality, then why should they seek it? Why would God give eternal *zoe* to humans, if they already possess it?

It is the gift of eternal zoe (*being alive forever*) that is by definition - immortality. Humans do not innately possess immortality.

24

Defining "Perish" and "Destroy"

Strong's Concordance defines the Greek word *apollumi* to mean "to destroy, utterly destroy, to lose" The word occurs ninety-two times in various forms in the New Testament. There are well over twenty occurrences in the New Testament where this word or some derivation of it has been translated as "perish," "perishing," "perished," etc. It is also frequently translated as "destroyed" or "destruction."

For Strong's definition of apollumi see: https://biblehub.com/greek/622.htm

Before we get much further, let's revisit the two viewpoints we have been discussing throughout this book.

TRADITIONAL VIEWPOINT

The "Traditional" view is the belief that hell is a place of everlasting torment, burning, darkness, and separation from God, where unbelievers will spend eternity. The Traditional view believes the second death does not mean physical death but rather signifies eternal spiritual separation from God. This would also include everlasting suffering. The Traditional view will sometimes explain that "perish" means "to ruin," as when Jesus describes the old wine skin that is "destroyed or ruined" when new wine is poured into it. Certainly "ruined" would be a suitable description of an inanimate wineskin that has been destroyed, from a practical perspective. But does the concept of "ruin" describe how Jesus meant to use *apollumi* in John 3:16 when referring to the fate of unbelievers?

> **John 3:16** For God so loved the world, that he gave his only Son, that whoever believes in him should not **perish (apollumi)** but have eternal life (zoe). (ESV)

Jesus has contrasted life (*zoe*) with death and destruction throughout the gospel according to John. How could *apollumi* mean anything other than death and destruction here in John 3:16? If Jesus is contrasting opposites here, what is the opposite of eternal zoe (being alive forever), if it is not eternal death?

CONDITIONAL IMMORTALITY

"Conditionalists" is the term associated with those Christians that hold to the belief that man is mortal. They believe the Bible does not teach that man "has a soul" but that man "is a soul" and that the soul (*psuche*) is mortal. Immortality is not an innate aspect of man's nature. They believe that a person receives immortality via the gift of eternal *zoe* when that person wholeheartedly believes the truth about Jesus' identity and purpose.

Romans 2:7 To those who by patience in well-doing seek for glory and honor and **immortality**, he will give **eternal life (zoe)**. (ESV)

They believe a person's immortality is *conditional* upon this gift of salvation. Immortality comes only from the impartation of the Holy Spirit into the believer.

They believe that the unbeliever is destroyed (or perishes) in the lake of fire. This means that the unbeliever ceases to exist at some point after being thrown into the lake of fire, which is called the second death (see Revelation 20:12-15).

Thus, Conditionalists hold to the belief that when any person dies (passes away from their earthly life), that is their first death. They believe that all people will be resurrected from the dead, either to eternal zoe or to judgment. See John 5:29.

> **John 5:29** "and they will come out—those who have done good things to a **resurrection of life (zoe)**, but those who have practiced evil things to a **resurrection of judgment**. (LEB)

Those who are resurrected to judgment will at some point be cast into the lake of fire (Gehenna) where they will ultimately perish (a permanent, second death from which there is no resurrection).

As we look closely at Jesus' teaching on *Hades* and *Gehenna*, we can see that the New Testament teaches conditionalism.

Let us look at a few of the scriptures where Jesus speaks of "perishing" and "destroying."

> **Luke 21:12-19** But before all this they will lay their hands on you and persecute you, delivering you up to the synagogues and prisons, and you will be brought before kings and governors for my name's sake. This will be your opportunity to bear witness. Settle it therefore in your minds not to meditate beforehand how to answer, for I will give you a mouth and wisdom, which none of your adversaries will be able to withstand or contradict. You will be delivered up even by parents and brothers and relatives and friends, and some of you they will put to death. You will be hated by all for my name's sake.
>
> But, not a hair of your head will **perish**. By your endurance, you will gain your **lives (psuche)**. (ESV)

In Luke 21:12-18, Jesus explains to his followers that the day is coming when many of them will be betrayed, and some will be put to death. Jesus reassures them, however, that not a hair of their heads will *perish*.

Please explain how this makes sense if you try to explain it from a traditional point of view? Jesus just told this crowd that some of them are definitely going to be killed. In order to give them confidence and comfort in the face of execution, he assures them that not a hair of their head will perish. This is not merely a reference to just their hair, but an expression that the dying person can hold onto, to assure them that ultimately, they (their psuche) will not perish.

So, just what is the word perish referring to here? Ruin? Eternal torment in hell? No, of course not.

Jesus's use of perish in this verse is not even speaking of the first death! This is obvious because he is speaking about people who are going to be killed. Jesus is quite plainly assuring them that they will not ultimately perish (remain dead). He is assuring those who are going to die for their faith, that they will be resurrected from the dead.

They can have certain hope that their *psuche* will be saved, for eternal zoe (resurrection from the dead to live forever). By their endurance (even to the point of enduring execution), they will gain their lives (psuche). They will gain them back from the dead at the resurrection.

Refer to the screenshot of the Greek-English Interlinear from Luke 21:16-19 on the following page.

21:16

ΠΑΡΑΔΟΘΗΣΕΣΘΕ paradothEsesthe — G3860 — vi Fut Pas 2 Pl — YE-SHALL-BE-BEING-BESIDE-GIVEN — ye-shall-be-being-given-up

ΔΕ de — G1161 — Conj — YET

ΚΑΙ kai — G2532 — Conj — AND also

ΥΠΟ hupo — G5259 — Prep — by

ΓΟΝΕΩΝ goneOn — G1118 — n_Gen Pl m — parents

ΚΑΙ kai — G2532 — Conj — AND

ΑΔΕΛΦΩΝ adelphOn — G80 — n_Gen Pl m — brothers

ΚΑΙ kai — G2532 — Conj — AND

ΣΥΓΓΕΝΩΝ suggenOn — G4773 — a_Gen Pl m — TOGETHER-generateds relatives

ΚΑΙ kai — G2532 — Conj — AND

ΦΙΛΩΝ philOn — G5384 — a_Gen Pl m — FOND-ones friends

ΚΑΙ kai — G2532 — Conj — AND

ΘΑΝΑΤΩΣΟΥΣΙΝ thanatOsousin — G2289 — vi Fut Act 3 Pl — THEY-SHALL-BE-(causing-to)-DIE they-shall-be-...ing-...-death

ΕΞ ex — G1537 — Prep — OUT

ΥΜΩΝ humOn — G5216 — pp 2 Gen Pl — OF-YOU(P) of-ye

21:17

ΚΑΙ kai — G2532 — Conj — AND

ΕΣΕΣΘΕ esesthe — G2071 — vi Fut vxx 2 Pl — YE-SHALL-BE

ΜΙΣΟΥΜΕΝΟΙ misoumenoi — G3404 — vp Pres Pas Nom Pl m — beING-HATED

ΥΠΟ hupo — G5259 — Prep — by

ΠΑΝΤΩΝ pantOn — G3956 — a_Gen Pl m — ALL

ΔΙΑ dia — G1223 — Prep — THRU because-of

ΤΟ to — G3588 — t_Acc Sg n — THE

ΟΝΟΜΑ onoma — G3686 — n_Acc Sg n — NAME

ΜΟΥ mou — G3450 — pp 1 Gen Sg — OF-ME

21:18

ΚΑΙ kai — G2532 — Conj — AND

ΘΡΙΞ thrix — G2359 — n_Nom Sg f — HAIR

ΕΚ ek — G1537 — Prep — OUT

ΤΗΣ tEs — G3588 — t_Gen Sg f — OF-THE

ΚΕΦΑΛΗΣ kephalEs — G2776 — n_Gen Sg f — HEAD

ΥΜΩΝ humOn — G5216 — pp 2 Gen Pl — OF-YOU(P) of-ye

ΟΥ ou — G3756 — Part Neg — NOT

ΜΗ mE — G3361 — Part Neg — NO

ΑΠΟΛΗΤΑΙ apolEtai — G622 — vs 2Aor Mid 3 Sg — SHOULD-BE-beING-destroyED should-be-perishing

21:19

ΕΝ en — G1722 — Prep — IN

ΤΗ tE — G3588 — t_Dat Sg f — THE

ΥΠΟΜΟΝΗ hupomonE — G5281 — n_Dat Sg f — UNDER-REMAINing endurance

ΥΜΩΝ humOn — G5216 — pp 2 Gen Pl — OF-YOU(P) of-ye

ΚΤΗΣΑΣΘΕ ktEsasthe — G2932 — vm Aor midD 2 Pl — YE-SHALL-BE-ACQUIRING

ΤΑΣ tas — G3588 — t_Acc Pl f — THE

ΨΥΧΑΣ psuchas — G5590 — n_Acc Pl f — souls

ΥΜΩΝ humOn — G5216 — pp 2 Gen Pl — OF-YOU(P) of-ye

---

16 And ye shall be betrayed both by parents, and brethren, and kinsfolks, and friends; and [some] of you shall they cause to be put to death.

17 And ye shall be hated of all [men] for my name's sake.

18 But there shall not an hair of your head perish.

19 In your patience possess ye your souls.

Notice that the last verse contains the word *psuche*. By looking at the Greek text, we can see that this could be read as:

By your endurance you shall be acquiring your psuche.

In other words, Jesus is telling these believers that even though they may be put to death, to not fear. He encourages them to stand firm (endure), assuring them they shall be acquiring (retaining or possessing) their *psuche*.

This makes absolute sense from what we have learned about *psuche* and *zoe* from Jesus' teachings.

Jesus is saying that if one of these believers is killed, they will certainly not perish (remain dead) but will with certainty, acquire their *psuche*. In other words, their psuche will live again.

On the other hand, these verses begin to get really crazy if you believe that perishing means "ruin". If "perish" is not referring to remaining dead with no hope of resurrection (in this verse), then just what do you think it means? Remember, perish in this verse is not referring to their first death. Their first death is already assumed. Perish, in this instance can only be referring to "remaining dead with no hope of resurrection".

If you hold to the traditional view, how do you explain where Jesus says that by enduring, these executed believers shall be acquiring their psuche?

This passage only make sense when you understand *perish* is linked to the prior statement where Jesus says, "some of you they will put to death". Jesus is assuring them that their psuche will not ultimately perish, they will get their psuche back (at the resurrection).

Matt. 10:28 And do not fear those who kill the body but cannot kill the soul (psuche). Rather fear him who can **destroy (apolesai)** both **soul (psuche)** and body in hell (Gehenna). (ESV)

Jesus makes it clear that the unbeliever's *psuche* will be destroyed in *Gehenna*.

Jesus is referring to the "killing" or "utter destruction" of their *psuche*, as he connects this destruction of the *psuche* to the killing of the body in the first part of this verse. He makes the killing of the *psuche* equivalent to the killing of the body. The body is dead, not ruined. The body is dead, just as the *psuche* of the unbeliever will be after it is thrown into *Gehenna* and destroyed.

Jesus is describing the death and destruction of a person's mortal soul (*psuche*) in the lake of fire, which is the second death.

The apostle John, in the book of Revelation defines the lake of fire as "the second death". John specifically chose this term, because that is exactly what he meant. The second death is physical death of the body and psuche. They are both destroyed. The psuche perishes, it dies forever.

John 10:10 The thief comes only to steal and kill and **destroy (apollumi)**. I came that they may have life (zoe) and have it abundantly. (ESV)

In John 10, Jesus explains that the thief comes to kill and *destroy (apollumi)* the sheep. Jesus' purpose, on the other hand, is quite different and directly opposed to that of the thief.

Jesus has come to rescue the sheep from this fate of death and destruction. Jesus has come to give them *zoe (the state of being alive)*. Zoe is the opposite of being dead. Jesus simply came to rescue man from the impending certainty of death, that Satan instigated by his role in lying to Eve in the Garden of Eden, which lead to Adam and Eve being cast from the garden and losing access to the tree of zoe, which would have enabled them to live forever.

Later in John 10:28, Jesus reiterates this statement:

John 10:28 I give them eternal life (zoe), and they will never **perish (apollumi)**. (ESV)

As you may recall from our earlier study of John, the English word "never" does not exactly reproduce the meaning in the original Greek (see the original Greek text on the following page)

The screen shot on the following page is a repeat of the Greek text in John 10:28 that was previously displayed in the chapter on John 10.

Read the English word for word translation below the Greek (John 10:28). Does it say "**never perish?**"

10:28	KAΓω	ZωHN	AIωNION	ΔIΔωMI	AYTOIC	KAI	OY	MH
	kagO	zOEn	aiOnion	didOmi	autois	kai	ou	mE
	G2504	G2222	G166	G1325	G846	G2532	G3756	G3361
	pp 1 Nom Sg Con	n_Acc Sg f	a_Acc Sg f	vi Pres Act 1 Sg	pp Dat Pl m	Conj	Part Neg	Part Neg
	AND-I	LIFE	eonian	AM-GIVING	to-them them	AND	NOT	NO

AΠOλωNTAI	EIC	TON	AIωNA	KAI	OYX	APΠACEI	TIC
apolOntai	eis	ton	aiOna	kai	ouch	harpasei	tis
G622	G1519	G3588	G165	G2532	G3756	G726	G5100
vs 2Aor Mid 3 Pl	Prep	t_Acc Sg m	n_Acc Sg m	Conj	Part Neg	vi Fut Act 3 Sg	px Nom Sg m
THEY-SHOULD-BE-beING-destroyED	INTO	THE	eon	AND	NOT	SHALL-BE-SNATCHING	ANY anyone

AYTA	EK	THC	XEIPOC	MOY
auta	ek	tEs	cheiros	mou
G846	G1537	G3588	G5495	G3450
pp Acc Pl n	Prep	t_Gen Sg f	n_Gen Sg f	pp 1 Gen Sg
them	OUT	OF-THE	HAND	OF-ME

28 And I give unto them eternal life; and they shall never perish, neither shall any [man] pluck them out of my hand.

John 10:28 may be better translated as:

I give them eternal life (zoe), and **they in no way should-be-being-destroyed into the eon**.

Jesus contrasts what he said in the first half of the sentence with his statement in the second half. Jesus gives them eternal *zoe*. The result is that the sheep will in no way be destroyed into the eon.

Jesus makes a clear, simple contrast with opposites. His sheep will receive eternal *zoe* from him, and because of this, they will "in no way" exist in a state of being destroyed unto the eon. Even though they will die a first death, they will not remain dead (destroyed) into the eon. They will be resurrected to being alive forever – eternal zoe.

DESTROY

Ultimately, Satan's end game is the destruction of man. It is no coincidence that Satan is called the "Destroyer" in Revelation 9:11.

> **Rev. 9:11** They have as king over them the angel of the bottomless pit. His name in Hebrew is Abaddon, and in Greek he is called **Apollyon [root is apollumi]**. (ESV)

The bottomless pit is not a reference to hades or gehenna, but more likely is referring to tartaroo, which is covered in another chapter.

Though Satan is the thief that has come to steal, kill, and destroy, we have the assurance that Jesus has come to overcome Satan's work of destruction of men's psuche, and instead bring eternal life to the psuche of believers.

Some believers who are still living on the day of Jesus' return will not suffer an earthly death but will join those believers who have already died. Paul refers to those believers who have previously died as "those who have fallen asleep" and the "dead in Christ". For more on this, see 1 Thessalonians 4:13-18.

IF THE DEAD ARE NOT RAISED, THEN WE WILL PERISH

> **1 Cor. 15:16-18** For if the dead are not raised, not even Christ has been raised. And if Christ has not been raised, your faith is futile and you are still in your sins. Then, those also who have fallen asleep in Christ have **perished (apollumi)**. (ESV)

Paul's emphasis here is that if Jesus has not been raised, then our faith is basically useless, since no one will be raised from the dead. Believers would just remain in their sins (in a status of death). Thus, those believers who have already died an earthly death (fallen asleep) would have perished (died with no hope of ever living again).

Questions for you if you hold to the traditional view:

- If you hold to the traditional view that *apollumi* means "ruin" and infers *eternal torment* in hell, then how do you explain this verse? Does it make sense that Paul would be saying that believers would be ruined in hell? Of course not, perish here is referring to remaining dead, never living again.
- If Jesus did not raise from the dead, then what happens to believers? Are they floating in the twilight zone? What do you honestly think it means when Paul says the implication of Jesus not raising from the dead means that all believers would "still be in their sins". If you are not sure what this means, go back and reread the chapter on John 8 – Dying in Sin. If you are still in your sins, that means you remain under the sentence of death. Paul is saying these believers would just remain dead with no hope of resurrection.

Paul's use of the word "perished" means that the dead believers would never resurrect from death. To perish would mean that their death is permanent.

Thanks be to God that is not the case!

Jesus did rise from the dead, is eternally alive at this very moment, and is our certain hope of eternal *zoe*!

DESTRUCTION

The Greek work apoleia (destruction) also comes from the root apollumi (perish, destroy).

For the Greek definition and listing of uses of these two words see the links below:

Apollumi (utterly destroy, perish, lose) -https://biblehub.com/str/greek/622.htm

Apoleia (destruction) - https://biblehub.com/str/greek/684.htm

The word destruction is used frequently in the New Testament. Please review the verses below which show the use of this word.

> **Matthew 7:13** Enter by the narrow gate. For the gate is wide and the way is easy **that leads to destruction**, and those who enter by it are many. For the gate is narrow and the way is hard **that leads to life (zoe)**, and those who find it are few (ESV)

Jesus uses a metaphor of two gates, one which leads to destruction (eternal death), with the other gate leading to zoe (eternal zoe). These two gates are contrasted as opposites. Destruction is permanent death. Zoe refers to future eternal zoe, (being raised from the dead to live forever). Notice the terminology that Jesus uses here... *leads to zoe*. Entering by the narrow gate *leads* to resurrection from the dead to live forever.

The unsaved will be resurrected from the dead to face judgment, which will at some point result in them being thrown into the lake of fire, which John defines as the second death in the book of Revelation. Jesus uses the word Gehenna (in the synoptic gospels) to refer to this event where the wicked will be destroyed in this lake of fire.

Romans 9:21-23 Or does the potter not have authority over the clay, to make from the same lump a vessel that is for honorable use and one that is for ordinary use? And what if God, wanting to demonstrate his wrath and to make known his power, endured with much patience vessels of wrath prepared for **destruction**? And he did so in order that he could make known the riches of his glory upon vessels of mercy that he prepared beforehand for glory (LEB)

In the verses above, Paul is referring to the destruction of those who are under God's wrath. (vessels of wrath prepared for destruction).

Philippians 1:27-28 Only let your manner of life be worthy of the gospel of Christ, so that whether I come and see you or am absent, I may hear of you that you are standing firm in one spirit, with one mind striving side by side for the faith of the gospel, and not frightened in anything by your opponents. This is a clear sign to them of their **destruction**, but of your salvation, and that from God. (ESV)

Philippians 3 :18-20 For many, of whom I have often told you and now tell you even with tears, walk as enemies of the cross of Christ. **Their end is destruction**, their god is their belly, and they glory in their shame, with minds set on earthly things. But our citizenship is in heaven, and from it we await a Savior, the Lord Jesus Christ (ESV)

In both sections of verses above, Paul is stating to the Philippians that those who oppose the gospel of Christ will be destroyed.

Peter also speaks of the destruction of those who deny Jesus. In the verses below I have highlighted the words perish and destruction which originate from the root word apollumi. The other instances of the destruction come from a similar Greek word.

2 Peter 2:1-3 But false prophets also arose among the people, just as there will be false teachers among you, who will secretly bring in destructive heresies, even denying the Master who bought them, bringing upon themselves swift **destruction**. And many will follow their sensuality, and because of them the way of truth will be blasphemed. And in their greed they will exploit you with false words. Their condemnation from long ago is not idle, and their **destruction** is not asleep (ESV)

2 Peter 3:3-16 Above all knowing this, that in the last days scoffers will come with scoffing, following according to their own desires and saying, "Where is the promise of his coming? For ever since the fathers fell asleep, all things have continued just as they have been from the beginning of creation." For when they maintain this, it escapes their notice that the heavens existed long ago and the earth held together out of water and through water by the word of God, by means of which things the world that existed at that time was **destroyed** by being inundated with water. But by the same word the present heavens and earth are reserved for fire, being kept for the day of judgment and **destruction** of ungodly people.

Now, dear friends, do not let this one thing escape your notice, that one day with the Lord is like a thousand years, and a thousand years is like one day. The Lord is not delaying the promise, as some consider slowness, but is being patient toward you, because he does not want any to **perish**, but all to come to repentance. But the day of the Lord will come like a thief, in which the heavens will disappear with a rushing noise, and the celestial bodies will be destroyed by being burned up, and the earth and the deeds done on it will be disclosed.

Because all these things are being destroyed in this way, what sort of people must you be in holy behavior and godliness, while waiting for and hastening the coming of the day of God, because of which the heavens will be destroyed by being burned up and the celestial bodies will melt as they are consumed by heat! But according to his promise, we are waiting for new heavens and a new earth in which righteousness resides. Therefore, dear friends, because you are waiting for these things, make every effort to be found at peace, spotless and unblemished in him. And regard the patience of our Lord as salvation, just as also our dear brother Paul wrote to you, according to the wisdom that was given to him, as he does also in all his letters, speaking in them about these things, in which there are some things hard to understand, which the ignorant and unstable distort to their own **destruction**, as they also do the rest of the scriptures. (LEB)

In the following verses from the Book of Acts, Peter is preaching to a crowd that contained members from the mob that had influenced the decision to crucify Jesus.

Acts 3:15-23 and you killed the Author of life (zoe), whom God raised from the dead. To this we are witnesses...

..."And now, brothers, I know that you acted in ignorance, as did also your rulers. But what God foretold by the mouth of all the prophets, that his Christ would suffer, he thus fulfilled. Repent therefore, and turn back, that your sins may be blotted out, that times of refreshing may come from the presence of the Lord, and that he may send the Christ appointed for you, Jesus, whom heaven must receive until the time for restoring all the things about which God spoke by the mouth of his holy prophets long ago. Moses said, 'The Lord God will raise up for you a prophet like me from your brothers. You shall listen to him in whatever he tells you. And it shall be that every **soul (psuche)** who does not listen to that prophet **shall be destroyed** from the people.' (ESV)

Notice what Peter tells them:

➢ They killed the "author of zoe", whom God raised from the dead.
➢ The resurrection of Jesus forms the very core of the message of salvation, specifically because Jesus will resurrect believers to eternal zoe, on the resurrection day.
➢ Any psuche that does not listen to that prophet (Jesus) shall be destroyed. They will be resurrected, not to live forever (eternal zoe), but to judgment. At the judgment they will be destroyed in the lake of fire, also known as the second (permanent) death.

Peter does not say anything about eternal torment. He is simply stating that the obstinate unbeliever will be destroyed.

25

Where Did Things Go Wrong?

If what we have concluded about *psuche* and *zoe* are in fact what Jesus taught, then we should expect to see some indication that Christians in the early church held to this teaching.

This is exactly what we find.[7]

Early church leaders frequently wrote about gaining eternal *zoe* and being saved from the penalty of death.

What do we not find? We don't see any reference to the "immortality of the soul" or "everlasting torment" until late in the second century AD.

PAUL'S WARNING

> **Col. 2:8** See to it that no one takes you captive by philosophy and empty deceit, according to human tradition, according to the elemental spirits of the world [this can also read as the "fundamental beliefs of the world system"], and not according to Christ. (ESV)

The apostle Paul warned against allowing existing philosophies, traditions, and belief systems to infiltrate and take captive the sound doctrine according to Christ. While this warning may not be specifically directed against the false teaching that we have exposed in this book, it was indeed the influence of human traditions and beliefs that were responsible for the divergence from Jesus' teaching that we have seen.

SHOULDN'T WE RESPECT TRADITION?

Traditions are typically very good things and have a great deal of value as people pass on values and beliefs from one generation to another. However, when a tradition is based on a false assumption, it should be respectfully challenged.

Tradition can also be a bad thing. Greek tradition held to the belief in the immortality of the soul for many centuries before the birth of Christianity. This belief became an invasive, insidious virus that spread into Christianity by the beginning of the third century AD. As many Greeks became Christians,

---

[7] Glenn Peoples, " History of Hell | Hell before Augustine," AfterLife, Last access 5-3-22, https://www.afterlife.co.nz/articles/history-of-hell/

some of their Greek traditions infiltrated the church. Some of these beliefs heavily influenced incorrect Christian doctrines that remain to this day.

As we saw in the verse above, Paul made a stern warning about this possibility in his letter to the Colossians church.

What if Martin Luther (out of a sense of respect) had deferred to the traditions of his day? Would he have still proceeded with posting his *Ninety-Five Theses*? Would he still have taken a defiant stand against what was one of the strongest traditions and forces in the history of the world?

Our goal should be to respect tradition in as far as it complies with the truth that we see in God's word. If it does not, then we are bound to respectfully disagree.

What if Peter and John had listened to the high priest, priests, and Jewish council and kept their mouths shut when commanded to do so by this very council? If they had indeed kept quiet and observed the tradition of the elders, we would have no gospel at all today.

> **Acts 4:19-20** But, Peter and John answered them, "Whether it is right in the sight of God to listen to you rather than to God, you must judge, for we cannot but speak of what we have seen and heard." (ESV)

INFILTRATION OF THE BELIEF OF THE "IMMORTAL SOUL"

One of the most damaging world views that infiltrated and captivated the church is the error of believing that man has an immortal soul. Man does not have a soul; *he is a soul*. Also, man is mortal, not immortal.

The concept of the "immortal soul" was not taught by Jesus, the New Testament authors, the apostles, nor the Apostolic Fathers.

Let's define "Apostolic Fathers." The term "Apostolic Fathers" is not a biblical term but has been historically used to describe those early church leaders who taught the teachings of Christ as they learned them from the apostles. In other words, they had not personally heard the teachings of Jesus but had sat at the feet of the apostles who had and were now passing on these teachings. This was the first generation removed, so to speak, from the apostles.

We have many writings of the Apostles, which have been accepted as part of the New Testament. Writings of the Apostolic Fathers were not accepted into the canon of the New Testament and rightfully so, as these men were not personal witnesses of Jesus' life, death, resurrection, and teaching. However, their writing does give us an accurate understanding as to what they believed in their time.

The concept of the "immortal soul" does not appear in early church writings until 150 years after the birth of the church. By this time, the Greek culture (the widely predominant culture surrounding Christianity during the first several centuries) began to influence and infiltrate Christian thought. Plato introduced the idea of the "immortal soul" many centuries earlier. This belief was widely and firmly held by the typical citizen of the Roman Empire. This belief deeply influenced Greek culture and permeated Christian beliefs during the first few centuries of the early church.

By the third century AD, the concept of the "immortal soul" had become widely accepted in Christian circles and powerfully influenced how scripture was interpreted. By the time Christianity was legalized by the Roman Empire in AD 311, the notion of "immortality" being a gift of God was held by the minority. The idea of the "immortal soul" became the official doctrine of the Roman Empire, which declared Christianity as its national religion by AD 380. About a century later, Augustine cemented the belief of the immortal soul as a bulwark of Christian doctrine. From this point forward, any effort to curb the idea of the "immortal soul" was heavily censored and even punishable as heresy.

There are many who have undertaken an astute study on the writings of the Apostolic Fathers and other prominent leaders in the first few centuries of the church. These studies reveal the slow emergence and infiltration of the fallacy of the "immortal soul" over the course of a couple centuries, displacing the clear teachings of Jesus and the New Testament writers.

You can find insights on the beliefs of early church fathers at the following webpage: EternalZoe.com/links. Navigate to the links under the category, "Early Church Beliefs on the Mortality of Psuche."

One of the most damaging world views that infiltrated the church

was the erroneous belief that man had an immortal soul.

The truth is, that man does not have a soul, man is a soul (psuche).

Also, the psuche of man is mortal, not immortal.

26

What is Hades?

The word *Hades* is sometimes translated as "hell" in English translations. Using the actual Greek word *Hades* would be a much better choice, to avoid conflation of this word with *Gehenna*. This is because the word *Gehenna* is almost always translated as "hell." Since some English translations use the word "hell" for translating both *Hades* and *Gehenna*, (especially the older translations) these 2 words are often conflated in the minds of readers.

This is much like the issue of translating both *zoe* and *psuche* as "life." This conflation and oversimplification of the scriptures has masked the important differences that existed in these original words. The consequences of these conflations has resulted in several disastrous misunderstandings.

If you would like to see evidence of where this conflation of Hell and Hades takes place, the following link shows a wide variety of English translations of Matthew 16:18.

https://www.biblegateway.com/verse/en/Matthew%2016:18

WE NEED CLARITY, NOT CONFLATION

This truly confuses the issue of the afterlife, as the words *Hades* and *Gehenna* are not the same. Neither Jesus nor any New Testament author would have ever thought of equating these two words. On the contrary, they used different words because they represented different venues/events that take place in the afterlife! Yet, mainstream Christian teaching frequently conflates these words with no effort to clarify their important differences.

But this is nothing new. This conflation has existed for millennia. A perfect example of this is the Apostle's creed that includes the following statement about Jesus, "he descended into Hell". This statement does not specify whether it is speaking of Hades or Gehenna. This statement can mean a lot of different things to a person depending on which paradigm they are influenced by.

This lack of clarity has led to a wide variety of opinions and arguments over the centuries as to just exactly what this statement in the Apostle's creed means. By the way, the Apostle's creed did not come from the Apostles, but was merely a statement (or creed) put together a couple hundred years after the last apostle had passed away.

But I digress, we are not studying the Apostle's Creed, we are studying the Bible. I only brought it up to illustrate how this conflation of Hades and Gehenna has been so influential.

We will see what really happened to Jesus during his time in Hades, later in this chapter.

Most traditionalists don't know the difference between Hades, Hell (Gehenna), nor even tartaroo for that matter. (Tartaroo is covered in a later chapter). Most Christians have no idea that there is a temporary place of the dead (Hades) that is destroyed after the final resurrection, and that then (and only then) Gehenna comes into the picture as the place of destruction for those resurrected to judgment. This true depiction of Hades and Gehenna is consistent throughout the New Testament.

Hades is equivalent to the Hebrew word *Sheol*, which is used throughout the Hebrew Old Testament. In the Old Testament, Sheol is portrayed as the place of the dead and nothing more. In fact, Sheol is often depicted as simply the "grave." It was never portrayed as a place of torment, nor a place of paradise, nor depicted as some sort of dichotomous realm. In fact, Sheol is never depicted as a place where there is any consciousness, but rather it is just depicted as the place of, or condition of, being dead.

Note: The incorrect portrayal of Hades as a dichotomous realm of conscious souls did not occur until the period between the Old and New Testaments, and originated from within Jewish folklore during this period.

In the New Testament, the Greek word *Hades* means the "unseen" and is a general term for the abode of *all* the dead, or the condition of being dead. Hades is considered an exact equivalent to the Hebrew word *sheol*. Neither hades or sheol is ever depicted as the place where only the unsaved go. Both are depicted as the place of *all* dead people.

THE CONNECTION BETWEEN DEATH AND HADES

Each time *Hades* is mentioned in the book of Revelation, *Hades* and death are always associated with each other. This makes sense. After a person dies, they enter *Hades*, which is a venue, or a phase of waiting until the resurrection.

> **Rev. 6:7-8** When he opened the fourth seal, I heard the voice of the fourth living creature say, "Come!" And I looked, and behold, a pale horse! And its rider's name was Death, and **Hades** followed him. (ESV)

Notice the interesting statement that Jesus makes in the verse below. *Jesus holds the keys to death and Hades.* This is hugely significant. Jesus will set believers free from death and *Hades* and give them Eternal Life.

There is no way out of Hades without Jesus freeing that person from death. On resurrection day, Jesus will free all who have trusted and believed in him from the grip of Hades. These people will be raised from death to eternal zoe.

> **Rev. 1:17-18** When I saw him, I fell at his feet as though dead. But, he laid his right hand on me, saying, "Fear not, I am the first and the last, and the living one. **I died, and behold I am alive forevermore, and I have the keys of death and Hades**." (ESV)

Note: The traditional view misses the significant role of the destruction of death and Hades because it is blinded to its importance. This event goes hand-in-hand with the resurrection. Resurrection from Hades is the final solution to the sentence of death that mankind has been under since the Garden of Eden. Yet this pinnacle achievement of God's rescue of man, is robbed of its importance in the traditional view. The traditional view is so focused on "eternal torment in hell" that it misses the true focus that the Bible places on resurrection and the destruction of death and Hades.

> **Rev. 20:11-15** Then, I saw a great white throne and him who was seated on it. From his presence earth and sky fled away, and no place was found for them. And I saw the dead, great and small, standing before the throne, and books were opened. Then, another book was opened, which is the book of life. And the dead were judged by what was written in the books, according to what they had done. And the sea gave up the dead who were in it, **death and Hades** gave up the dead who were in them, and they were judged, each one of them, according to what they had done. Then, **death and Hades** were thrown into the lake of fire. This is the second death, the lake of fire. And if anyone's name was not found written in the book of life (zoe), he was thrown into the lake of fire. (ESV)

On the day of the "great white throne" judgment, both death and *Hades* will be destroyed. *Hades* will cease to exist after this judgment that is described in the book of Revelation.

Remember, both death and *Hades* are thrown into the "lake of fire", which is the *second death.* The lake of fire is *Gehenna*. Each time Jesus used the word *Gehenna* in the synoptic gospels, he used it as a metaphor referring to the future lake of fire.

The first and second resurrection will both have occurred by the day of judgment. Nobody will be left in Hades, since both those rising to eternal zoe (first resurrection), and those resurrecting for the second resurrection will have been raised from Hades. (They will no longer be dead, as all will be resurrected at this point.)

Note: There are several stages to the first resurrection and all of them involve believers. Jesus permanently ends death for all who have believed in him, as they are resurrected to eternal zoe.

During the second resurrection (also known as the great white throne judgment), unbelievers (those whose names are not written in the book of zoe) are thrown into the lake of fire, which is aptly called the "second death". They will ultimately be destroyed, killed, dead forever. This would be known as "everlasting punishment," not "everlasting punishing." There is a difference.

THE RICH MAN AND LAZARUS (LUKE 16:19-31)

Hades became associated with torment partly because of Jesus' story of Lazarus and the rich man, in which the text mentions that the rich man looked up within *Hades* and saw Lazarus (see Luke 16:19-31 below).

> **Luke 16:19-31** Now a certain man was rich, and dressed in purple cloth and fine linen, feasting sumptuously every day. And a certain poor man named Lazarus, covered with sores, lay at his gate, and was longing to be filled with what fell from the table of the rich man. But even the dogs came and licked his sores. Now it happened that the poor man died, and he was carried away by the angels to Abraham's side. And the rich man also died and was buried. And in **Hades** he lifted up his eyes as he was in torment and saw Abraham from a distance, and Lazarus at his side. And he called out and said, 'Father Abraham, have mercy on me, and send Lazarus so that he could dip the tip of his finger in water and cool my tongue, because I am

suffering pain in this flame!' But Abraham said, 'Child, remember that you received your good things during your life, and Lazarus likewise bad things. But now he is comforted here, but you are suffering pain. And in addition to all these things, a great chasm has been established between us and you, so that those who want to cross over from here to you are not able to do so, nor can they cross over from there to us.' So he said, 'Then I ask you, father, that you send him to my father's house, for I have five brothers, so that he could warn them, in order that they also should not come to this place of torment!' But Abraham said, 'They have Moses and the prophets; they must listen to them.' And he said, 'No, father Abraham, but if someone from the dead goes to them, they will repent!' But he said to him, 'If they do not listen to Moses and the prophets, neither will they be convinced if someone rises from the dead.'" (LEB)

In this text, Jesus specifically refers to *Hades*, not *Gehenna*. Lazarus is depicted as being in Abraham's bosom while the rich man is in torment. There is a chasm separating them, but the scripture does not infer that the rich man is in Hades and Lazarus is in heaven. Rather, they are *both in Hades* with a chasm separating them. Hades is the interim place of the dead, before the resurrection and judgment day take place.

Neither Jesus nor any New Testament author would have

ever considered equating Hades with Gehenna.

On the contrary, they used different words because

they represented different things!

In Luke's account, the rich man is tormented in *Hades*. If you take this story literally, keep the following in mind. This torment of the rich man within Hades may last for millennia, but it will eventually come to an end. *Hades* will be destroyed on the day of judgment. See the following verse from the end of Revelation where on the day of judgment, the first two things to be thrown in the lake of fire, are death and *Hades*.

> **Revelation 20:4** Then **Death and Hades** were thrown into the lake of fire. This is the second death, the lake of fire. (ESV)

Upon being cast into the "lake of fire" *death* and *Hades* will be destroyed forever. Thus, this interim venue (*Hades*) will come to an end.

Note about Hades: Many believe this story of the rich man and Lazarus is literally true, and that Jesus was referring to a historical event involving the rich man, Lazarus and Abraham. Holding to this literal understanding has also contributed to the conflation of Hades and Gehenna. This is because (from a Traditionalist point of view) the torment in Hades appears to be identical to the torment that the Traditionalist believes will occur in Gehenna.

Others believe that Jesus was merely retelling a story from common Jewish folklore that originated during the intertestamental period. Jesus changes parts of the folktale to make an important point about the legalistic beliefs of the Pharisees in the crowd. There is evidence to support this.

The exact nature of what occurs during the period of Hades, is not something that I want to discuss at length here. What you may believe about this account of the rich man and Lazarus, as it is nowhere near as critical as understanding the resurrection from the dead to eternal zoe. You will be able to tell my leanings on the subject of Hades in the next few pages. But this argument is not a hill I want to die on, OK? The real issue is the resurrection from the dead (from Hades) to eternal zoe. You or I can be wrong on the exact nature of the interim period of Hades, but please, let's not be wrong on eternal zoe.

TWO PARADIGMS REGARDING *HADES*

As mentioned, there are some who argue that the story of the rich man and Lazarus is like a parable, with Jesus using an existing story from the cultural folklore of that time (the intertestamental period) to incriminate the Pharisees for their long-held view that wealth was sign of God's blessing, and that poverty or ill health was a sign of God's disfavor. After all, Luke 15 and 16 deal with Jesus speaking to the greed and presumptuous pride of the Pharisees. The story of the rich man and Lazarus is the final salvo that Jesus uses in Luke 16 to incriminate the Pharisees.

A similar story was commonly used by the Pharisees to indicate their assurance of going to Abraham's bosom, while almost everyone else would go to torment. This folklore was not based on scripture but was a popular belief during the Maccabean period. For instance, the terms "Abraham's bosom" and the idea of a chasm in the after-life is not described anywhere else in the Bible, yet was a popular notion among the Jews at that time.

If this is so, then Jesus turned this folktale on its head, rebuking the Pharisees. It is thought that Jesus intentionally used the "rich man" to allude to Caiphus (the high priest) as all the components in the story of the rich man as Jesus tells the story, would be interpreted by the Jews in the crowd as referring to Caiphus, the high priest.

However, others believe this story of *Hades* is an actual account of an "intermediate holding place" of the dead. They believe the story of the rich man and Lazarus should be taken literally as an actual historical event.

An exact understanding of what happens during the interim period of *Hades* is not essential to understanding Jesus' teachings on *eternal zoe, death, and immortality.*

My focus is on Jesus' ultimate purpose, which is to save man from eternal death and give him eternal life. I do not want to get distracted by a debate over the exact nature of this interim period of the after-life (Hades), and miss the main focus of Jesus' teachings throughout the gospels.

HADES IS NOT GEHENNA (DON'T CONFLATE THEM)

But one thing is for certain: *Hades* is not *Gehenna*. *Hades* is clearly going to be destroyed on the day of judgment. *Hades* is therefore an interim state and is not indicative (in any way) of what takes place in *Gehenna* on the day of judgment after Hades is destroyed.

Many who hold to the traditional view use this story of the rich man and Lazarus as the foundation of their teaching that when a person dies, they immediately go to heaven or hell. The traditional view conflates *Gehenna* and *Hades* as essentially saying that they are the same thing. This is a perfect example of how powerful and influential the traditional paradigm is and how it twists and weaves multiple concepts together in order to fit its distorted understanding.

One thing is for certain: Hades is not Gehenna.

Hades is clearly going to be destroyed on the day of judgment.

SOUL SLEEP

"Soul sleep" is the idea that the dead are asleep and are later awakened on the resurrection day. Those who hold to the idea of "soul sleep" believe that the dead are asleep. Therefore, they would not have any sensation of suffering nor of well-being. There is a great deal of support in the Old and New Testament for this belief. If you take the story of the rich man and Lazarus literally then it is likely that you would reject this idea of soul sleep.

I have listed a few scriptures below, from the New Testament that support the idea of "soul sleep". Notice that the gospel writers consistently show Jesus as depicting someone who had passed away as being asleep. Indeed, the apostle Paul also refers to believers who are already dead as being asleep.

Matthew 9:24 he said, "Go away, for the girl is not dead but **sleeping**." And they laughed at him. (ESV)

Mark 5:39 And when he had entered, he said to them, "Why are you making a commotion and weeping? The child is not dead but **sleeping**." (ESV)

Luke 8:52 And all were weeping and mourning for her, but he said, "Do not weep, for she is not dead but **sleeping**." (ESV)

John 11:11-15 He said these things, and after this he said to them, "Our friend Lazarus has fallen **asleep**, but I am going so that I can awaken him." So the disciples said to him, "Lord, if he has fallen **asleep**, he will get well." Now Jesus had been speaking about his death, but they thought that he was speaking about real **sleep**. So Jesus then said to them plainly, "Lazarus has died, and I am glad for your sake that I was not there, so that you may believe. But let us go to him. (LEB)

1 Corinthians 15:6 Then he appeared to more than five hundred brothers at one time, most of whom are still alive, though some have fallen **asleep**. (ESV)

1 Corinthians 15:17-18 And if Christ has not been raised, your faith is futile and you are still in your sins. Then those also who have fallen **asleep** in Christ have perished. (ESV)

1 Corinthians 15:20 But in fact Christ has been raised from the dead, the first fruits of those who have fallen **asleep** (ESV)

1 Corinthians 15:50-52 I tell you this, brothers: flesh and blood cannot inherit the kingdom of God, nor does the perishable inherit the imperishable. Behold! I tell you a mystery. We shall not all **sleep**, but we shall all be changed, in a moment, in the twinkling of an eye, at the last trumpet. For the trumpet will sound, and the dead will be raised imperishable, and we shall be changed. (ESV)

1 Thessalonians 4:13-15 Brothers, we do not want you to be uninformed about those who **sleep** in death, so that you will not grieve like the rest, who are without hope. 14 For since we believe that Jesus died and rose again, we also believe that God will bring with Jesus those who have fallen **asleep** in Him. 15 By the word of the Lord, we declare to you that we who are alive and remain until the coming of the Lord will by no means precede those who have fallen **asleep**.

1 Thessalonians 5:9-10 For God has not destined us for wrath, but to obtain salvation through our Lord Jesus Christ, who died for us so that whether we are awake or **asleep** we might live with him. (ESV)

Look at this verse from Daniel in the Old Testament. Daniel speaks of many who are asleep in the earth who will awaken to everlasting life, shining like the stars forever and ever. Unlike those who will wake to shame and everlasting contempt (destruction in Gehenna).

> **Daniel 12:2-3** And many of **those who sleep in the dust of the earth shall awake**, some to everlasting life, and some to shame and everlasting contempt. And those who are wise shall shine like the brightness of the sky above; and those who turn many to righteousness, like the stars forever and ever. (ESV)

Again, I do not want to wade into this argument about Hades, (this interim period or place of the dead), as that is not the focus of this book. I just want to make you aware of "Soul Sleep" in case you have never heard of it.

However, if you quickly dismiss the idea of "soul sleep", then what do you do with the verses above? Do you think that Paul's statement regarding believers that have fallen asleep, is an accurate depiction of the immediate heaven experience that you think believers will experience after death? In other words, does "sleep" describe the experience that you expect to experience immediately after you die and go to heaven?

NOTABLE CONDITIONALISTS

Four of the great reformers of Christianity who were Conditionalists (who also held to the belief of "soul sleep") are listed below:

- **John Wycliffe**: translated the Bible into Middle English from Latin in 1382.
- **John Huss**: A famous priest and reformer who preferred trusting in the scriptures rather than the pope, was burned at the stake by the Catholic church in 1415.
- **William Tyndale**: the first person to translate the New Testament from the original Greek into English. This happened about the same time as the invention of the printing press. His printed Bibles spread all over Europe. Tyndale was executed (strangled and then burned at the stake) by Henry VIII for producing this translation. His execution was an attempt by Henry VIII to meld his relationship with the powerful Catholic church who sought to kill Tyndale.
- **Martin Luther**: the most notable reformer, usually credited with starting the reformation, although the works of others like Wycliffe, Huss and Tyndale certainly contributed to the environment in which this occurred.

Martin Luther's boldly stood against the Pope's declaration that the soul was immortal. [8]

It is noteworthy that John Calvin (another reformer who came onto the scene while Luther was still alive) *severely* attacked the position of "soul sleep" that these other prominent reformers had held to. Calvin wrote a vicious pamphlet as a young man attacking those who held to "soul sleep" entitled "Psychopannychia". At the end of the day, due to Calvin's aggressive, prolific and tenacious writing (and the fact he was the last in this long line of influential reformers) his doctrine won out for the long term.[9]

Most Protestants hold Calvin and Luther in the same high esteem yet are completely unaware of their strong difference on this belief.

Calvin can be credited (infamously) with overtaking the great work of these men who had correctly clarified the message (Conditionalism) of the gospel. Calvin was one of the strongest proponents of the idea of "eternal torment in hell." Had Calvin not viciously attacked the beliefs of these other men, then Conditionalism may have become the predominant belief throughout Protestant Christianity today.

---

[8] Leroy Edwin Froom, "Martin Luther's Views on Conditionalism and Soul Sleep," Truth According to Scripture, Accessed 5/3/22,
https://www.truthaccordingtoscripture.com/documents/death/froom/luther-conditionalism.php#.YnHQVtrMLIV

[9] Afterlife, "Immortality of the soul in the bible?," May 25, 2010,
https://www.afterlife.co.nz/2010/05/immortality-of-the-soul-in-the-bible/

JESUS WENT TO *HADES* WHEN HE WAS CRUCIFIED

On the day of Pentecost, the apostle Peter preached to a large crowd, many of whom would become believers in Christ upon being convicted by his sermon. Peter begins by explaining who Jesus was. Then he continues by explaining that they (the crowd) had killed him. Yet God raised him from the dead, because it was impossible for Jesus to be held by death.

> **Acts 2:22-24** "Men of Israel, hear these words: Jesus of Nazareth, a man attested to you by God with mighty works and wonders and signs that God did through him in your midst, as you yourselves know—this Jesus, delivered up according to the definite plan and foreknowledge of God, you crucified and killed by the hands of lawless men. God raised him up, loosing the pangs of death, because it was not possible for him to be held by it." (ESV)

Peter continues his sermon by quoting from King David (from Psalm 16:9-11).

> **Acts 2:25-32** "For David says concerning him, 'I saw the Lord always before me, for he is at my right hand that I may not be shaken; therefore my heart was glad, and my tongue rejoiced; my flesh also will dwell in hope. For you will not abandon my soul (psuche) to Hades, or let your Holy One see corruption. You have made known to me the paths of life (zoe); you will make me full of gladness with your presence.'"
>
> "Brothers, I may say to you with confidence about the patriarch David that he both died and was buried, and his tomb is with us to this day. Being therefore a prophet, and knowing that God had sworn with an oath to him that he would set one of his descendants on his throne, he foresaw and spoke about the resurrection of the Christ, that he was not abandoned to Hades, nor did his flesh see corruption. This Jesus God raised up, and of that we all are witnesses." (ESV)

Peter points out that King David is dead and buried. (In other words, David has not been resurrected). Peter explains that God promised David that he would someday set one of David's descendants upon David's throne. This man would be known as the "Holy One," better known as the Messiah (Hebrew) or the Christ (Greek).

Peter also explains that David prophesied that God would not leave (abandon) Jesus' *psuche* in *Hades*. In other words, God would raise Jesus from the dead.

---

[10] Afterlife, "Immortality of the soul in the bible?," May 25, 2010,
https://www.afterlife.co.nz/2010/05/immortality-of-the-soul-in-the-bible/

In addition, Jesus' flesh did not see corruption (Jesus' body did not decay). This certainly would not be true about David as Peter explains that David's tomb was still with them.

In summary, Peter's sermon about Jesus contained these main points:

> The crowd participated in killing Jesus, according to the plan and foreknowledge of God the Father.
> God did not leave Jesus' *psuche* in *Hades*. (Jesus was resurrected)
> God did not allow Jesus' body to decay. (Jesus was resurrected)

We can see that Peter understood *Hades* as a place of the dead. He doesn't explain anything else about *Hades*, just that God was not going to abandon Jesus's *psuche* in Hades. Jesus's resurrection from death (being raised from *Hades*) is the focal point of Peter's sermon. Everything else in his sermon hinges upon Jesus's resurrection from hades.

Peter clarifies David's prophecy, explaining that

God would not leave Jesus' psuche in Hades.

In other words, God would raise Jesus from the dead.

WHAT HAPPENED TO JESUS IN HADES?

Remember, Hades is the place of the dead. When Jesus died on the cross, he died. It's that simple. He was dead, completely dead. This fact is what makes his resurrection from the dead so pivotal. Jesus's purpose for coming to earth as a human was so that he could die. He predicted this many times, and even spoke of laying down his psuche in John 10. He also spoke of the fact (in John 10) that the had the authority to take it (his psuche) up again. Jesus was raised from the dead by the power of the Holy Spirit. But his psuche died from the time of his last breath, until he was resurrected.

This is the crux of the gospel. If you miss this fact, then you miss the gospel message and you are likely spinning the gospel message as something totally different than what Jesus intended. Jesus's death was a substitute for our death. Then his resurrection from the dead, was the ultimate victory over death. His resurrection is a prelude, a guarantee of our own resurrection from the dead to eternal zoe.

WHAT PAUL SAYS ABOUT *HADES* AND MORTALITY

Now that you know a bit more about *Hades* and man's mortality, let us take a closer look at what Paul says in 1 Corinthians 15. There is an important word here that we have missed.

1 Cor. 15:50-57 But I say this, brothers, that flesh and blood is not able to inherit the kingdom of God, nor can corruption inherit incorruptibility. Behold, I tell you a mystery: we will not all fall asleep, but we will all be changed, in a moment, in the blink of an eye, at the last trumpet. For the trumpet will sound, and the dead will be raised imperishable, and we will be changed.

For it is necessary for this perishable body to put on incorruptibility, and this mortal body to put on immortality. But whenever this perishable body puts on incorruptibility and this mortal body puts on immortality, then the saying that is written will take place:

"Death is swallowed up in victory.

55 Where, O **death** is your victory? (**the actual Greek word is Hades, not death**!) Where, O death, is your sting?

Now the sting of death is sin, and the power of sin is the law. But thanks be to God, who gives us the victory through our Lord Jesus Christ! (LEB)

Notice the actual Greek-English Interlinear text on the following page. Notice that "Hades" is defined as the "unseen" or "unperceived".

1 Corinthians 15:55 The Greek word in 15:55 is not "death" but *Hades*. This verse reads more accurately as, "Oh *Hades*, where is your victory?"

15:55	ΠΟΥ	ΣΟΥ	ΘΑΝΑΤΕ	ΤΟ	ΚΕΝΤΡΟΝ	ΠΟΥ	ΣΟΥ	ΑΔΗ	ΤΟ	
	pou	sou	thanate	to	kentron	pou	sou	hadE	to	
	G4226	G4675	G2288	G3588	G2759	G4226	G4675	G86	G3588	
	Part Int	pp 2 Gen Sg	n_ Voc Sg m	t_ Nom Sg n	n_ Nom Sg n	Part Int	pp 2 Gen Sg	n_ Voc Sg m	t_ Nom Sg n	
	?-where	OF-YOU	DEATH!	THE	PIERCer	?-where	OF-YOU	UN-PERCEIVED !	THE	
	where ?				sting	where ?		unseen !		

NIKOC	
nikos	
G3534	
n_ Nom Sg n	
CONQUEST	
victory	

55 O death, where [is] thy sting? O grave, where [is] thy victory?

The point Paul is making here, is that *Hades* will not have victory over the believer. The believer will be resurrected from *Hades*. (This is obvious from reading the entirety of 1 Corinthians 15:50-57 shown on the previous page.)

This is a major deviation from the Traditionalist view. The traditional view is that *Hades* is a place of torment for the unbeliever. Therefore, it is no surprise that *Hades* was not translated literally in this verse, as this would not fit the Traditionalist paradigm.

HADES CANNOT PREVENT BELIEVERS FROM ESCAPING DEATH

Toward the end of Jesus' ministry, he asks his closest disciples a very important question. He asks them, "Who do people say that I am?"

They give him an answer, and then Jesus turns the question directly to them . . . "Who do **you** say that I am? "

Jesus' ministry up to this point has been a living testimony to his closest disciples, revealing who he really was. They had not only listened to his teaching for nearly three years but had personally witnessed his miracles and observed his day-to-day living.

Now, Jesus presents this vital question directly to them: "Do you believe in me?" See the following conversation from the gospel according to Matthew.

> **Matt. 16:13-18** Now when Jesus came to the region of Caesarea Philippi, he began asking his disciples, saying, "Who do people say that the Son of Man is?" And they said, Some say John the Baptist, but others Elijah, and others Jeremiah or one of the prophets." He said to them, "But who do you say that I am?" And Simon Peter answered and said, "You are the Christ, the Son of the living God!" And Jesus answered and said to him, "Blessed are you, Simon son of Jonah, because flesh and blood did not reveal this to you, but my Father who is in heaven. And I also say to you that you are Peter, and on this rock I will build my church, and the gates of **Hades** will not overpower it! (LEB)

Many English New Testaments (Including the ESV) translate *Hades* into English as "hell." This is a huge mistake! *Hades* is not *Gehenna* in any way imaginable. This lack of clarity in translation contributes to this conflation problem we are dealing with.

Now, back to the context of the verses above. Peter answers Jesus' question by making a firm statement of faith that he believes Jesus is the Messiah, the Son of the living God. Based upon Peter's confession of faith, Jesus then states that his church will be built upon this truth (the truth that Jesus is the Messiah, the Son of the living God).

GATES OF HADES - DON'T MISS THIS IMPORTANT DETAIL!

Jesus then says that the gates of *Hades* will not overcome the church!

I often hear this verse being incorrectly used to refer to the realm of Satan and his demonic forces. This incorrect assumption then presumes that this so-called realm of Satan (*Hades*) would therefore not have enough power to overcome Christ's church. In other words, many Christians use this verse to portray hades or "hell" as Satan's headquarters, or his base of operations.

This is not at all what this verse is saying! Satan has nothing to do with *Hades* other than the fact that it is his deception of Adam and Eve that has put us all into the certainty of death that we are born into.

Let me repeat this: Satan has nothing to do with *Hades*, other than the fact that he has been successful in getting all of us to enter Hades (because all humans enter Hades when they die) when our temporal life on earth is over. Remember, in John chapter 8 Jesus referred to Satan as a murderer from the beginning. Satan has in essence murdered all mankind. We are born into a state of impending death that has existed since mankind was expelled from the Garden of Eden, and lost access to the tree of zoe.

Satan stands as both the deceiver and the accuser of all mankind. Satan's ultimate goal at this point is to continue to deceive mortals in order to prevent them from believing in Jesus.

Satan does not have a headquarters located in *Hades*, or *Gehenna* for that matter. Satan's headquarters is the world you currently live in. His reign of darkness covers the whole earth. It is only through the "light of life" (zoe) that Jesus provides to the believer that one can escape this darkness.

Back to the verse. Jesus says that *Hades* will not overcome the church (those that are believers). *This is because the gates of Hades will not be able to prevent believers from escaping the sentence of death!* Jesus will free believers from *Hades* to receive eternal *zoe*.

There will also be no more dying from that point on, hence the destruction of death. There will no longer be a state of the "unseen" dead (*Hades*), as there will not be anyone to inhabit such a state. Everyone will have been resurrected to receive Eternal Life, or resurrected to judgment and subsequently cast into the lake of fire, which is the second death.

Think back to the verse just quoted from King David, in Acts 2. As with many prophecies from the Old Testament, there are two fulfillments. However, there is something very unique about this prophecy (Psalm 16:9-11). The second fulfillment (Jesus's resurrection) took place *before* the first fulfillment. Normally double fulfillments indicate that the first fulfillment occurred during the time and in the context of the Old Testament. This would be considered a type or shadow of the ultimate fulfillment which would generally come later through Jesus.

In this case the first fulfillment (David's resurrection) has yet to occur. Though David has not yet been resurrected, he expressed his complete confidence that this will happen at some point in the future. He speaks of his assurance that God will not abandon him to *Hades*. He was confident, based on the fact that God had shown him the path to *zoe*. We do not know exactly what God revealed to David, but it was enough for David to rest in confidence.

Remember that in John 10:10, Jesus said he had come so that his sheep might have *zoe*. Jesus has come to end the sentence of death once and for all for those who believe in him.

Jesus says that Hades will not overcome the church.

This is because the gates of Hades will not be able to

keep believers from escaping the sentence of death.

Jesus will free believers from death and Hades to receive eternal zoe.

ONE FINAL COMMENT REGARDING *HADES*: WHAT IT IS *NOT*

Hades is not "purgatory" in any sense whatsoever.

Purgatory was a concept fabricated by men that evolved over a period of several centuries. By the eleventh century AD, purgatory was a belief firmly held by the Roman Catholic Church. According to this belief man must undergo a purging of sin after death (or purification) in a place called "purgatory" before being allowed into heaven.

There are so many things wrong with this belief, it would take me a long time to go into them all—but primarily, no such a place is never mentioned in the Bible.

The belief in purgatory has generated subsequent errors that are even more disturbing. The notion of being able to purchase "indulgences" for those that have died became prevalent in the Roman Catholic Church by the fifteenth century. The purchased "indulgence" would supposedly enable the dead person in question to pass through purgatory much more quickly.

The notion of those still alive being able to purchase "indulgences" in order to expedite forgiveness or purification of someone in purgatory was one of the primary reasons that drove Martin Luther (a Catholic priest at the time), to produce his Ninety-Five Theses against the Roman Catholic Church. There is no biblical support for "purgatory" or "indulgences."

27

What is Tartaroo?

There is one other word that is translated as "hell" one time in the New Testament. This occurs in 2 Peter 2:4, when Peter speaks of the angels that sinned long ago.

> **2 Pet. 2:4** For if God did not spare angels when they sinned, but cast them into hell **(tartaroo)** and committed them to chains of gloomy darkness to be kept until the judgment. (ESV)

Peter is referring to a temporary place of confinement for some fallen angels (demons). They are to be kept there either until the day of judgment that takes place after the second resurrection, or until the judgment event that takes place in Revelation 9, where we see creatures that are released from the abyss to torment those who do not have the seal of God on their foreheads. Notice in Rev 9:11 these creatures coming forth from the abyss have as king over them one known as Apollyon. ("The destroyer" likely a reference to Satan).

In either case *Tartaroo* is plainly a place where these demons are confined with chains of gloomy darkness. What these chains consist of is unknown and irrelevant. The point here is that these particular demons have been taken out of action and are being held there until another time.

> **Revelation 9:1-11** And the fifth angel blew the trumpet, and I saw a star that had fallen from heaven to the earth, and the key of the shaft of the **abyss** was given to him. 2 And he opened the shaft of the **abyss**, and smoke went up from the shaft like smoke from a great furnace, and the sun and the air were darkened by the smoke from the shaft. 3 And out of the smoke locusts came to the earth, and power was given to them like the scorpions of the earth have power. 4 And it was told to them that they should not damage the grass of the earth or any green plant or any tree, except those people who do not have the seal of God on their foreheads. 5 And it was granted to them that they should not kill them, but that they would be tormented five months, and their torment is like the torment of a scorpion when it stings a person. 6 And in those days people will seek death and will never find it, and they will long to die, and death will flee from them.
>
> 7 And the appearance of the locusts was like horses prepared for battle, and on their heads were something like crowns similar in appearance to gold, and their faces were like men's faces, 8 and they had hair like the hair of women, and their teeth were like the teeth of lions, 9 and they had breastplates like iron breastplates, and the sound of their wings was like the sound of many horse-drawn chariots running into battle. 10 And they have tails similar in appearance to scorpions, and stings, and their power to injure people for five months is in their tails. 11 **They have as king over them the angel of the abyss**, whose name in Hebrew is Abaddon, and in Greek he has the name Apollyon. (LEB)

The verses below record when Jesus encountered a man possessed by a legion of demons. When confronted by Jesus, the demons pleaded with him not to send them into the abyss. This is likely a reference to *tartaroo*.

This is evidently a place the demons greatly feared. Why Jesus spared these particular demons from this fate at that time is not clear.

> **Luke 8:26-33** And they sailed to the region of the Gerasenes, which is opposite Galilee. And as he got out on the land, a certain man from the town met him who had demons and for a considerable time had not worn clothes and did not live in a house, but among the tombs. And when he saw Jesus, he cried out, fell down before him, and said with a loud voice, "What do I have to do with you, Jesus, Son of the Most High God? I beg you, do not torment me!" For he had commanded the unclean spirit to come out of the man. For it had seized him many times, and he was bound with chains and shackles and was guarded, and breaking the bonds he would be driven by the demon into the deserted places. So Jesus asked him, "What is your name?" And he said, "Legion," because many demons had entered into him. And they began imploring him that he would not order them to depart into the **abyss**. Now there was a large herd of pigs feeding there on the hill, and they implored him that he would permit them to enter into those pigs. And he permitted them. So the demons came out of the man and entered into the pigs, and the herd rushed headlong down the steep slope into the lake and were drowned. (LEB)

28

What is *Gehenna*?

The word *Gehenna* occurs twelve times in the New Testament. Eleven of these are used by Jesus in his teachings. All eleven occur in the Synoptic gospels.

GEHENNA WAS USED AS A METAPHOR, BUT IT IS A REAL PLACE

Gehenna is the actual name of a valley located just outside of Jerusalem. In the mind of the Jew in Jesus' day, *Gehenna* was associated with a prophetic curse of judgment. In fact, although Gehenna was peaceful in Jesus' day, it's infamous history was abhorrent to them.

JESUS' USE OF APOCALYPTIC TERMINOLOGY

Jesus heavily quotes from the Old Testament throughout the gospels. His reference to Old Testament scripture and prophecies would always reflect the true intended thrust of those scriptures, even if the contemporary Jewish view of those same scriptures was incorrect.

> When Jesus quoted from Old Testament prophecies, he reflected the true intended thrust of those scriptures, regardless of any contemporary misunderstanding that may have existed.

In fact, when Jesus alludes to Gehenna, he often combines two separate apocalyptic prophecies from the Old Testament. He mixes these two prophecies that both entail massive destruction of wicked men. Gehenna itself is a direct reference to one of these dreadful prophecies of death and destruction. The other prophecy mixed in with some of the Gehenna verses comes directly from the last chapter of the prophetic book, Isaiah.

Even if we are clueless about what Jesus is talking about in our contemporary times (2000 years after Jesus spoke these words), Jesus was very intentional when he pulled two very graphic prophecies about death, judgment and slaughter from the Old Testament. He knew exactly what he was doing. He was not creating and injecting some totally new concept on the fly. When Jesus used these two prophecies together, he intended to point to the ultimate day of judgment, which will involve massive slaughter, death and destruction. Neither of these prophecies from the Old

Testament depict long term suffering or torment of those that are judged. Rather, they clearly depict a massive slaughter resulting in countless dead corpses.

When Jesus alludes to Gehenna, he often combines two

separate apocalyptic prophecies from the Old Testament.

He mixes these two prophecies of massive slaughter of wicked men,

in order to emphasize this totally destructive nature of Gehenna.

For example, when Jesus spoke of *Gehenna*, he occasionally added phrases from Isaiah 66 to emphasize this totally destructive nature of *Gehenna*. The traditional view argues that these phrases indicate "never ending torment", such as being continuously eaten by worms, where the person is always eaten, but never devoured, and always burning, but never consumed by the fire. Whereas in fact, these phrases from Isaiah denote numerous corpses laying around (after a judgment of slaughter) that are being consumed by maggots and burning pires of dead bodies.

Many Jews that heard Jesus mention *Gehenna* would have indeed connected it to the prophecy of judgement (a judgement of death and destruction) from the book of Jeremiah. These Jews would never have associated Jesus' statements about *Gehenna* with "eternal torment". They would have understood he was talking about a judgment of death.

Knowledgeable Jews that heard Jesus use the word Gehenna

would have known of the Valley of Hinnom's infamous reputation and its

association with judgment of massive slaughter and utter destruction.

They would not have associated it with eternal suffering or torment.

LAKE OF FIRE – THE SECOND DEATH

Jesus used the word *Gehenna* as a metaphor to refer to what John refers to in the Book of Revelation as the "lake of fire." The phrase "lake of fire" is used several times by John in the book of Revelation. John defines this **lake of fire** as the **second death**. The second death will occur after the resurrection to judgment. Those whose names are not in the book of zoe, will be cast into the lake of fire. This second death is permanent. There is not going to be another resurrection. These people will be destroyed.

Rev. 20:14-15 Then, death and Hades were thrown into the lake of fire. This is the second death, the lake of fire. And if anyone's name was not found written in the book of life (zoe), he was thrown into the lake of fire. (ESV)

Rev. 21:8 But as for the cowardly, the faithless, the detestable, as for murderers, the sexually immoral, sorcerers, idolaters, and all liars, their portion will be in the lake that burns with fire and sulfur, which is the second death (ESV)

The gospel according to Matthew records seven instances of *Gehenna*, while three occur in the gospel according to Mark, and one occurs in the gospel according to Luke.

The other instance occurs in the book of James, when *Gehenna* is used by James, the brother of Jesus. The apostle John never used the word *Gehenna* in his gospel or in any of his writings. Nor did Paul use it in any of his writings.

In Matthew, Jesus uses the word *Gehenna on four separate occasions.* In two of these instances, Jesus uses *Gehenna* multiple times in the same conversation.

I've listed each occurrence below:

Matt. 5:22 But, I say to you that everyone who is angry with his brother will be liable to judgment; whoever insults his brother will be liable to the council; and whoever says, 'You fool!' will be liable to the **hell (Gehenna)** of fire." (ESV)

Matt. 5:27-30 "You have heard that it was said, 'You shall not commit adultery.' But, I say to you that everyone who looks at a woman with lustful intent has already committed adultery with her in his heart. If your right eye causes you to sin, tear it out and throw it away. For it is better that you lose one of your members than that your whole body be thrown into hell (Gehenna). And if your right hand causes you to sin, cut it off and throw it away. For it is better that you lose one of your members than that your whole body go into **hell (Gehenna)**." (ESV)

Matt. 10:28 "And do not fear those who kill the body but cannot kill the soul (psuche). Rather fear him who can destroy both soul (psuche) and body in **hell (Gehenna)**." (ESV)

Matt. 18:7-9 "Woe to the world for temptations to sin! For it is necessary that temptations come, but woe to the one by whom the temptation comes! And if your hand or your foot causes you to sin, cut it off and throw it away. It is better for you to enter life (zoe) crippled or lame than with two hands or two feet to be thrown into the eternal fire. And if your eye causes you to sin, tear it out and throw it away. It is better for you to enter life (zoe) with one eye than with two eyes to be thrown into the **hell (Gehenna)** of fire." (ESV)

Matt. 23:15 "Woe to you, scribes and Pharisees, hypocrites! For you travel across sea and land to make a single proselyte, and when he becomes a proselyte, you make him twice as much a child of **hell (Gehenna)** as yourselves." (ESV)

Matt. 23:33 "You serpents, you brood of vipers, how are you to escape being sentenced to **hell (Gehenna)**?" (ESV)

In Mark's gospel, Jesus uses the word Gehenna 3 times in a single conversation.

Mark 9:42-48 And whoever causes one of these little ones who believe in me to sin, it is better for him if instead a large millstone is placed around his neck and he is thrown into the sea. And if your hand causes you to sin, cut it off! It is better for you to enter into life (zoe) crippled than, having two hands, to go into **hell (Gehenna)** - into the unquenchable fire! And if your foot causes you to sin, cut it off! It is better for you to enter into life (zoe) lame than, having two feet, to be thrown into **hell (Gehenna)**! And if your eye causes you to sin, tear it out! It is better for you to enter into the kingdom of God with one eye than, having two eyes, to be thrown into **hell (Gehenna)**, 'where their worm does not die and the fire is not extinguished.' (LEB)

Luke's gospel records Jesus using Gehenna once, very similar to the verse in Matthew 10:28

Luke 12:4-5 "I tell you, my friends, do not fear those who kill the body, and after that have nothing more that they can do. But, I will warn you whom to fear: fear him who, after he has killed, has authority to cast into **hell (Gehenna)**." (ESV)

Finally, James uses the word Gehenna once in his letter.

James 3:5-6 So also the tongue is a small member, yet it boasts of great things. How great a forest is set ablaze by such a small fire! And the tongue is a fire, a world of unrighteousness. The tongue is set among our members, staining the whole body, setting on fire the entire course of life, and set on fire by **hell (Gehenna)**. (ESV)

ETYMOLOGY OF THE WORD *GEHENNA*

The history of *Gehenna* goes back to the days of the kingdom of Judah seven to eight centuries earlier. The nation of Judah during that time had adopted the pagan rituals of Baal worship from the nations surrounding them. One of these rituals associated with Baal worship included the sacrifice of children upon the red-hot altar of Baal (and Moloch) as these living babies were sacrificed (killed) in the fire.

This practice took place in an area that became known as Topheth, within the Valley of Hinnom. By the time of Jesus, this Valley of Hinnom became known as *Gehenna* in the Greek language.

God responded to this horrific practice of child sacrifice with a most severe prophecy of judgment. See the following verses from the Old Testament, which depicts this idolatry of Judah and God's response.

2 Chron. 28:1-3 Ahaz was twenty years old when he began to reign, and he reigned sixteen years in Jerusalem. And he did not do what was right in the eyes of the Lord, as his father David had done, but he walked in the ways of the kings of Israel. He even made metal images for the Baals, and he made offerings in the **Valley of the Son of Hinnom** and burned his sons as an offering, according to the abominations of the nations whom the Lord drove out before the people of Israel. (ESV)

Ahaz was the king of Judah (the southern kingdom of Israel) for sixteen years, around 730 BC. Ahaz succumbed to pressure from Assyria to adopt the worship of Baal, which included burning his sons alive on an idol to Baal. This took place in the Valley of Ben Hinnom (later known in Greek as *Gehenna*).

> **2 Chron. 33:1-6** Manasseh was twelve years old when he began to reign, and he reigned fifty-five years in Jerusalem. And he did what was evil in the sight of the Lord . . . And he burned his sons as an offering in the **Valley of the Son of Hinnom**, and used fortune-telling and omens and sorcery, and dealt with mediums and with necromancers. He did much evil in the sight of the Lord, provoking him to anger. (ESV)

King Manasseh continued with this detestable practice of sacrificing children in the fire in the Valley of Ben Hinnom. He was the grandson of Ahaz.

Josiah was the grandson of Manasseh. Josiah actually made an earnest effort to turn the kingdom of Judah back to worshipping the true God and to do away with the idolatrous practices of his father Amon and his grandfather Manasseh.

This section is a bit long but is a very interesting and powerful story about King Josiah, who was dedicated to repenting and restoring Judah to faithfully following the true God.

> **2 Kings 23:1-16** Then, the king sent, and all the elders of Judah and Jerusalem were gathered to him . . . And he read in their hearing all the words of the Book of the Covenant that had been found in the house of the Lord. And the king stood by the pillar and made a covenant before the Lord, to walk after the Lord and to keep his commandments and his testimonies and his statutes with all his heart and all his soul, to perform the words of this covenant that were written in this book. . . .
>
> . . . And he deposed the priests whom the kings of Judah had ordained to make offerings in the high places at the cities of Judah and around Jerusalem; those also who burned incense to Baal, to the sun and the moon and the constellations and all the host of the heavens. . . . **And he defiled Topheth, which is in the Valley of the Son of Hinnom**, that no one might burn his son or his daughter as an offering to Molech. (ESV)

We see where Josiah desecrated Topheth. This desecration likely involved the breaking of idols and altars into pieces and then burning them into ashes or grinding them into dust. The desecration would also involve filling the area with dead men's bones or burning the bones first and then spreading the ashes over the area. In any case, this desecration and infamous history would be recalled in the minds of many Jews when Jesus mentioned Gehenna.

Josiah was the last "righteous" king that Judah had. After Josiah's death, the nation of Judah basically fell away and abandoned seeking God and his word.

THE PROPHECY OF THE DESTRUCTION OF JUDAH

Jeremiah was a prophet in Judah from about 630-580 BC. During this time, he makes a prophecy regarding the destruction of Judah. Listen to the harsh words of judgment that God places upon Judah.

> **Jer. 7:30-34** "For the sons of Judah have done evil in my sight, declares the Lord. They have set their detestable things in the house that is called by my name, to defile it. And they have built the high places of **Topheth, which is in the Valley of the Son of Hinnom**, to burn their sons and their daughters in the fire, which I did not command, nor did it come into my mind. Therefore, behold, the days are coming, declares the Lord, when it will no more be called **Topheth, or the Valley of the Son of Hinnom**, **but the Valley of Slaughter**; for they will bury in Topheth, because there is no room elsewhere. And the dead bodies of this people will be food for the birds of the air, and for the beasts of the earth, and none will frighten them away. And I will silence in the cities of Judah and in the streets of Jerusalem the voice of mirth and the voice of gladness, the voice of the bridegroom and the voice of the bride, for the land shall become a waste." (ESV)

Jeremiah again pronounces judgment upon Judah. Notice what Jeremiah says about the "Valley of Ben Hinnom" (*Gehenna*). Remember, *Gehenna* is the word that Jesus uses as a metaphor for the judgement of the lake of fire, the second death.

> **Jer. 19:1-15** Thus said Yahweh, "Go and buy a potter's earthenware jar, and take some of the elders of the people, and some of the leaders of the priests, and go out to the Valley of Ben Hinnom, which is at the entrance of the Gate of the Potsherd, and proclaim there the words that I speak to you. And you shall say, 'Hear the word of Yahweh, O kings of Judah and inhabitants of Jerusalem. Thus says Yahweh of hosts, the God of Israel: "Look, I am about to bring disaster upon this place so that everyone who hears it his ears will ring. Because they have forsaken me, and they have defaced this place, and they have made smoke offerings in it to other gods whom they have not known, they, nor their ancestors, nor the kings of Judah, and they have filled up this place with the blood of the innocent, and they have built the high places of Baal, to burn their children in the fire, burnt offerings to Baal, which I commanded not, and I ordered not, and it did not come to my mind.
>
> "Therefore look, days are about to come," declares Yahweh, "when this place will no longer be called **Topheth or the Valley of Ben Hinnom, but the Valley of the Slaughter.** And I will lay waste the plans of Judah and Jerusalem in this place, and I will bring them to ruin by the sword before their enemies, and by the hand of those who seek their life, and I will give their dead bodies as food to the birds of heaven and to the animals of the earth. And I will make this city a horror, and an object of hissing, everyone who passes by it will be appalled, and will hiss because of all its wounds. And I will cause them to eat the flesh of their sons, and the flesh of their daughters, and each one will eat the flesh of his neighbor in the siege and in the distress which their enemies and those who seek their life inflict on them.'"

"Then you shall break the jar before the eyes of the men who go with you. And you shall say to them, 'Thus says Yahweh of hosts: "So I will break this people and this city as one breaks the vessel of the potter, so that it is not able to be repaired again. And in Topheth they will bury until there is no room to bury. Thus will I do to this place," declares Yahweh, "and to its inhabitants, to make this city like Topheth. And the houses of Jerusalem and the houses of the kings of Judah will be unclean like the place of Topheth, all the houses where they made smoke offerings upon their roofs to all the host of heaven, and where they poured out libations to other gods."'"

Then Jeremiah came from Topheth, where Yahweh had sent him to prophesy, and he stood in the courtyard of the house of Yahweh and said to all the people, "Thus says Yahweh of hosts, the God of Israel, 'Look, I am about to bring to this city and upon all its towns all the disaster that I have pronounced against it, because they have hardened their neck to not hear my words.'" (LEB)

The context of all these verses from the prophets is one of judgment, a massive slaughter with complete and utter destruction. There is no allusion to everlasting torment, only countless dead corpses.

The context of these prophecies is one of judgment,

a massive slaughter with complete and utter destruction.

There is no connotation of everlasting torment,

only countless dead corpses.

WHERE THE WORM NEVER DIES AND FIRE NEVER GOES OUT

The following verse from Mark show Jesus use of the phrases: "where the worm never dies and where the fire is not quenched."

Mark 9:42-48 "Whoever causes one of these little ones who believe in me to sin, it would be better for him if a great millstone were hung around his neck and he were thrown into the sea. And if your hand causes you to sin, cut it off. It is better for you to enter life (zoe) crippled than with two hands to go to hell (Gehenna) to the unquenchable fire. And if your foot causes you to sin, cut it off. It is better for you to enter life (zoe) lame than with two feet to be thrown into hell (Gehenna). And if your eye causes you to sin, tear it out. It is better for you to enter the kingdom of God with one eye than with two eyes to be thrown into hell (Gehenna), '**where their worm does not die and the fire is not quenched.**'" (ESV)

Reminder: Jesus inserts quotes from Old Testament scriptures frequently during in his teachings. These quotes from the Old Testament are prophecies of doom, slaughter, and utter destruction—not eternal torment.

WHERE JESUS GOT THESE PHRASES

> **Isaiah 66:24** And they shall go out and look on the dead bodies of the men who have rebelled against me. For their worm shall not die, their fire shall not be quenched, and they shall be an abhorrence to all flesh. (ESV)

Jesus quotes this idea of "their worm shall not die, and their fire is not quenched" from this very last verse of the book of Isaiah.

Notice that Isaiah is not talking about people who are suffering forever in torment. He is clearly speaking of dead corpses after a great and terrible slaughter.

The idea of "their worm shall not die" is referring to the maggots that will consume the dead corpses that are laying everywhere after a great slaughter. In other words, the idea is that their destruction will be complete; there will be no end to the worms, until there is no more decaying flesh for them to eat. There is no portrayal of worms eating a conscious person. There is no idea conveyed of suffering but rather of complete destruction.[11]

The idea of "their worm shall not die" is referring to the maggots that will consume the dead corpses that are laying around everywhere after a great slaughter.

Similarly, the idea of "their fire shall not be quenched" is also referring to the final destruction of those dead corpses upon the battlefield. Corpses will be burned until they are utterly and totally gone. The fire that burns them will not be quenched. This is not referring to some sort of eternal fire but rather an unquenchable fire that will not be extinguished until all the dead bodies have been completely burned up (utterly destroyed) by the fire. Again, there is no idea conveyed of suffering or of eternal torment. Dead corpses do not feel pain.

The scripture above speaks of those who will go out and look upon dead bodies. There is nothing implied here about conscious people that are still alive and being tormented. Rather, the observers are looking upon dead and decaying bodies that are being eaten by maggots, or being burned in pyres in order to get rid of the dead stinking corpses (i.e. abhorrent).

Jesus' use of this phrase is not alluding to eternal torment but to a day of judgment and slaughter, which was prophesied in the very last verse of Isaiah.

Note: Jesus is tying this prophecy by Isaiah (Isaiah 66:24) to the prophecies made by Jeremiah (Jeremiah 7:30-34 and 19:1-15). Jeremiah spoke of the judgment that will take place in the Valley

---

[11] Edward Fudge, "The Fire That Consumes," [Video] EdwardFudge.com, Accessed 5/3/22, https://edwardfudge.com/category/videos/the-fire-thatconsumes/

of Hinnom (Gehenna). Neither of these prophecies involved eternal torment. Certainly, there may be some temporary suffering in such a slaughter, but those who are being slaughtered will ultimately die. Their corpses as depicted are completely consumed (destroyed). They will no longer exist.

These quotes from the Old Testament are prophecies of doom,

slaughter, and utter destruction - not eternal torment

WEEPING AND GNASHING OF TEETH

The traditional view often claims that the phrase "weeping and gnashing of teeth" used by Jesus, proves that the damned will undergo eternal pain and suffering in Hell. In reality, there is no imperative that this phrase indicates eternal suffering. It is only chosen to mean that by the traditional view. Jesus uses this phrase 7 times, 6 of which occur in the Gospel of Matthew, and one time in Luke. Twice in Matthew (both in Matthew chapter 13), it is accompanied by the phrase "thrown into the fiery furnace". Being in a fiery furnace certainly could cause pain. But the emphasis of these verses is not on suffering, but rather is focused on being burned up.

In 3 other instances where "weeping and gnashing of teeth" is used in Matthew, it is associated with being cast into outer darkness. One time it is connected to being cut into pieces and put with the hypocrites.

In every instance this phrase is most likely referring to the intense anger, regret, and sorrow of those who have been left out (or cast out) of the kingdom of God.[12] Let's look at the instance where Jesus uses this phrase in Luke and then we will look at one of fiery furnace verses in Matthew.

> **Luke 13:24-30** "Strive to enter through the narrow door. For many, I tell you, will seek to enter and will not be able. When once the master of the house has risen and shut the door, and you begin to stand outside and to knock at the door, saying, 'Lord, open to us,' then he will answer you, 'I do not know where you come from.' Then, you will begin to say, 'We ate and drank in your presence, and you taught in our streets.' But, he will say, 'I tell you, I do not know where you come from. Depart from me, all you workers of evil!' **In that place there will be weeping and gnashing of teeth**, when you see Abraham and Isaac and Jacob and all the prophets in the kingdom of God but you yourselves cast out. And people will come from east and west, and from north and south, and recline at table in the kingdom of God. And behold, some are last who will be first, and some are first who will be last." (ESV)

Notice the other phrase: "when you see... yourselves cast out." It is the realization of their plight that triggers their weeping and gnashing of teeth, not suffering or torment.

---

[12] Edward Fudge, "gnashing of teeth," EdwardFudge.com, Accessed 5/3/22, https://edwardfudge.com/2014/01/gnashing-of-teeth/

Weeping and gnashing of teeth does not allude to physical pain or eternal torment. Gnashing of teeth indicates extreme rage, while weeping indicates sorrow and regret.

> **Matt. 13:40-42** Just as the weeds are gathered and burned with fire, so will it be at the end of the age. The Son of Man will send his angels, and they will gather out of his kingdom all causes of sin and all law-breakers, and throw them into the fiery furnace. In that place there will be **weeping and gnashing of teeth**. (ESV)

The traditional view will argue that the verse above indicates that weeping and gnashing of teeth are due to pain and suffering in the fiery furnace. I can see where that might seem to make sense if you were determined to take that path, but even if it indicates pain and suffering, it does not convey pain that goes on forever.

However, this verse does describe the destruction that is going to take place on the day of judgment. There will indeed be weeping and gnashing of teeth, as rage and despair overtake those who are about to be destroyed. How long those who are thrown into the fiery furnace will suffer before they are destroyed is not mentioned. But the complete destruction of these people is certain. They will not be tormented forever. There is no way to substantiate the claim that this verse proves eternal torment in hell.

If you go back and read all of Matthew 13, Jesus uses multiple parables to talk about the kingdom of heaven, bearing fruit, and the harvest at the end of the age. In two of the parables, he uses the illustration of weeds that are gathered by the angels to be burned. Let me ask you… does the metaphor of burning up weeds represent eternal torment? Do weeds that are being burned undergo eternal burning? Or are they burned up, and then gone?

Jesus uses this metaphor of burning weeds to segue into how his angels will gather all causes of sin and all law-breakers and throw them into the fiery furnace. Jesus segues by saying, "Just as the weeds are gathered and burned with fire, so it will be at the end of the age".

Several years ago, after moving into a home with a yard full of tall weeds in the backyard, my son and I gathered and burned a large pile of limbs and weeds in our backyard. I could not get the fire to start so I stupidly had my son pour a small amount of gasoline on the pile, and then light it. Fortunately, my son was fine, though startled by the subsequent big ball of fire, and fortunately our house and fence did not burn down. But within a few minutes, there was nothing left of branch nor weed. They were totally burned up, only some ashes remained.

The idea of burning weeds or chaff up at the end of the age, is a very visual illustration of destruction, of being burned up. As Edward Fudge calls it, it is a "consuming fire". [13]

---

[13] Edward Fudge, "The Fire That Consumes," [Video] EdwardFudge.com, Accessed 5/3/22, https://edwardfudge.com/category/videos/the-fire-thatconsumes/

Ps. 112:10 The wicked man sees it and is angry; **he gnashes his teeth and melts away**; the desire of the wicked will perish! (ESV)

As you can see in this Psalm, the phrase "he gnashes his teeth" is used as an expression of intense anger, not as a reference to pain. This is a direct reference to the anger of the wicked man, who sees the blessing of the man who fears the Lord.[14]

Notice that the wicked man melts away, and his desires will perish.

Acts 7:54 Now, when they heard these things they were enraged, and **they ground their teeth at him**. (ESV)

Here in the book of Acts, we see the Jews becoming so angry at Stephen that they ground their teeth (gnashing) at him. In their intense anger they stoned Stephen to death.

LEARNING THE VOCABULARY OF JUDGMENT (BY EDWARD FUDGE)

I highly recommend the video (part 4) of the lecture series, "The Fire that Consumes," by Edward Fudge that discusses the "Vocabulary of Judgment" used in the Bible, [15]

Fudge does a thorough job of reviewing multiple scriptures regarding many of the topics discussed in Part 3 of this book. The video quality is not great, but the audio is fine, and the content is excellent.

THE ULTIMATE QUESTION ABOUT HELL

In Revelation 20, the apostle John states that on the final day of judgment those people whose names are found in the book of *zoe* will be given Eternal *zoe*. Those whose names are not found in the book of *zoe* will be thrown into the lake of fire, which is the second death.

> **Rev. 20:13-15** And the sea gave up the dead who were in it, death and Hades gave up the dead who were in them, and they were judged, each one of them, according to what they had done. Then, death and Hades were thrown into the **lake of fire**. This is the second death, the lake of fire. And if anyone's name was not found written in the book of life (zoe), he was thrown into the **lake of fire**. (ESV)

So, the question about hell comes down to this. Based on what you have learned about *psuche* and *zoe*, how do *you* define the "second death"?

---

[14] Edward Fudge, "gnashing of teeth," EdwardFudge.com, Accessed 5/3/22, https://edwardfudge.com/2014/01/gnashing-of-teeth/

[15] Edward Fudge, "The Fire That Consumes, Part 4" [Video] EdwardFudge.com, Accessed 5/3/22, https://edwardfudge.com/category/videos/the-fire-thatconsumes/

Would you agree with the traditional view, which defines the "second death" as spiritual death? According to the traditional view this spiritual death lasts forever and would include being separated from God, being cast into hell as a place of never-ending torture, continuous burning, continuously being eaten by worms, and everlasting darkness.

Would you agree with the traditional view, which redefines Jesus' repeated use of the word "perishing" to mean "spiritual death" as just defined.

Note: It is important to remember that we are already separated from God. We are all initially in a state of impending eternal death. To review this, go back and see the section on John 5:24-26, in the chapter on John 5. The consistent proleptic use of death that Jesus frequently uses (as well as John and Paul in their New Testament writing) is referring to eternal physical death, not spiritual death.

Maybe it would be best to take Jesus and John at their word. Let's return to understanding that the term "second death" means the second death. Likewise, perish means perish and destruction means destruction. Let's not twist these words to fit a distorted paradigm.

CLARIFYING SATAN'S CONNECTION TO *GEHENNA*

Satan is not directly connected to *Gehenna*, as is frequently portrayed by the traditional view. However, it **will** be Satan's ultimate destination.

I mentioned earlier that *Gehenna* is not a headquarters for Satan. It is not his dwelling place, as it has been depicted for centuries. However, it will become his final destination, where he and his angels will be punished.

Keep in mind that this is not their place today; they currently have free range throughout the world of men, seeking to deceive and enslave men to darkness. (There is a slight exception to this, see the chapter on Tartaroo). Satan and his demons seek to keep mankind enslaved on the path to death.

> **Rev. 20:10** . . . and the devil who had deceived them was thrown into the lake of fire and sulfur, where the beast and the false prophet were, and they will be tormented day and night forever and ever. (ESV)

But, the devil's (Satan's) time is coming, when he will be thrown into the lake of fire. It appears that Satan and his angels will be tormented forever.

But this is not the case for humans.

DIFFERENCE BETWEEN HUMANS AND ANGELS

Let's take a brief look at a statement that Jesus makes about angels, that may give us some insight into Satan's nature. (We will look at this in more detail later, as it gives us some important clarity about Jesus' humanity). In Luke 20:34-36, Jesus makes a comment about those who are worthy to participate in the age to come, and the resurrection (to eternal zoe).

Luke 20:34-36 And Jesus said to them, "The sons of this age marry and are given in marriage, but those who are considered worthy to attain to that age and to the resurrection from the dead neither marry nor are given in marriage, **for they cannot die anymore, because they are equal to angels and are sons of God, being sons of the resurrection.** (ESV)

Jesus says those believers will be like the angels, <u>for they cannot die anymore</u>. They are equal to the angels (only in that sense). They have become children of God, children of the resurrection.

This gift of immortality upon their resurrection, will make the child of God like the angels, in the sense that they can no longer die!

Upon their resurrection, the gift of immortality will make the

children of God like the angels, in the sense that they can no longer die

---

Humans have existed under a sentence of death, since Adam and Eve were banished from the Garden of Eden and the Tree of Life (zoe). Only God, Jesus, and the Holy Spirit have zoe within themselves. They are the "source" of zoe, that can be "given" to another creature.

It seems plausible that the angels were given immortality when they were created, although no angel has "zoe" inherent within them, in other words, they cannot bestow "zoe" upon any other creature.

The earlier verse from Luke seems to indicate that angles are not capable of dying. Thus, Jesus statement that those believers who are considered worthy to attain to the resurrection will be like the angels in the sense that they can no longer die makes complete sense, when you understand the purpose of the resurrection.

The saving effect of the resurrection is that it resurrects us from death! The effect of that is that we can no longer die. We will be given immortality via the gift of zoe into the ages. At the resurrection believers will be raised from dead to live again, this time forever.

As an after-thought, it could be that the reason that Satan and his angels will be tormented forever is because as angels they were created with (given) immortality.

This seems to be a plausible explanation, although the Bible is not emphatically clear about this. There are some who believe that Satan and his angels will be destroyed in the lake of fire. I am not going to lose any sleep over this either way. God, in his perfect wisdom and justice will see that Satan and his demons (fallen angels) will get what they deserve.

29

Zoe For All Men

Romans 5:17-18 For if, because of one man's trespass, death reigned through that one man, much more will those who receive the abundance of grace and the free gift of righteousness reign in life (zoe) through the one man Jesus Christ. Therefore, as one trespass led to condemnation for all men, so one act of righteousness leads to justification and life (zoe) for all men. (ESV)

Question: If one trespass of Adam lead to condemnation for all men, then just exactly what does this "condemnation" consist of?

Was this condemnation supposed to be "hell"? Did God pronounce an "eternity of torment" for Adam and Eve, that then progressed on down to all men? No, not at all.

What was the punishment for Adam? It was this... ***death***.

Adam's access to the "Tree of Life" was taken away. He and Eve were banished from the garden. God told them their destiny was that they would die and return to dust and ashes. From dust they came and to dust they would return.

This has been the state of man ever since. It is only through Jesus' death, substituted for our death that this sentence was taken away, for those whose believe in Jesus as Messiah, Lord and Savior.

As a result of believing in the one man's (Jesus') act of righteousness, people are justified by this act of faith and receive the *gift of zoe*. Remember, zoe means "being alive". So, when Paul is speaking of the one act of righteousness that leads to zoe, he is referring to the believer's assurance of being resurrected from the dead to live again, this time for eternity. This expectation of eternal zoe comes from the gift of the indwelling Holy Spirit. It is the Holy Spirit (Spirit of Christ) that gives zoe.

This impartation of the Holy Spirit into the psuche of the believer takes place when a person's belief results in their being born again. The zoe of God begins to live within the psuche of the believer from that moment on. This *zoe* preserves that person's *psuche* for eternal *zoe*. The believer is now immortal in essence, as they are indwelt by the immortal Holy Spirit that is the source of zoe. The believer has exchanged the status of death for the assurance of eternal *zoe*.

If you read Romans chapter 5 in it's entirety, you will see why the "resurrection" plays such an important part in this chapter. It is the resurrection of Jesus, that displayed Jesus' power and victory over death. It is Jesus' resurrection that gives the believer assurance of their own resurrection. You see, it is not "eternal torment" that is the issue here, nor anywhere else in Paul's writings. Remember, Paul never mentions Gehenna (hell) in any of this writing. *That's because "eternal torment" is a non-issue*. Eternal torment is a straw-man. Eternal torment is a distortion of truth injected by Satan to detract from the real argument of Jesus. Satan has always been and always will be a deceiver, twisting any truth coming from God.

If Satan cannot just outright deceive a person from believing in Jesus, then he will do the next best thing. He will twist and distort the real message of Christ, so that people will be confused about the original message. This distortion alone contributes to reducing fruit in the life of the believer and is a major deterrence to unbelievers accepting the message of salvation that is available through Jesus.

SOMETHING TO PONDER

Think about this for a minute… the traditional view almost assumes a missing gospel narrative. It's like there must be a missing segment of Jesus' teaching from the gospels that would clear up the confusion brought about by the traditional view. This missing section might go something like this:

> Jesus said to his disciples, "By the way, I know you understand that the punishment for man's disobedience in the Garden of Eden was death. I just want to clarify that this death was not referring to physical death. Absolutely not. Don't get confused. The whole dust-to-dust thing was merely a metaphorical statement that really meant "spiritual death". Ok, do you understand? Don't get the obvious statements in Genesis mixed up with the real meaning that I am just now going to share with you.'

> 'Just so you understand, this spiritual death really means being separated from God forever, and will also include unspeakable torture, including continuously being eaten alive but never consumed, and being continuously seared by fire that never goes out (nor burns up) in order that the wicked person will suffer intensely for all eternity.

> So just to clarify, the Father chose to use a different narrative throughout the Old Testament to describe the fate of the wicked which is over and over again described as slaughter, destruction, death, perishing, etc.. The Father chose to wait until I arrived on Earth to clarify what he meant by all these statements and to add a caveat to this fate of the wicked. So, just to clarify, in addition to death, or actually in place of physical death… I'm sorry this sounds confusing, but what the Father really meant to say was that the fate of the wicked is actually eternal torment in hell, and has little or nothing to do with physical death, even though physical death is what is conveyed throughout the Old Testament.'

> 'Any questions?" After this teaching Jesus' disciples left to ponder his words, some would never return.

Note: Obviously, the above scenario did not happen. I just added it here as a prompt to take another look at what the gospel really teaches.

30

Revelation 14 & 20

There are a few verses in Revelation that the traditional view insists proves beyond a shadow of doubt that "hell" is a place of eternal suffering for the unsaved. They contend that these verses are so obvious in their support for ECT (eternal conscious torment) that they need no further exegesis. But is this true? Do these verses really support ECT?

Earlier I mentioned that Jesus frequently made statements that were direct references to imagery and prophecy from the Old Testament. Indeed, without understanding these connections it is impossible to have an accurate understanding of what Jesus meant.

This also holds true for many statements made by New Testament authors and certainly holds true for the apostle John. Nowhere is this more evident than in the book of Revelation, where John uses vivid imagery to depict future events.

To accurately understand this prophetic imagery in Revelation 14 & 20, we must understand the direct connections that John is making from the Old Testament.

John did not pull these prophetic images of symbolism out of his hat. The ideas of "fire and sulfur", "day and night", as well as "smoke that rises forever" seen in Rev. 14:10-11 did not originate with John. Rather, John is making a direct parallel with imagery seen in the Old Testament.

IMAGERY FROM GENESIS 19 & ISAIAH 34 FOUND IN REVELATION

Pulling from Genesis 19, we see John using imagery found in the destruction of Sodom and Gomorrah. Then from Isaiah 34, John recalls imagery from Isaiah's prophecy of the utter and complete destruction of the nation of Edom. In both Old Testament accounts, the imagery is one of complete destruction of people. Both scenes depict a massive, final slaughter, not a scene of eternal torment or everlasting suffering. The final depiction in both Genesis and Isaiah shows smoke rising as an indicator of this utter destruction.

One would be hard-pressed to say these Old Testament scriptures point to eternal suffering of people or a nation. Rather, these people were clearly killed and destroyed.

If a person was unaware that John is making a direct parallel between Revelation 14:10-11, 20:10 and Isaiah 34 (as well as Genesis 19) then it's not hard to see where that person might logically conclude that these verses in Revelation are referring to eternal suffering in "hell".

In the following paragraphs, I've included three sections of verses from Revelation 14, Genesis 19 and Isaiah 34. We will see how these Old Testament scriptures are inextricably linked to these apocalyptic statements in Revelation.

REVELATION 14:9-11

And another angel, a third, followed them, saying with a loud voice, "If anyone worships the beast and its image and receives a mark on his forehead or on his hand, 10 he also will drink the wine of God's wrath, poured full strength into the cup of his anger, and he will be tormented with fire and sulfur in the presence of the holy angels and in the presence of the Lamb. 11 And the smoke of their torment goes up forever and ever, and they have no rest, day or night, these worshipers of the beast and its image, and whoever receives the mark of its name." (ESV)

GENESIS 19:23-29

The sun had risen on the earth when Lot came to Zoar. Then the Lord rained on Sodom and Gomorrah sulfur and fire from the Lord out of heaven. And he overthrew those cities, and all the valley, and all the inhabitants of the cities, and what grew on the ground. But Lot's wife, behind him, looked back, and she became a pillar of salt.

And Abraham went early in the morning to the place where he had stood before the Lord. And he looked down toward Sodom and Gomorrah and toward all the land of the valley, and he looked and, behold, the smoke of the land went up like the smoke of a furnace. So it was that, when God destroyed the cities of the valley (ESV)

ISAIAH 34:9-10

And its streams shall be changed to pitch and its soil to sulfur, and its land shall become like burning pitch. Night and day it shall not be quenched; its smoke shall go up forever. From generation to generation it shall be in ruins; forever and ever there will be no one who passes through her. (LEB)

Let's look at three specific parts of Revelation 14:10-11

FIRST - HE WILL BE TORMENTED WITH FIRE AND SULFUR

In Revelation 14:10 John speaks of being "tormented with fire and sulfur". John is pulling imagery from both Genesis 19 and Isaiah 34. Genesis shows us that fire and sulfur rained down on Sodom and Gomorrah. This resulted in the destruction of those cities. There was indeed torment experienced by the people in those cities that occurred during the destruction, but the people in those cities were destroyed. Abraham sees the smoke from the destruction the following morning. In other words, by the time Abraham saw the smoke, the suffering and destruction were already complete.

In Isaiah 34, we also see sulfur and burning associated with the destruction of Edom. Likewise, there would no doubt torment may have been associated with the destruction of this nation, but it would have been transient (even if it took years) as that nation was eventually totally destroyed.

Thus, the fire and sulfur imagery associated with Revelation 14 and 20 is not unique to Revelation but is a direct pull from apocalyptic imagery of God's judgment upon man found in the Old Testament. There is absolutely no imperative to associate the references of "fire and sulfur burning" in Revelation with the erroneous concept of eternal torment in "hell". Revelation just does not support this idea.

SECOND - SMOKE OF THEIR TORMENT GOES UP FOREVER AND EVER

In Genesis, Abraham sees the smoke rising the next day indicating the destruction and slaughter of Sodom and Gomorrah.

In Isaiah, the verse indicates that upon the fulfillment of this prophecy, the smoke generated by the destruction of Edom rises forever. Isaiah's prophecy about the destruction of Edom was written about 2 – 3 centuries before it was fulfilled. Edom's destruction was fulfilled however, about the 5th century BC. The smoke associated with this destruction is no longer visible today. Therefore, the imagery associated with the smoke rising forever is not to be taken literally (as with most symbolism found in Revelation) rather the symbolism of the smoke rising forever simply attests to the complete "finality" of the judgment.

In other words, in Isaiah's account the smoke rising forever from Edom's burning is not due to Edom continuing to burn forever but is symbolic as a sign of Edom's everlasting destruction. Her destruction was complete and it is final. There is not a chance of her return.

If this is not convincing, then let's look at another verse where John uses this same phrase "smoke goes up forever and ever".

THE UTTER DESTRUCTION OF BABYLON

This imagery of smoke rising and "smoke rising forever" is mentioned again in Revelation 18 and 19. Revelation 18 repeatedly speaks of the city of Babylon and the sexual immorality that she has committed with the nations. I point out this reference to Babylon's sexual immorality, so that it will be clear to you when we see John referring to the destruction of the "prostitute" (in Revelation 19), that you will understand he is referring back to Babylon.

> **Revelation 18:2-3** "Fallen, fallen is Babylon the great, and it has become a dwelling place of demons and a haunt of every unclean spirit and a haunt of every unclean bird and a haunt of every unclean and detested animal. For all the nations have drunk from the wine of the passion of her sexual immorality, and the kings of the earth have committed sexual immorality with her, and the merchants of the earth have become rich from the power of her sensuality." (LEB)

In 18:8-10 Babylon is shown to be destroyed and being burned up with fire. The smoke from Babylon's destruction is evident for all to see.

> **Revelation 18:8-10** Because of this her plagues will come in one day - death and mourning and famine— and she will be burned up with fire, because the Lord God who passes judgment on her is powerful!" And the kings of the earth will weep and mourn over her, those who committed sexual immorality and lived sensually with her, when they see the smoke of her burning, 10 standing far off because of the fear of her torment, saying, "Woe, woe, the great city, Babylon the powerful city, because in one hour your judgment has come!" (LEB)

Notice that torment is indeed experienced by those being destroyed in verse 15 (below). The violent nature of this massive and utter destruction would involve suffering, even though it may be brief. Also notice the brevity of the destruction, as this passage mentions (twice) that the destruction only takes one hour. Perhaps this is a symbolic period of time or maybe it's a literal hour, but it certainly indicates finality, and a short period of time.

> **Revelation 18:15-20** The merchants of these things, who became rich from them, will stand far off, weeping and mourning because of the fear of her torment, saying, "Woe, woe, the great city, dressed in fine linen and purple cloth and scarlet cloth, and adorned with gold and precious stones and pearls, because in one hour such great wealth has been laid waste!" And every shipmaster and every seafarer and sailors and all those who labor on the sea stood far off and began to cry out when they saw the smoke of her burning, saying, "Who is like the great city?" And they threw dust on their heads and were crying out, weeping and mourning, saying, "Woe, woe, the great city, in which all those who had ships on the sea became rich from her prosperity, because in one hour she has been laid waste! "Rejoice over her, heaven and the saints and the apostles and the prophets, because God has pronounced your judgment on her!" (LEB)

The ESV renders verse 17 as "What city was like the great city?", indicating past tense, and is referring to Babylon.

> **Revelation 18:15-20** For in a single hour all this wealth has been laid waste." And all shipmasters and seafaring men, sailors and all whose trade is on the sea, stood far off and cried out as they saw the smoke of her burning, "What city was like the great city?" And they threw dust on their heads as they wept and mourned, crying out, "Alas, alas, for the great city where all who had ships at sea grew rich by her wealth! For in a single hour she has been laid waste. (ESV)

Moving to Revelation 19, John now refers to Babylon as the prostitute. We see the host of heaven crying out in praise at the destruction of Babylon. The key verse to take notice of is verse 3, which says the "smoke from her goes up forever and ever". This is the same imagery we saw in Revelation

14:10-11. We also just saw the destruction of Babylon clearly depicted as being complete (finished) in Revelation 18 (taking one hour and the resulting smoke from Babylon's destruction).

The fact that her smokes rises forever and ever does not indicate everlasting torment, nor everlasting burning. Rather it is symbolic of Babylon's everlasting destruction, a disastrous event that is completed and finished. Also, notice the phrase "forever and ever" also comes from Isaiah 34:10. In each instance the phrase is indicative of a judgment that has concluded, and is incapable of being undone.

> **Revelation 19:1-3** "Hallelujah! Salvation and glory and power belong to our God, for his judgments are true and just; for he has judged the great prostitute who corrupted the earth with her immorality and has avenged on her the blood of his servants." 3 Once more they cried out, "Hallelujah! The smoke from her goes up forever and ever." (ESV)

Thus, the phrase "smoke goes up forever and ever" found in Revelation is symbolic of everlasting destruction (finality), not everlasting torment. This phrase does not in any way support the traditional concept of eternal torment in "hell".

Again, if you look at the phrase "the smoke of her burning" from Rev 18, this smoke is what the sailors can see from afar, during and after the one hour of Babylon's (aka the great prostitute in Rev. 19) destruction.

THIRD - THEY HAVE NO REST, DAY OR NIGHT

The phrase "they shall have no rest day or night" is found in both Rev 14:11 and Rev 20:10. Isaiah 34 and Revelation chapters 14, 18, 19 & 20 share these common themes: fire, burning, sulfur, smoke, as well as "day and night". John makes repeated direct parallels in Revelation to Isaiah's apocalypse. And just as Jesus does in the synoptic gospels when he speaks of Gehenna, John sometimes mixes these apocalyptic themes. They are not always word for word parallels, but rather phrases that are symbolic of destruction and the inescapable certainty of destruction for those that are being judged.

In Isaiah 34, we see Isaiah using the phrase, "Night and day it shall not be quenched", as he refers to the non-stop burning of the land which cannot be put out, until the fire is done consuming those whom God has appointed for destruction.[16]

Some traditionalists will concede that there is no definitive proof that the phrase "fire and sulfur", nor the phrase "smoke of their torment rising forever" are referring to eternal torment. Yet they will tenaciously hold their ground on the phrase "they have no rest day or night" as undeniably indicating eternal torment in "hell".

Why would John so clearly connect to imagery from Genesis and Isaiah 34 which points to a judgment of slaughter and destruction and then randomly take the phrase "day and night" from Isaiah 34, and change its context from meaning "no respite, relief or rescue from the impending

---

[16] Edward Fudge, "The Fire That Consumes," [Video] EdwardFudge.com, Accessed 5/3/22, https://edwardfudge.com/category/videos/the-fire-thatconsumes/

violent slaughter" to a totally different meaning of "being tortured for ever and ever"? Understanding that John is referring to a judgment of slaughter is straightforward once you realize the imagery that John connects to from Isaiah 34.

MEANING OF THE PHRASE "NO REST DAY OR NIGHT"

In Revelation 6, we see John describing the dreadful intensity of God's judgment. It depicts the fact that there is no escape, and no rest to be found from the judgment that is in progress. This is the same concept of "there is no rest day or night".

> **Revelation 6:16-17** And they said to the mountains and to the rocks, "Fall on us and hide us from the face of the one who is seated on the throne, and from the wrath of the Lamb, because the great day of their wrath has come, and who is able to stand?" (LEB)

We can see the dread in this scenario where people are desperately and vainly searching for refuge. There is no place for them to hide. This is clearly an environment where there would be no rest day or night. This is not some vague or intangible idea. If you were to read news articles about cities that were under siege (2018-2020) in Syria (or anywhere there are active war zones), you can see that people and families caught in the cross hairs of battle must deal with this dreadful reality 24 hours a day, often with nowhere to run or seek refuge, nor hope of rescue. This scenario is a real nightmare that is experienced today in some parts of the world.

John indicates the future judgment depicted in Revelation 14-20 will be worse than this, on a large scale that will inevitably result in total destruction of the wicked.

Thus, the idea of "no rest night and day" is not referring to torture that is never ending. Rather it is speaking of a dreadful scenario where those seeking shelter and rescue from an impending slaughter can find no haven day or night from their approaching doom.

RESULT OF JUDGMENT – CORPSES, NOT ETERNAL TORMENT

In the first few verses of Isaiah 34, Isaiah clearly points out the ultimate result of God's judgment in this apocalyptic chapter is the slaughter of the nation that he judges. We see images of a great slaughter with lots of dead corpses. There is no depiction of people that are still alive being tormented.

> **Isaiah 34:2-3** For the anger of Yahweh is against all the nations, and his wrath is against all their armies; he has put them under a ban, he has given them up for slaughter. And their slain shall be cast out; as for their corpses, their stench shall go up. (LEB)

REVELATION 20:10

> **Revelation 20:10** And the devil who deceived them was thrown into the lake of fire and sulfur, where the beast and the false prophet also are, and they will be tormented day and night forever and ever. (LEB)

In Revelation 20:10 we see some of the same terminology that we've seen in Revelation 14, such as burning fire and sulfur, as well as tormenting day and night forever.

There are some important things to understand about this specific verse. It is not speaking about humans. Anytime humans are spoken of with regard to the final judgment they are destroyed. For example, in verse 9 (see below), those people that are part of the nations that have been deceived by Satan will be "consumed by fire from heaven." The word "consumed" indicates destruction, leaving nothing but ashes, it does not refer to eternal torment.

> **Revelation 20:7-10** And when the thousand years are completed, Satan will be released from his prison 8 and he will go out to deceive the nations that are at the four corners of the earth, Gog and Magog, to assemble them for battle, whose number is like the sand of the sea. 9 And they went up on the broad plain of the earth and surrounded the fortified camp of the saints and the beloved city, and fire came down from heaven and consumed them. 10 And the devil who deceived them was thrown into the lake of fire and Sulphur, where the beast and the false prophet also are, and they will be tormented day and night forever and ever. (LEB)

Later in Revelation 20:14, John depicts the final end of those humans that are going to be resurrected to judgment. He shows that they will be consumed in the lake of fire, which John clearly defines in verse 14 as the second death, **"This is the second death—the lake of fire"** (LEB). This instance is speaking of humans, not Satan or his angels (demons). Notice that the humans are "consumed" by the lake of fire. Consumed means they are burned up. There is nothing left of them after they are consumed.

Death and hades are also seen as being cast into the lake of fire, symbolizing the end of death and hades. (Neither death nor hades are living beings, see the chapter on "What is Hades").

> **Revelation 20:14** And Death and Hades were thrown into the lake of fire. This is the second death—the lake of fire. 15 And if anyone was not found written in the book of life, he was thrown into the lake of fire. (LEB).

On the other hand, the devil and his angels could be quite capable of receiving eternal torment as the Bible seems to indicate they were created immortal. Thus, it may be possible that they could undergo eternal torment should God choose not to destroy them. Notice in Revelation 20:10 (above) the Devil is thrown into the lake of fire, and in this instance the lake of fire is not identified as the second death, perhaps that is because Satan will not die there.

Notice the remark that Jesus makes below (Luke 20:34-36) about those who are considered worthy of participating in the age to come and the resurrection. He points out that they will be like the angels because:

➢ Just like angels, they will be incapable of dying
➢ Because they are sons of God
➢ Because they are sons of the resurrection

223

Inversely, these verses would indicate that if someone is not considered worthy (i.e. because they rejected Jesus) then that person would stay in a mortal condition, thus remain quite capable of dying.

> **Luke 20:34-36** And Jesus said to them, "The sons of this age marry and are given in marriage, 35 but those who are considered worthy to attain to that age and to the resurrection from the dead neither marry nor are given in marriage, 36 for they are not even able to die any longer, because they are like the angels and are sons of God, because they are sons of the resurrection. (LEB)

Notice also in Matthew 25:41 where Jesus speaks of the destiny of the unsaved. He says these people (mortal humans) will be cast into the eternal fire prepared for the devil and his angels. Perhaps this eternal fire is intended to torment the devil and his demons forever. But there is no impetus for us to believe this is the sentence of mortal humans.

> **Matthew 25:41** Then he will also say to those on his left, 'Depart from me, you accursed ones, into the eternal fire that has been prepared for the devil and his angels! (LEB)

Why would Jesus find it necessary to point out that this fire was prepared for the devil and his angels? Perhaps because of its eternal nature. A few verses later in Matthew 25:46 Jesus says those humans going into the eternal fire will go into eternal punishment, unlike the saved who will receive eternal zoe. The Traditional view believes that eternal punishment is "eternal punishing." But that is a huge presumption strongly influenced by the Traditional paradigm. There is no mandate to interpret this verse that way. Rather, eternal punishment indicates a punishment whose "effect" lasts forever. In other words, the punishment is not reversible. It never ends, in the sense that it is final. There is no longer an opportunity for those who are destroyed to receive eternal life. There will be a resurrection from a person's first death. There is no remedy or resurrection from the second death. It is final.

> **Matthew 25:46** And these will depart into eternal punishment, but the righteous into eternal life. (LEB)

Unlike the righteous who will be raised to eternal zoe and experience an immortal existence like the angels, the lost will be destroyed forever. Would this not be considered eternal punishment? If you consider the highest level of punishment that humans can receive in a court of law currently, it is "capital punishment" also known as execution. If a person is executed for a heinous crime today, do we expect to ever see that person again? Do we expect them to suddenly show up again? No, of course not. Their punishment is never ending, it is everlasting. That person is not continuing to be tormented or punished. Their punishment is final, with no hope of being reversed.

DON'T LET THE TAIL WAG THE DOG

My argument for conditional immortality is not dependent on Revelation 14 and 20, although these two sections of verses do support conditional immortality.

224

If as traditionalists, we dig in our heels and take our stand on these two verses, it is like the tail wagging the dog. As Christians we cannot take a stance on doctrine based on a couple verses without looking at what the rest of the Bible says. My concern is that someone reading this book will focus on arguing about these two sections of verses in Revelation, and brush aside the rest of this book.

Please carefully read Parts 1 & 2 of this book, before thoughtfully making decisions on any of the material in Part 3. Parts 1 & 2 lay a foundation for understanding Part 3. Jesus' teaching on life and death, was Jesus primary focus. Gehenna was only used as a metaphor for the final destruction of wicked men.

VERSES SUPPORTING "DESTRUCTION" OF THE WICKED BY FIRE

Matthew 13:24-30 He put another parable before them, saying, "The kingdom of heaven may be compared to a man who sowed good seed in his field, but while his men were sleeping, his enemy came and sowed weeds among the wheat and went away. So when the plants came up and bore grain, then the weeds appeared also. And the servants of the master of the house came and said to him, 'Master, did you not sow good seed in your field? How then does it have weeds?' He said to them, 'An enemy has done this.' So the servants said to him, 'Then do you want us to go and gather them?' But he said, 'No, lest in gathering the weeds you root up the wheat along with them. Let both grow together until the harvest, and at harvest time I will tell the reapers, "Gather the weeds first and bind them in bundles to be burned, but gather the wheat into my barn." (ESV)

Matthew 13:36-43 Then he left the crowds and went into the house. And his disciples came to him, saying, "Explain to us the parable of the weeds of the field." He answered, "The one who sows the good seed is the Son of Man. The field is the world, and the good seed is the sons of the kingdom. The weeds are the sons of the evil one, and the enemy who sowed them is the devil. The harvest is the end of the age, and the reapers are angels. Just as the weeds are gathered and burned with fire, so will it be at the end of the age. The Son of Man will send his angels, and they will gather out of his kingdom all causes of sin and all law-breakers, and throw them into the fiery furnace. In that place there will be weeping and gnashing of teeth. Then the righteous will shine like the sun in the kingdom of their Father. He who has ears, let him hear. (ESV)

What happens to weeds when they are burned? They are destroyed. They are consumed by the fire and no longer exist. There is no support in the above verses for eternal torment.

Malachi 4:1-3 For behold, the day is coming, burning like an oven, when all the arrogant and all evildoers will be stubble. The day that is coming shall set them ablaze, says the Lord of hosts, so that it will leave them neither root nor branch. 2 But for you who fear my name, the sun of righteousness shall rise with healing in its wings. You shall go out leaping like calves from the stall. 3 And you shall tread down the wicked, for they will be ashes under the soles of your feet, on the day when I act, says the Lord of hosts. (ESV)

What happens to the arrogant and evildoers? They will be like stubble that is set ablaze, so that there is no root or branch remaining (i.e., destruction with no chance of returning). The result (in verse 3) depicts that all that is left of the arrogant and evildoers is ashes. This indicates complete and final destruction, not everlasting torment.

> **Jude 7** just as Sodom and Gomorrah and the surrounding cities, which likewise indulged in sexual immorality and pursued unnatural desire, serve as an example by undergoing a punishment of eternal fire. (ESV)

Sodom and Gomorrah serve as examples of punishment by eternal fire. The inhabitants of these two cities were destroyed as we discussed earlier in the section on Genesis 19. These people were not tormented forever, they were killed, destroyed. The example of punishment by eternal fire is not a fire that burns for eternity, but rather a fire whose consuming nature results in destruction that is final.[17] Sodom and Gomorrah's destruction from burning is indeed permanent, but the burning was completed in a day or two. Remember, Abraham saw the smoke from their destruction the following morning from a distance.

On the other hand, if you hold to the view that eternal fire means a fire that burns for eternity, then point to the fire that destroyed Sodom and Gomorrah! Jude says it is an example of eternal fire. If this is the case, then it must still be burning somewhere, and we should be able to still see this fire and its smoke rising.

> **2 Peter 2:4-6** For if God did not spare angels when they sinned, but cast them into hell (tartaroo) and committed them to chains of gloomy darkness to be kept until the judgment; if he did not spare the ancient world, but preserved Noah, a herald of righteousness, with seven others, when he brought a flood upon the world of the ungodly; if by turning the cities of Sodom and Gomorrah to ashes he condemned them to extinction, making them an example of what is going to happen to the ungodly (ESV)

Peter gives us two examples of the destruction of the ungodly, not their eternal torment. In this first example, he points out that Sodom and Gomorrah were condemned to extinction (destroyed). He states this is an example of what is going to happen to the ungodly. If the ungodly were going to be tormented forever in hell, he would have stated this much differently.

> **2 Peter 3:5-7** For they deliberately overlook this fact, that the heavens existed long ago, and the earth was formed out of water and through water by the word of God, and that by means of these the world that then existed was deluged with water and perished. But by the same word the heavens and earth that now exist are stored up for fire, being kept until the day of judgment and <u>destruction</u> of the ungodly. (ESV)

In this second example, Peter points out that those in the world at the time of the flood were destroyed (they perished). Then he goes on to point out that in the same manner the present world

---

[17] Edward Fudge, "The Fire That Consumes," [Video] EdwardFudge.com, Accessed 5/3/22, https://edwardfudge.com/category/videos/the-fire-thatconsumes/

is being kept until the day of judgment, when the ungodly will be destroyed (not tormented) by fire.

There are many other verses depicting the destruction of the wicked by fire, that are covered elsewhere in this book.

Note: The traditional paradigm blurs the mention of sinful angels in Tartaroo (2 Peter 3:5-7), with the judgment of the flood and the judgment of Sodom and Gomorrah. For a clear understanding of this verse on Tartaroo, see the previous chapter in this book on Tartaroo. By conflating the nature of the temporary imprisonment of the fallen angels in Tartaroo with the two destructive judgments of men, as well as conflating the word Tartaroo with Gehenna (as is often done in mainstream Christian teaching), the traditional view generates an untold amount of confusion just from these few verses.

31

Resurrection... the Main Thing

How do you explain the important role that the Bible gives to the resurrection? Why does the Bible say it was important that Jesus was resurrected from the dead?

Was Jesus resurrected to save believers from hell? Or death?

Traditionalists often claim Jesus went to hell when he died (i.e., *hell as they define it*), but the Bible does not say that anywhere! The traditional view asserts that Acts 2:22-36, states that Jesus went to hell after he died on the cross.

In Acts 2:22-36, Peter is quoting from Psalm 16. Peter indicates that King David was prophesying about Jesus in Psalm 16. David prophesies that God would not leave Jesus' body to decay, nor leave him in *Sheol*. The Hebrew word *Sheol* is equivalent to the Greek word Hades. Psalm 16 (written in Hebrew) uses the word Sheol, while Acts 2 (written in Greek) uses the word Hades.

Sheol in the Old Testament was generally interpreted as the place of the dead or the grave. Peter does not use the word "Gehenna" in Acts 2 but uses the Greek word Hades (just as Psalm 16 uses the word Sheol). This is important to understand. Gehenna and Hades are not equivalent in any way. Yet, many bibles translate both words into the English word "hell". Those who hold to the traditional view will sometimes use the word hell and hades interchangeably (and inconsistently) in order to support their confusing views.

Look closely at David's statement. Peter's main point in quoting from David in this passage from Psalm 16, is to point out that David *died*, and that his *tomb still remains*. In other words, David is still dead, and still in his tomb. Thus, David's body did indeed decay, and he is still in Hades. Peter's emphasis is that David's prophesy is not referring to David himself, but rather to the resurrection of Jesus from the dead.

When Jesus died, God indeed did not abandon Jesus' psuche to Hades, nor did his body decay (see corruption). God raised Jesus from the dead on the third day.

Peter's emphasis on the resurrection of Jesus was to show Jesus' victory over death. Hell (Gehenna) has nothing to do with this section of scripture.

Peter's emphasis in Acts 2:22-36 was on the Resurrection of Jesus,

in order to show Jesus' victory over Death.

Acts 2:24-31 God raised him up, having brought to an end the pains of death, because it was not possible for him to be held by it. For David says with reference to him,

'I saw the Lord before me continually, for he is at my right hand so that I will not be shaken. For this reason my heart was glad and my tongue rejoiced greatly, furthermore also my flesh will live in hope, because you will not abandon my soul (psuche) in Hades, nor will you permit your Holy One to experience decay. You have made known to me the paths of life (zoe); you will fill me with gladness with your presence.'

"Men and brothers, it is possible to speak with confidence to you about the patriarch David, that he both died and was buried, and his tomb is with us until this day. Therefore, because he was a prophet and knew that God had sworn to him with an oath to seat one of his descendants on his throne, by having foreseen this, he spoke about the resurrection of the Christ, that neither was he abandoned in Hades nor did his flesh experience decay. (LEB)

RESURRECTION IS VICTORY OVER DEATH

Resurrection is the primary objective that Jesus accomplished. Jesus did not come to save people from eternal torment in hell, but rather to save people from eternal death (destruction).

Jesus resurrection is the pinnacle of the Bible. This is because Jesus has overcome and defeated death. The resurrection was the exclamation point of Jesus' mission, which he completed via his death on the cross, and subsequent resurrection from the dead.

See Paul's emphasis below, where Paul delineates the real issue (death), and the real solution (Jesus' resurrection from the dead).

If you hold to the traditional view of eternal torment in hell, then try to explain how your view of hell fits into this narrative.

I Corinthians 15:12-26 Now if Christ is proclaimed as raised from the dead, how can some of you say that there is no resurrection of the dead? But if there is no resurrection of the dead, then not even Christ has been raised. And if Christ has not been raised, then our preaching is in vain and your faith is in vain. We are even found to be misrepresenting God, because we testified about God that he raised Christ, whom he did not raise if it is true that the dead are not raised. For if the dead are not raised, not even Christ has been raised. And if Christ has not been raised, your faith is futile and you are still in your sins. Then those also who have fallen asleep in Christ have perished. If in Christ we have hope in this life only, we are of all people most to be pitied. But in fact Christ has been raised from the dead, the first fruits of those who have fallen asleep. For as by a man came death, by a man has come also the resurrection of the dead. For as in Adam all die, so also in Christ shall all be made alive. But each in his own order: Christ the first fruits, then at his coming those who belong to Christ. Then comes the end, when he delivers the kingdom to God the Father after destroying every rule and every authority and power. For he must reign until he has put all his enemies under his feet. The last enemy to be destroyed is death. (ESV)

There will indeed be a resurrection on the day of judgment. All mankind will be resurrected from the dead. Those whose names are written in the "Book of Life (zoe)" will be raised to eternal life (zoe). Those whose names are not in the book of zoe, will be destroyed in the lake of fire, which John aptly defines as the "second death" in the Book of Revelation. (Revelation 20:14, 21:8)

JESUS IS THE FIRSTBORN FROM THE DEAD

Jesus is the firstborn from the dead. Believers (as adopted children into the family of God), will follow by being resurrected on the day of resurrection.

Colossians 1:18 And he is the head of the body, the church. He is the beginning, the firstborn from the dead, that in everything he might be preeminent. (ESV)

Revelation 1:4-5 Grace to you and peace from him who is and who was and who is to come, and from the seven spirits who are before his throne, and from Jesus Christ the faithful witness, the firstborn of the dead, and the ruler of kings on earth (ESV)

32

Hell No – The Book of Acts

Let me ask you a question. If hell was the main problem that Jesus came to save us from, don't you think that this message would have been preached in the early church? Wouldn't we see a dire warning to those who had never heard the gospel, that they must escape the fires of hell?

Luke authored both the gospel of Luke as well as the book of Acts. He records one instance of Jesus teaching about Gehenna in the gospel of Luke. If Luke had held to the traditional view, don't you think he would have made painstaking efforts to record Paul or someone else teaching about eternal torment in Hell for unbelievers in the book of Acts?

Do you realize that the word hell (Gehenna) is never mentioned in the book of Acts? Neither Peter, nor Paul, nor Stephen, nor anyone else ever mentions hell, or eternal torment anywhere in the book of Acts. On the other hand, they frequently mention Jesus being raised from the dead, and the real hope of resurrection for those who believe.

However, the Greek word *Hades* is mentioned in Acts 2:27, with reference to a quote from the Old Testament, where King David prophecies that "God will not abandon Jesus' *psuche* in *Hades*". As you should know by now, *Hades* is the place of the dead. In the Old Testament, the Hebrew word "Sheol" (equivalent to the Greek word *Hades*) is often simply portrayed as the grave. I covered *Hades* in a previous chapter, but suffice to say, that *Hades* is the place of the dead. Some simply consider it to be no more than the grave where all mankind is in a state of sleep until the resurrection day. Others believe it is a place of both conscious torment and paradise. The condition of torment or paradise would depend on which side of the chasm a person would be located within *Hades*, as depicted in Jesus' story of the rich man and Lazarus in Luke 16. I am not taking sides on this *Hades* argument. This is an insignificant issue compared to the matter of death, *zoe* and the huge consequences due to the false understanding about *Gehenna*. Regardless of where you end up standing on hades, it is explicitly clear that hades is an *interim* state or venue for those that have died. Also, Hades will be destroyed on the day of judgment.

It is very important to take note of this fact: the Greek word *Hades* that is used in Acts 2, is NOT the Greek word *Gehenna*! There is a huge difference! I hear preachers occasionally saying that Jesus went to hell when he died, and then he was later resurrected. This is so wrong! Jesus did not go to hell. When Jesus died, he just simply died, his *psuche* was killed.

Trying to make Jesus' death into something else, diminishes from the powerful message that is portrayed in the book of Acts. Jesus was resurrected from *death*. It is only because of his resurrection from death, that any of us has hope of being raised from the dead.

Death is *THE* ultimate problem – not the notion of eternal torment in hell. Death is the enemy and will be the last enemy that Jesus destroys. Jesus' own death was a substitution for our death.

Resurrection from our death via Jesus' gift of Eternal Zoe, is the final solution to this problem of death.

1 Corinthians 15:26 The last enemy to be abolished is death. (LEB)

Death is the ultimate problem!

Death is the last enemy that Jesus will destroy.

Jesus own death was a substitution for our death.

Resurrection from our death via Jesus' gift of Eternal Zoe,

is the final solution to this problem of death.

Death is the problem that Paul emphasizes repeatedly in the book of Acts. When God raised Jesus from Hades, it was his *psuche* that was resurrected.

Acts 2:22-33 "Israelite men, listen to these words! Jesus the Nazarene, a man attested to you by God with deeds of power and wonders and signs that God did through him in your midst, just as you yourselves know— 23 this man, delivered up by the determined plan and foreknowledge of God, you executed by nailing to a cross through the hand of lawless men. 24 God raised him up, having brought to an end the pains of death, because it was not possible for him to be held by it. 25 For David says with reference to him, 'I saw the Lord before me continually, for he is at my right hand so that I will not be shaken. 26 For this reason my heart was glad and my tongue rejoiced greatly, furthermore also my flesh will live in hope. 27 because you will not abandon my soul (psuche) in Hades, nor will you permit your Holy One to experience decay. 28 You have made known to me the paths of life; you will fill me with gladness with your presence.' 29 "Men and brothers, it is possible to speak with confidence to you about the patriarch David, that he both died and was buried, and his tomb is with us until this day. 30 Therefore, because he was a prophet and knew that God had sworn to him with an oath to seat one of his descendants on his throne, 31 by having foreseen this, he spoke about the resurrection of the Christ, that neither was he abandoned in Hades nor did his flesh experience decay. 32 This Jesus God raised up, of which we all are witnesses. 33 Therefore, having been exalted to the right hand of God and having received the promise of the Holy Spirit from the Father, he has poured out this that you see and hear. (LEB)

In Acts chapter 2, we see the very first sermon (by Peter) that occurs after Jesus' resurrection, on the day of Pentecost. Peter points out that Jesus was killed, but that God would not abandon Jesus' *psuche* to Hades.

Peter is quoting from Psalm 16, where King David states his own confidence that God will not abandon his *psuche* to Hades. David was speaking of the grave, or unseen place of the dead. David was confident that God would not leave him there. His confidence was based upon the fact that God had shown him the path to life (zoe).

Acts 3:14-15 But you denied the Holy and Righteous One, and asked for a murderer to be granted to you, and you killed the Author of life (zoe), whom God raised from the dead. To this we are witnesses. (ESV)

In another sermon by Peter, he is preaching to an audience containing many people who had been responsible for condemning Jesus to death. He indeed accuses them of killing the "author of zoe". This is an interesting statement. According to Helps Word Studies, the Greek word "archegon" translated here as "author", does not strictly mean "author," but rather "a person who is originator or founder of a movement and continues as the leader". Do you see the connection? Jesus is the originator of zoe, in two ways. First, it is his resurrection from the dead, that is the origin of our hope of resurrection from the dead. Secondly, it is his zoe living within us via the life-giving Holy Spirit that will one day resurrect us from the dead.

Peter also states that God raised Jesus from the dead, and that he was a personal witness of this resurrection.

This is the approach we should all consider. It is indeed our sin... yours and mine, that condemned Jesus to death. It was God's plan to atone for our death sentence, by killing Jesus, and then resurrecting him. It is only because Jesus was resurrected, declaring victory over death, that you and I have hope of eternal life. His resurrection and zoe provide you and I with hope beyond the grave. This is the message throughout the Book of Acts.

Acts 3:22-24 Moses said, 'The Lord God will raise up for you a prophet like me from your brothers. You shall listen to him in whatever he tells you. And it shall be that every soul who does not listen to that prophet shall be destroyed from the people.' And all the prophets who have spoken, from Samuel and those who came after him, also proclaimed these days. (ESV)

The above verse contains a quote from Moses. Moses is prophesying that anyone who does not listen to the future prophet (referring to Jesus) shall be destroyed. Does that sound like eternal torment? Or does that sound like *destruction*?

In the following verses we see:

> ➢ The resurrection of Jesus
> ➢ The salvation that is directly tied to resurrection
> ➢ The connection of resurrection to zoe

Neither hell, nor eternal torment are ever mentioned.

Acts 4:1-2 And as they were speaking to the people, the priests and the captain of the temple and the Sadducees came upon them, 2 greatly annoyed because they were teaching the people and proclaiming in Jesus the resurrection from the dead. (ESV)

Acts 4:8-12 Then Peter, filled with the Holy Spirit, said to them, "Rulers of the people and elders, if we are being examined today concerning a good deed done to a crippled man, by what means this man has been healed, let it be known to all of you and to all the people of Israel that by the name of Jesus Christ of Nazareth, whom you crucified, whom God raised from the dead—by him this man is standing before you well. This Jesus is the stone that was rejected by you, the builders, which has become the cornerstone. And there is salvation in no one else, for there is no other name under heaven given among men by which we must be saved." (ESV)

Acts 11:15-18 As I began to speak, the Holy Spirit fell on them just as on us at the beginning. And I remembered the word of the Lord, how he said, 'John baptized with water, but you will be baptized with the Holy Spirit.' If then God gave the same gift to them as he gave to us when we believed in the Lord Jesus Christ, who was I that I could stand in God's way?" When they heard these things they fell silent. And they glorified God, saying, "Then to the Gentiles also God has granted repentance that leads to life (zoe)." (ESV)

As you know by now, zoe means "the state of being alive", as opposed to being dead. In Acts 11, we see that God granted repentance that leads to zoe. Zoe is used here to refer to future eternal zoe. Peter is specifically referring to the assurance of resurrection from the dead to live again, this time to live forever (eternal zoe).

Note: In the verses below, the comments inside parenthesis are mine.

Acts 13:36-41 For David, after he had served the purpose of God in his own generation, fell asleep and was laid with his fathers and saw corruption (*corruption means decay of David's body*), but he whom God raised up (*specifically referring to the resurrection of Jesus from the dead*) did not see corruption. Let it be known to you therefore, brothers, that through this man forgiveness of sins is proclaimed to you, and by him everyone who believes is freed from everything from which you could not be freed by the law of Moses.

Beware, therefore, lest what is said in the Prophets should come about: "'Look, you scoffers, be astounded and perish (*utterly destroyed*); for I am doing a work in your days, a work that you will not believe, even if one tells it to you.'" (ESV)

Acts 13:46-48 And Paul and Barnabas spoke out boldly, saying, "It was necessary that the word of God be spoken first to you. Since you thrust it aside and judge yourselves unworthy of eternal life (eternal *zoe, i.e., being alive forever*), behold, we are turning to the Gentiles. For so the Lord has commanded us, saying,

"'I have made you a light for the Gentiles, that you may bring salvation to the ends of the earth.'" And when the Gentiles heard this, they began rejoicing and glorifying the word of the Lord, and as many as were appointed to eternal life (eternal zoe) believed. (ESV)

Paul is telling the audience that Jesus was resurrected, that indeed God raised him and that his body did not decay. He warns the scoffers that they will perish (be killed/destroyed). He then speaks of *eternal zoe*.

Notice that Paul did not speak of going to hell or experiencing eternal torment, but rather that the scoffers would perish (be killed/destroyed*).*

The following verses speak of the hope of the resurrection which is only available because of Jesus' resurrection and victory over death. There is no mention of hell or eternal torment. This is because death is the issue. Eternal torment was not mentioned, because it was not even on the radar at that time. This false belief of eternal torment did not begin to infiltrate into Christian doctrine until 150 to 200 years later.

> **Acts 17:30-32** The times of ignorance God overlooked, but now he commands all people everywhere to repent, because he has fixed a day on which he will judge the world in righteousness by a man whom he has appointed; and of this he has given assurance to all by raising him from the dead." Now when they heard of the resurrection of the dead, some mocked. But others said, "We will hear you again about this." (ESV)

> **Acts 23:6** Now when Paul perceived that one part were Sadducees and the other Pharisees, he cried out in the council, "Brothers, I am a Pharisee, a son of Pharisees. It is with respect to the hope and the resurrection of the dead that I am on trial." (ESV)

> **Acts 24:20-21** Or else let these men themselves say what wrongdoing they found when I stood before the council, other than this one thing that I cried out while standing among them: 'It is with respect to the resurrection of the dead that I am on trial before you this day.'" (ESV)

> **Acts 25:18-19** When the accusers stood up, they brought no charge in his case of such evils as I supposed. Rather they had certain points of dispute with him about their own religion and about a certain Jesus, **who was dead, but whom Paul asserted to be alive**. (ESV)

Remember, death is the problem that Paul emphasizes in the book of Acts. Then he always presents Jesus' substitutionary death and resurrection as the solution to the problem. In the verses below, Paul is preaching to Festus and King Agrippa.

> **Acts 26:22-29** Therefore I have experienced help from God until this day, and I stand here testifying to both small and great, saying nothing except what both the prophets and Moses have said were going to happen, **that the Christ was to suffer and that as the first of the resurrection from the dead, he was going to proclaim light both to the people and to the Gentiles**."

And as he was saying these things in his defense, Festus said with a loud voice, "You are out of your mind, Paul! Your great learning is driving you insane!" But Paul said, "I am not out of my mind, most excellent Festus, but am speaking words of truth and rationality. For the king knows about these things, to whom also I am speaking freely, for I am not convinced that these things in any way have escaped his notice, because this was not done in a corner. Do you believe the prophets, King Agrippa? I know that you believe."

But Agrippa said to Paul, "In a short time are you persuading me to become a Christian?" And Paul replied, "I pray to God, whether in a short time or in a long time, not only you but also all those who are listening to me today may become such people as I also am, except for these bonds!" (LEB)

It was Paul's preaching of the resurrection of the dead, that prompted Festus to accuse Paul of being insane. The idea of the resurrection of the dead seemed impossible to Festus, and Paul risked his life by preaching such an implausible idea. Yet, Paul is not afraid of dying. He is determined to preach the good news of Jesus' salvation for all who will listen and hopefully believe.

Note: Notice that Paul says Jesus, "as the first of the resurrection from the dead, he was going to proclaim light to both the people and to the Gentiles. Darkness in some scriptures can refer to the death sentence that all mankind has lived under since the fall of Adam. Paul's statement of "Jesus proclaiming light" may very well be referring to the darkness of death.

33

The Romans Road from Death to Zoe

In Christian circles we often refer to the "Romans Road to Salvation," a series of a half dozen verses that are a useful tool for evangelism due to Paul's letter to the church at Rome clearly laying out the gospel. A Christian can quickly explain the message of salvation by sequencing through these verses in Romans that summarize the gospel. I am not taking issue with this at all. I wholeheartedly agree that these verses are great for this purpose.

What I am suggesting, is that due to the traditional paradigm clouding our ability to see, we have been blinded as to what Romans is truly saying.

If you will carefully read through Romans taking notice of what Paul says is the real issue facing mankind, you will see that "life and death" is a consistent emphasis throughout the book. You never see Paul mention eternal torment in hell or anything that even closely resembles that. Romans is often thought of as Paul's most concise letter, as fully containing the message of the gospel. Wouldn't we expect him to mention the idea of eternal torment in hell somewhere in Romans if this idea were true?

As we progress through Romans, take note of what Paul consistently says about "zoe" and "death".

Note: If you have just jumped into this book, you might miss the significance of these life and death statements. If you do not understand how zoe is used consistently by Paul in his letters, then I would strongly recommend going back and reading Part 1 of this book, especially chapter 4 on the Nuances of Zoe. Zoe at its core simply means "the state of being alive". It is the opposite of being dead, and in most cases in Romans the word zoe when being used solo is implicitly referring to eternal zoe (resurrection from the dead to being alive forever).

One other thing to keep track of as you read through Romans. Paul repeatedly contrasts the righteousness that is available through observing the law, versus the righteousness that comes from God as a gift to believers. The first righteousness available by keeping the law, is essentially impossible to attain. This is contrasted against the righteousness available from God as a gift, not requiring observing the law, but requires faith. The law would have given zoe (eternal life) to those who observed it, but due to man's sin, this path to eternal life is impossible to achieve. But the gift of righteousness from God, paid for by the blood of Jesus and his death, justifies the believer with the result being the believer's assurance of being raised from the dead to live forever (eternal life).

Even if you have read Romans a hundred times, due to the powerful influence of the traditional paradigm you would have likely missed this narrative about zoe (life) that permeates Romans. You would have likely taken the word "life" or "live" and attributed the idea of a lifestyle or "way of living out the gospel in your life" as the idea being conveyed. This preconceived incorrect notion prevents you from seeing the clear and simple message that is portrayed throughout Romans. The message is about life (eternal life - being raised from the dead to live forever), versus death (the second, permanent death).

WHAT KIND OF DEATH?

The following pages will display several verses from Romans. When they speak of death, ask yourself, "what is this referring to"? If these verses are not referring to physical death, then how do you explain what they mean?

Don't you think Paul was building a case in the book of Romans that could stand on its own? Did he expect readers in the first century to cross reference his comments in Romans with other passages throughout the Bible in order to be able to understand what he meant? No of course not, he was being as complete and clear as he could.

> **Romans 2:6-12** who will reward each one according to his works: 7 to those who, by perseverance in good work, seek glory and honor **and immortality, eternal life,** 8 but to those who act from selfish ambition and who disobey the truth, but who obey unrighteousness, wrath and anger. 9 There will be affliction and distress for every human being who does evil, of the Jew first and of the Greek, 10 but glory and honor and peace to everyone who does good, to the Jew first and to the Greek. 11 For there is no partiality with God. 12 For as many as have sinned without law will also **perish** without law, (LEB)

Consider verse 7 in the verses above. If mankind already possesses immortality, then why should they seek it? God gives eternal zoe (resurrection from the dead to being physically alive forever) to these people who by perseverance in good work, seek honor and immortality. Eternal zoe is by definition, "immortality".

On the other hand, those who do not receive eternal zoe, will perish as seen in verse 12.

Perish means they will die at the second death. They will not be resurrected to eternal zoe, rather they will be resurrected to judgment and destruction. This destruction (the second death) lasts forever.

> **Romans 4:17** (just as it is written, "I have made you the father of many nations") before God, in whom he believed, **the one who makes the dead alive** and who calls the things that are not as though they are (LEB)

In 4:17, Paul points out that God is the one "who makes the dead alive". Why does he include this point? It is because Paul is building his case for God resurrecting the dead. The Greek word for "dead" actually means "dead ones", it is plural and is pointing to those believers that God is going to resurrect from the dead.

Romans 4:22-25 Therefore it was credited to him for righteousness. 23 But it was not written for the sake of him alone that it was credited to him, 24 but also for the sake of us to whom it is going to be credited, to those who believe in the one who raised Jesus our Lord from the dead, 25 who was handed over on account of our trespasses and was raised up in the interest of our justification. (LEB)

Paul goes on to emphasize that we believe in the one who raised Jesus from the dead (v24), who was killed on account of our trespasses, and was raised from the dead in the interest of our justification (v25).

Paul is beginning to lay the foundation in Romans 4 for the need for righteousness through faith, and justification which leads to resurrection. Let's examine key points that he makes in 4:22-25:

1. Righteousness (right standing before God) is credited to the believer because of the believer's faith in the one who was raised from the dead (Jesus).
2. Jesus was handed over to be killed on account of our sins.
3. Jesus was raised from the dead (resurrected) in the interest of justifying the believer. In other words, it was Jesus' death on account of our sins, that justified our account, allowing our sins to be covered by his blood, enabling us to stand righteous before God. Our sins have been atoned for.
4. This justification means Jesus' righteousness has been attributed to the believer, (in lieu of the believer's own worthless right-standing before God). Believers are justified by their faith, not by their own works or merit.

Remember that Paul mentioned in v17 that God makes the dead ones alive. This was an introductory statement about God resurrecting believers from the dead. Now in verses 22-25 he shows the necessity of Jesus dying for our sins and being resurrected as prerequisite for our own resurrection.

Notice Paul's consistency with this point, in his second letter to Corinth:

2 Corinthians 3:4-6 Now we possess such confidence through Christ toward God. 5 Not that we are adequate in ourselves to consider anything as from ourselves, but our adequacy is from God, 6 who also makes us adequate as servants of a new covenant, not of the letter, but of the Spirit, for the letter kills, but the Spirit gives **life (zoe)**.

Notice that it is the Spirit (Holy Spirit, aka Spirit of Christ) that gives zoe. It is the Spirit that gives us (believers) the assurance of resurrection from the dead (eternal zoe) while we are still currently alive in this age and will also ultimately raise us from the dead with new imperishable bodes to live forever. Paul will bring this up again shortly and explain in more detail.

Romans 5 and 6 are full of references to zoe (being alive) and death. I am only going to cover a few verses out of these two chapters, but I would highly encourage you to read these two chapters in a single sitting on your own. As you read through Romans 5 & 6, notice the contrast that Paul continually makes between life (zoe) and death.

Romans 5:5-6 and hope does not disappoint, because the love of God has been poured out in our hearts through the Holy Spirit who was given to us. 6 For while we were still helpless, yet at the proper time Christ died for the ungodly. (LEB)

Even though we were helpless (or powerless) to do anything about our death sentence, we are not disappointed, because the Holy Spirit is being given to us (imparting zoe unto us). At the proper time Jesus died for the ungodly. This is a direct reference to you and me, despite what we might think of ourselves, we are basically ungodly. This is the message of good news, the message of the gospel.

Romans 5:7-11 For only rarely will someone die on behalf of a righteous person (for on behalf of a good person possibly someone might even dare to die), 8 but God demonstrates his own love for us, in that while[e] we were still sinners, Christ died for us. 9 Therefore, by much more, because we have been declared righteous now by his blood, we will be saved through him from the wrath. 10 For if, while we were enemies, *we were reconciled to God through the death* of his Son, by much more, having been reconciled, *we will be saved by his life (zoe)*. 11 And not only this, but also we are boasting in God through our Lord Jesus Christ, through whom we have now received the reconciliation. (LEB)

Let's analyze 5:7-11:

1. Jesus died for us, even though we were unrighteous.
2. We have been declared righteous by his blood (which he shed when he died on the cross).
3. This saves us from wrath. That is, the wrath that began the death sentence of all mankind since Adam was cast out of the garden of Eden and lost access to the tree of zoe (the tree of being alive). Adam's sin began the death sentence for all mankind. Jesus came to rescue (redeem) us from this death sentence.
4. Even though we were enemies of God, we were reconciled to God through the death of his Son. This reconciliation is speaking of being justified and made righteous before God.
5. How much more, having been reconciled, will we be saved by his life (zoe). This is speaking of Jesus' resurrection from the dead, to life (zoe).

Think of this as two aspects to our salvation

1. Reconciliation: First our sentence of death is taken away due to Jesus stepping in and taking our death sentence for us. His death in our stead puts us in right standing (his death justifies us, making us righteous) before God.
2. Then in addition to removing our death sentence, we will be saved by Jesus' zoe. There are a few aspects to this "zoe" as well.
   a. It is Jesus living again by being raised from the dead to zoe, that paves the way to our own future resurrection from the dead.
   b. It is Jesus's zoe that lives within the psuche of the believer (through the indwelling Holy Spirit) that gives them assurance of resurrection from the dead to live forever.
   c. It is this same zoe of Christ (though the Holy Spirit) that will powerfully resurrect dead believers to live forever.

Remember that Jesus told Nicodemus in John 3, that he must be born again, because flesh and blood cannot inherit the Kingdom of God. It is the indwelling Holy Spirit (the Spirit of Jesus) that conveys the zoe of Christ into the psuche of the believer causing them to be born a second time, this time not of the flesh, but of the Spirit. It is at that point that we become children of God.

Just to be clear, the Holy Spirit and Spirit of Christ are used interchangeably in the New Testament. It is the zoe of Christ that lives within a person that assures them of being resurrected to eternal zoe.

Notice the following points from 5:12-21 (below):

1. by the trespass of the one man (Adam), death reigned through the one man (Adam)
2. much more will those who receive the abundance of grace and of the gift of righteousness reign in life (zoe) through the one, Jesus Christ
3. therefore, as through one trespass came condemnation to all people
4. so also, through one righteous deed came justification of life (zoe) to all people
5. so that just as sin reigned in death, so also grace would reign through righteousness to eternal life (eternal zoe) through Jesus Christ our Lord

Romans 5:12-21 Because of this, just as sin entered into the world through one man, and death through sin, so also death spread to all people because all sinned. 13 For until the law, sin was in the world, but sin is not charged to one's account when there is no law. 14 But death reigned from Adam until Moses even over those who did not sin in the likeness of the transgression of Adam, who is a type of the one who is to come. 15 But the gift is not like the trespass, for if by the trespass of the one, the many died, by much more did the grace of God and the gift by the grace of the one man, Jesus Christ, multiply to the many. 16 And the gift is not as through the one who sinned, for on the one hand, judgment from the one sin led to condemnation, but the gift, from many trespasses, led to justification. 17 *For if by the trespass of the one man, death reigned through the one man, much more will those who receive the abundance of grace and of the gift of righteousness reign in life through the one, Jesus Christ.* 18 Consequently therefore, as through one trespass came condemnation to all people, so also through one righteous deed came justification of life to all people. 19 For just as through the disobedience of the one man, the many were made sinners, so also through the obedience of the one, the many will be made righteous. 20 Now the law came in as a side issue, in order that the trespass could increase, but where sin increased, grace was present in greater abundance, 21 so that just as sin reigned in death, so also grace would reign through righteousness to eternal life through Jesus Christ our Lord. (LEB)

In the verses above Paul repeatedly emphasizes the deliverance from death, via the gift of righteousness which assures us of life (eternal zoe - resurrection from the dead to live forever).

If we try to explain the death and condemnation seen in Romans 5, by asserting that it is a symbolic reference to spiritual death and "eternal torment in hell" then we have essentially changed the meaning and focus of this chapter. We rob it of its powerful life-saving message and its clearly stated purpose. There is no connection in Romans 5 with eternal torment in hell, just as there is no connection with this false notion anywhere in the Book of Romans.

THE FINALITY OF SIN IS ULTIMATELY - DEATH

Romans 6:1-16 What therefore shall we say? Shall we continue in sin, in order that grace may increase? 2 May it never be! How can we who died to sin still live in it? 3 Or do you not know that as many as were baptized into Christ Jesus were baptized into his death? 4 Therefore we have been buried with him through baptism into death, in order that just as Christ was raised from the dead through the glory of the Father, so also we may live a new way of life. 5 For if we have become identified with him in the likeness of his death, certainly also we will be identified with him in the likeness of his resurrection, 6 knowing this, that our old man was crucified together with him, in order that the body of sin may be done away with, that we may no longer be enslaved to sin. 7 For the one who has died has been freed from sin.

8 Now if we died with Christ, we believe that we will also live with him, 9 knowing that Christ, because he has been raised from the dead, is going to die no more, death no longer being master over him. 10 For that death he died, he died to sin once and never again, but that life he lives, he lives to God. 11 So also you, consider yourselves to be dead to sin, but alive to God in Christ Jesus.

12 Therefore do not let sin reign in your mortal body, so that you obey its desires, 13 and do not present your members to sin as instruments of unrighteousness, but present yourselves to God as those who are alive from the dead, and your members to God as instruments of righteousness. 14 For sin will not be master over you, because you are not under law, but under grace.

15 What then? Shall we sin because we are not under law but under grace? May it never be! 16 Do you not know that to whomever you present yourselves as slaves for obedience, you are slaves to whomever you obey, whether sin, leading to death, or obedience, leading to righteousness? (LEB)

What is Paul saying in v16? He is saying that sin leads to death. That's it. Death is the end game for the unsaved. Paul is not leaving anything out or expecting you to read between the lines thinking that the end game is "eternal conscious torment" in "hell" as the traditional view believes.

Let me suggest an exercise. As you read thru Romans chapters 5 and 6, highlight the words die, died, and death. Count them. How many times do these words appear? What are they talking about? What is the solution to this death? What is the contrast that Paul consistently makes with death?

Take a look at verse 4 and 5. The LEB translates this as "a new way of life". I believe this verse is speaking about something far more important than a new way of life. The Greek reads more accurately as "we in newness of zoe (being alive) should be walking". This is speaking of one of two things:

1. This is either referring to walking in the assurance of eternal life (being raised from the dead to live forever). There would obviously be a change in our behavior if we keep this precious assurance in the forefront of our thoughts as we walk through the remainder of our days in this age.
2. Or it is implicitly referring to eternal life.

Part of the problem with the traditional view of immortality, is that it compels us to miss the point on the zoe vs death statements in Romans. This powerful paradigm prevents us from seeing outside the box so to speak. We even miss the importance of Paul's teaching on the resurrection from death to eternal zoe, which is the capstone of Romans. The traditional view takes many of the instances of the word life (zoe) in Romans (and elsewhere in the Bible) and change the focus of the word from the intended focus on being alive, to say instead it is a way of life, or a deeper level of spiritual life, or even a higher quality of life. Zoe is never used in the New Testament to refer to a quality of life. At its core zoe means being alive. About 10% of the time zoe is used in the New Testament it is generically referring to a person's lifetime (the time they are alive) or the course of their life. But about 90% of the time zoe is implicitly or explicitly referring to eternal life, or the assurance the believer has of being raised from the dead to eternal life.

If you hold to the traditional view, then let me ask you this... Why was it a big deal for Jesus to die, and then be resurrected? What did he actually accomplish by this? How did this save you from hell? What is the significance of a saved person's future resurrection from the dead? You likely believe that the saved person is already in heaven. If so, then what is the purpose of the resurrection? Is it merely for the person who is already living as a spirit in heaven to get a body? This study creates a lot of questions. Please do not give up, this is important to understand. If you come to a clear understanding of what is going on about life, death and the resurrection in Romans, it will radically change your understanding of the Bible and what it is saying from Genesis to Revelation.

***

Romans 6:21-23 Therefore what sort of fruit did you have then, about which you are now ashamed? **For the end of those things is death.** 22 But now, having been set free from sin and having been enslaved to God, you have your fruit leading to sanctification, **and its end is eternal life.** 23 For **the compensation due sin is death, but the gift of God is eternal life in Christ Jesus** our Lord. (LEB)

Romans 6:23 For the **wages of sin is death**, but the free gift of God is eternal life in Christ Jesus our Lord. (ESV)

The famous verses above are very straightforward and should be simple to understand. Yet, due to the incredibly strong paradigms of the "immortal soul" and "everlasting torment in hell", we are inclined to twist these plain, powerful verses into a lie. As a result, we have created a jumbled-up mess, a confusing doctrine that resembles a pretzel. The incredibly interesting (and devastating)

245

thing about the traditional paradigm is that it resembles the truth just enough, that it convinces the believer they see the big picture when in reality, they have missed the big picture. The traditional paradigm is like a slight-of-hand magician who does a trick by getting us to look where the action is not taking place, so we think we see something, when in reality we missed seeing what is really going on. The trickster is Satan, and he is an expert on twisting truth. His original twist of the truth, in his lie to Eve, "you shall not surely die", continues today with an even more insidious twist to it.

Romans 6:21-23 depicts a fork in the road that either leads to death or leads to eternal zoe. That's it, it is simple and uncomplicated. There is no depiction of everlasting torture, being eaten forever by worms, or being continually burned by fire forever and ever.

Romans 6:23 portrays a fork in the road that either leads to death or leads to eternal zoe. It is simple statement.

There is no depiction of everlasting torture, being eaten forever by worms, or being eternally burned by fire.

END MEANS "END"!

Paul uses the word "end" to emphasize the outcome of both of these events. The end of wicked fruit is death. Whereas the end for those deemed righteous by faith is eternal zoe.

- for the end of those things is death
- and its end is eternal life

The traditional view does not view death as the end. In fact, according to the traditional view, the next step (after death) for the unsaved would be their concept of eternal torment in hell, <u>which has no end</u>. The traditional view attempts to explain the second death as referring to "spiritual death". This notion of spiritual death entails eternal separation from God (spiritual death), in addition to physical torture that lasts forever.

On the other hand, zoe is always used to refer to being physically alive, when referring to humans in the New Testament. It is contrasted repeatedly in the New Testament against death, i.e., physical death. The idea of spiritual death was concocted by the traditional view in an attempt to make the narrative of life and death fit its paradigm. One aspect of this paradigm is the incredibly powerful and influential belief in the immortality of the human soul. This one belief drives many of the contorted explanations of the traditional paradigm. This belief heavily undermines the true message that was the central focus of both Jesus and the New Testament authors.

Romans 7:4-5 So then, my brothers, you also were brought to death with respect to the law through the body of Christ, so that you may belong to another, to the one who was

246

raised from the dead, in order that we may bear fruit for God. 5 For when we were in the flesh, sinful desires were working through the law in our members, to bear fruit for death. (LEB)

Sinful desires bear fruit for what? Death? Or eternal torment in hell?

Romans 7:24 Wretched man that I am! Who will rescue me from this body of **death**? (LEB)

Rescue from what? Death or Hell? If death is not the ultimate issue, why does Paul keep bringing it up? Why didn't he say "rescue me from hell"?

Romans 8:1-2 Consequently, there is now no condemnation for those who are in Christ Jesus. 2 For the law of the Spirit of life (zoe) in Christ Jesus has set you free from the law of sin and death. (LEB)

Notice there are two laws. The English word law comes from the Greek word "nomos". It is often referring to the law of Moses. But it can also refer to a "principle", or premise that predicts an expected outcome. Although Paul has been repeatedly talking about the law of Moses in Romans, it is this second definition that Paul is using here. He is talking about two principles that have a predictable outcome.

1. The law of sin and death (The premise that if you sin, you will die).
2. The law of the Spirit of zoe in Christ Jesus (The premise that if you believe, you will receive eternal zoe by the power of the zoe-giving Spirit of Jesus)

This contrast has been going on for several chapters in Romans. The verse above is a summary of these two laws or principles. One is the law of sin which ultimately ends in death. The other law is the one introduced by Jesus that frees men from this law of sin and death. It is the Holy Spirit that gives zoe, thereby saving a person's psuche from death. The Holy Spirit (aka Spirit of Jesus) will raise believers from the dead to eternal zoe. This law of the Spirit that gives zoe, overrides the law that sentences us to death. Jesus assures believers of being resurrected from the dead to live forever (aka eternal zoe).

The traditional view will often say that the Old Testament never mentions Hell. This is true, if you are referring to the definition of Hell that is held to by the traditional view. The problem is that this definition of hell as being a place of eternal torment is not accurate. It is a false premise. On the other hand, the Old Testament consistently contrasts life and death, life for the faithful and death for the wicked. In Ezekial chapter 18, scripture lays out the law or premise of life and death for the person who practices injustice vs practicing right living. I would encourage you to read all of Ezekial 18. I am only including a few verses here.

Ezekial 18: 26-28 When the righteous turns from his righteousness, and he does injustice, then he will die because of them; because of his injustice that he did he will die! 27 And when the wicked turns from his wickedness that he did and he does justice and righteousness, he will preserve his life. 28 And if he sees and he returns from all of his transgressions that he did, surely he will live; he will not die!

Ezekial 18 is speaking of the end game, the future. It is not referring to a person's current life expectancy. It is referring to the ultimate end of man, either eternal life or eternal death. Going back to the premises of life and death that Paul set forth in Romans 8:1-2, these premises are not set in concrete. If a person repents, they can avert the law of sin and death. Ezekial 18 also speaks to this. Romans 8 and Ezekial 18 are pointing to the same ultimate end result.

Ezekial 18:27 also uses the phrase "he will preserve his life". The word life in this instance is the Hebrew word nephesh, which is an exact equivalent to the Greek word psuche. This statement is an exact match to what Jesus says in John 12:25 and what is said by the author of Hebrews in Hebrews 10:39.

> **John 12:25** The one who loves his life (psuche) loses it, and the one who hates his life (psuche) in this world preserves it for eternal life (zoe). (LEB)

> **Heb. 10:39** But we are not among those who shrink back to destruction, but among those who have faith to the preservation of our souls (psuche)! (LEB)

In John 12:25 we see the word "life" appearing three times. The first two instances come from the word psuche, and the last instance is from the word zoe. The meaning of John 12:25 is this: the person who hates his psuche in this world will preserve it (or keep it) for eternal zoe. In other words that person's psuche will be resurrected from the dead to live forever.

> **Romans 8:3-8** For what was impossible for the law, in that it was weak through the flesh, God did. By sending his own Son in the likeness of sinful flesh and concerning sin, he condemned sin in the flesh, 4 in order that the requirement of the law would be fulfilled in us, who do not live according to the flesh but according to the Spirit. 5 For those who are living according to the flesh are intent on the things of the flesh, but those who are living according to the Spirit are intent on the things of the Spirit. 6 For the mindset of the flesh is death, but the mindset of the Spirit is life (zoe) and peace, 7 because the mindset of the flesh is enmity toward God, for it is not subjected to the law of God, for it is not able to do so, 8 and those who are in the flesh are not able to please God. (LEB)

Again, notice the contrast between death and zoe in v5-6. Those whose minds are set on the flesh are trending towards death, while those whose minds are set on following the spirit are trending towards zoe and peace.

> **Romans 8:9-11** But you are not in the flesh but in the Spirit, if indeed the Spirit of God lives in you. But if anyone does not have the Spirit of Christ, this person does not belong to him. 10 But if Christ is in you, the body is dead because of sin, but the Spirit is life because of righteousness. 11 And if the Spirit of the one who raised Jesus from the dead lives in you, the one who raised Christ Jesus from the dead will also make alive your mortal bodies through his Spirit who lives in you. (LEB)

Paul now explains the process of the resurrection. He explains that it was the Spirit of God that raised Jesus from the dead. This same Spirit will also make our mortal bodies alive when we are resurrected. He also explains that this Holy Spirit (which is responsible for the believer's resurrection), already lives within the believer, while the believer is still alive in this age. This is referring to the indwelling Holy Spirit that begins to indwell the believer at the point they are born again.

Romans 8:12-13 So then, brothers, we are obligated not to the flesh, to live according to the flesh. 13 For if you live according to the flesh, you are going to die, but if by the Spirit you put to death the deeds of the body, you will live. (LEB)

The phrase "you will live", comes from a single Greek word that is a verb form of zoe that means "you shall be living" or "you shall be alive". This is a statement of the assurance that believers have of being resurrected from the dead to eternal zoe, to live forever. This is the opposite of what happens if you live according to the flesh, which is "you are going to die". This is not speaking of the first death that everyone experiences but is speaking of the second death.

POP QUIZ

Based on v13 above:

> What happens if we live according to the flesh?

   o We will _____.

> What happens if by the Spirit we put to death the deeds of the body?

   o We will _____.

Notice the two-step approach that Paul presents again in Romans 8. In v3 Paul showed us that God sent Jesus to die, to take our death sentence for us. Then in v11 Paul shows that the one who raised Jesus from the dead (i.e., God the father raised Jesus' psuche from the dead) will make alive our mortal bodies through his Spirit who lives within us. Merely removing our sentence of death is not enough, that is just the first step. In addition, we must also be given new life by being resurrected from the first death, to eternal zoe.

These two steps can be summarized as:

> **Step 1** – Jesus pays our death penalty for us, by dying in our stead, thereby allowing us to stand righteous before God.
> **Step 2** – God raises us from the dead to eternal zoe, by his Holy Spirit.

Notice there aren't any steps that mention eternal torment for the unsaved. The unsaved only face the certainty of the permanent second death. There may be some suffering that the unsaved experience as they die, but it is not everlasting.

Romans 11:13-15 Now I am speaking to you Gentiles. Therefore, inasmuch as I am apostle to the Gentiles, I promote my ministry, 14 if somehow I may provoke my people to jealousy and save some of them. 15 For if their rejection means the reconciliation of the world, what will their acceptance mean except life from the dead? (LEB)

Verse 15 is clearly stated. What is the nature of the reconciliation that Paul is talking about here? Is he talking about saving the Jews from hell? No, of course not. He is speaking of the same reconciliation he has been talking about all through Romans up to this point. Their reconciliation means being raised to zoe from the dead. The whole narrative in Romans focuses on resurrection from the dead, to zoe.

WHAT'S THE BIG DEAL?

I've had people ask me, "why is this a big deal?". It's like this is just a matter of semantics to them. Their question implies this assumption, that Jesus saves us from death or from hell, it's not such a big deal… it's just important that he saved us. It's not that important what he saved us from.

Really? It's just semantics?

Is it ok that we miss the central point of Jesus' reason for becoming a man and coming to earth? Is it ok that we misrepresent his purpose for dying on the cross? Is it acceptable that we are clueless about the significance of Jesus' resurrection? Furthermore, is it ok if we are clueless about the significance of our own resurrection? Is it ok that we miss the narrative that began in Genesis and runs all the way to the last chapter of Revelation, ending in God's victory over Satan and the death sentence that man has been under since Adam and Eve lost access to the tree of Zoe? Is there anything wrong about being blissfully unaware of the contrasts that Jesus, Peter, Paul and John focused on throughout the New Testament?

Is it ok that we totally miss Jesus' core teaching? Look, I realize this is an extensive study, that unwraps and clarifies a lot of fundamental teaching of the gospel. And I understand the reticence of those who do not want to undertake such a study. Some people even ask, "why does this have to be so complicated"? My response is that the truths that we have missed are not complicated at all. In fact, the core teaching of Jesus and the Bible is quite simple, and significantly less complicated than what we have accepted as sound doctrine for millennia. The complication does not come from these simple truths, but rather from untangling all the complex, interwoven half-truths that depend on each other for holding the tangled traditional paradigm together. If you can persevere through this study, in the end your understanding will be very clear and simple. You will no longer have to settle for all the complicated mess and incorrect assumptions that make up the traditional paradigm.

Going forward, you will see these simple truths popping up almost everywhere you read in the Bible, both in Old and New Testament. These are scriptures you have likely read before, but missed what they were really saying, due to the blinding effect of the traditional paradigm.

34

Take It at Face Value

Most scripture can be taken at face value. We must be careful not to attempt to explain what something means by shaping it to mean something else, just to fit a particular paradigm or tradition.

A FEW EXAMPLES THAT STATE THE OBVIOUS

2 Timothy 1:9-10 who saved us and called us with a holy calling, not according to our works but according to his own purpose and grace that was given to us in Christ Jesus before time began, but has now been disclosed by the appearing of our Savior Jesus Christ, who has abolished death and brought to light **life (zoe)** and **immortality** through the gospel (LEB)

- ➤ Jesus abolished the sentence of death for the believer
- ➤ Jesus brought zoe (the state of being alive) and immortality (the state of never dying) to light through the good news (gospel) of his teaching. Zoe and immortality are tied together. It is the zoe of Christ that imparts immortality to the believer. The Holy Spirit conveys zoe into a person when they become a believer.
- ➤ These statements by Paul to Timothy are proleptic. He is referring to both zoe and death as future events as if they are already in place. The sentence of death is what all mortals live under. Whereas zoe (the assurance of being raised from the dead to live forever) is a promise that breaks the certainty of eternal death.

John 3:16 For God so loved the world, that he gave his only Son, that whoever believes in him should not **perish (apollumi)** but have **eternal life (zoe)** (ESV)

- ➤ This verse is very straight forward, when you understand what Jesus said throughout the gospel of John.
- ➤ Perish means perish (being dead).
- ➤ Eternal zoe means living forever, which is the exact opposite (contrast) of perishing. Perish is speaking of permanent physical death, not spiritual death as some in the traditional view suggest.

Romans 6:23 For the wages of sin is death, but the free gift of God is eternal life (zoe) in Christ Jesus our Lord. (ESV)

> ➤ This is as simple to understand as it can possibly be. Paul would have never imagined that believers would eventually twist this verse into the horrible mindset that is so prevalent today.

When Paul wrote the above verse did he in the most complete manner he was capable of, express what he understood the gospel to be? Did he accidentally or intentionally leave out extremely important details?

Paul never mentions hell (Gehenna) in any of his writing. If eternal torment in hell was part of what believers were being saved from, don't you think he would have thought to mention that in the book of Romans, or 1st or 2nd Corinthians? Or any of his other books? Do you know Paul is credited with writing practically half of the books in the NT? Isn't it odd that he would not even mention hell or everlasting torment in any of these?

On the other hand, Paul frequently emphasizes death as the problem faced by mankind. He teaches about zoe that brings immortality to the believer, which is only available through Jesus, as the only solution to this problem of death. He talks repeatedly and clearly about resurrection from the dead to eternal zoe!

How do you explain this?

If you hold to the traditional view, then how do you explain "the wages of sin are death"?

If the wages of sin are truly death, then how do you explain how this punishment plays itself out? According to the traditional belief, everyone (both saved and unsaved) is going to be resurrected to live forever, so how can "the wages of sin are death" be a punishment? It's like there must be a verse that Paul left out somewhere that says, "the real wages of sin are being raised from the dead in order to be cast into hell where the sinner will be tortured forever. Death is not really the wage of sin, it's merely a temporary stop on the way to hell."

The traditional view attempts to explain this as "spiritual death", which includes permanent separation from God, and also includes eternal torture in hell. But spiritual death as punishment is not supported by the Old or New Testaments. Death is speaking of physical death, and in this case it is a proleptic statement about the second death, which is permanent. The traditional paradigm is incapable of accepting this because of powerful incorrect assumptions, including the belief that man has an immortal soul.

OTHER WRITERS

John (the apostle) wrote the Gospel of John, which is the foundation of the study of this book, as well as writing 1st, 2nd, 3rd John and the Book of Revelation. John never mentions hell (Gehenna) in any of these books. Yet he repeatedly speaks of death being the main issue.

Luke wrote the book of Acts (see the previous chapter), which details the history of the newly born church, which started shortly after Jesus' resurrection, and the decades to follow. Throughout all the book of Acts, which includes Peter's sermons, Stephen's sermon, and Paul's pleas and teachings throughout his missionary journeys, there is no mention of hell or eternal torment. If hell were the main issue that mankind was to be saved from, shouldn't Paul or Peter have mentioned that somewhere?

> **Matthew 10:28** And do not fear those who kill the body but cannot kill the soul (psuche), Rather fear him who can destroy (apollumi) both soul (psuche) and body in hell (Gehenna). (ESV)

The traditional view takes the word *destroy* (apollumi) in the above verse and twists it to mean "ruin" and uses that context to say that those who are not saved will be "ruined" by their eternal, excruciating torment in hell for eternity. If you try to interpret this verse in that way, then what do you do with the next verse (below) from Luke 13:1-5?

Note: The English words perish and destroy are each translated from the Greek word apollumi.

> **Luke 13:1-5** Now at the same time some had come to tell him about the Galileans whose blood Pilate had mixed with their sacrifices. And he answered and said to them, "Do you think that these Galileans were sinners worse than all the Galileans, because they suffered these things? No, I tell you, but unless you repent you will all **perish (apollumi)** as well! Or those eighteen on whom the tower in Siloam fell and killed them—do you think that they were sinners worse than all the people who live in Jerusalem? No, I tell you, but unless you repent, you will all **perish (apollumi)** as well!" (LEB)

If you interpret Luke 13:1-5 to mean *ruin*, you have to deal with the "likewise" statement that Jesus uses. Jesus uses these two recent newsworthy items of his day, to break the notion that his listeners held to, that bad things like this happened to people who were sinners, or that they deserved these untimely deaths.

Jesus is refuting this notion, by telling them that these people who were killed were not any worse than anyone else. He then goes on to tell his listeners that unless they repent they will **all likewise** perish (be destroyed). As we know from Jesus' teachings that we have seen in this book, all men exist in state of death and unless they believe they will die in their sin. They will not have hope of this death sentence being removed.

But, if perish (apollumi) should be interpreted as "ruin" as the traditional view would have us believe, then what does **likewise** mean? Did the Galileans that were killed suffer ruin? Did the eighteen that died when the tower fell on them suffer ruin? Of course not. They were all killed. They died. This is what Jesus is referring to. He does not imply in any way that these people were killed and then went on to eternal torment (ruin). Nor as some traditionalists define "perish" to mean "loss of well-being".

Finally let's chat about the idea of perish meaning "ruin". The traditional view will sometimes focus on Jesus' teaching where he talked about "not putting new wine into old wineskins, lest the wineskins will burst and be ruined (apollumi)". The traditional view insists that this verse can be used as a basis for interpreting perish to mean ruin when it is talking about people.

It makes sense to say that a wineskin is ruined when it is destroyed. The wineskin is not annihilated, in other words it still exists in a ruined state. But a wineskin is an inanimate object. On the other hand, if a living person perishes, that person dies. They are dead, even if their corpse exists in some state of decay for a period, there is no question that person is dead. They have perished. To say a dead person is ruined would be ridiculous.

So, the traditional view twists this (just as many other scriptures) to say that that perish is referring to the ruined state of a person's well-being, by their new life in hell where they will experience torture for eternity.

> **Matthew 7:13** Enter by the narrow gate. For the gate is wide and the way is easy that leads to **destruction**, and those who enter by it are many. For the gate is narrow and the way is hard that leads to **life (zoe),** and those who find it are few. (ESV)

If you didn't know that Jesus was speaking of *zoe* (the state of being alive) when the English word life is used here, then the meaning of this verse becomes enigmatic. Not only will you miss the fact that Jesus is speaking of zoe, he is also directly contrasting zoe to destruction which he does frequently during his ministry. We have seen this theme throughout the gospel of John, as well as in the synoptic gospels.

Jesus is again being very straightforward here. Enter by the narrow gate that leads to *zoe (The word "leads" is referring to future resurrection from the dead to zoe)*, or stay on the wide, easy path that leads to *destruction (speaking of future second death)*.

We must avoid reshaping this by insisting that *destruction* does not mean destruction. Instead of taking destruction for what it plainly means, the traditional view insists that destruction is alluding to everlasting suffering for those that took the easy and wide path.

Jesus is making a clear statement.

Enter by the narrow gate that leads to Zoe,

or stay on the wide & easy path

that leads to Destruction.

Aroma of Christ

> **2 Cor. 2:15-16** For we are the aroma of Christ to God among those who are being saved and among those who are perishing, 16 to those on the one hand an odor from death to death, and to those on the other hand a fragrance from life (zoe) to life (zoe). (LEB)

There are two aromas mentioned in the verses above. To those who are perishing, the aroma is from death to death, while those who are going to be saved the aroma is from life to life. What does this mean?

We have to understand the message that Paul uses throughout his letters, and in his teaching in the book of Acts. Paul consistently conveys that the issue is life (zoe) and death. He contrasts zoe and death throughout his letters.

Due to sin, all mankind initially exists under a sentence of death, (a state of impending judgment and death). Paul sometimes uses the word death proleptically to refer to this. He is not referring to a person's first death, but rather the certainty of being resurrected from the first death to judgment, which will result in the unsaved person dying a second, permanent death. Thus, the phrase from death to death, is referring to this unsaved person's current state of impending death that they live under, to their future, final, second death that will take place on the day of judgment. From death unto death.

For the saved person, we have seen that when a person becomes a believer, they cross over from the state of death to the state of zoe. So, the believer exists (during their current life on earth) already having the zoe of Christ living in them via the indwelling Holy Spirit. This gives the believer the assurance of being raised from the dead to eternal zoe (being alive forever). So, the believer has the aroma of current zoe (assurance of eternal zoe, due to the current indwelling zoe-giving Holy Spirit) unto future zoe (resurrection from the dead to eternal zoe). From life to life.

35

Insights about Angels & Conditionalism

This chapter contains two sections of scripture that give insight into man's mortality, and his need for a savior. Indeed, they show mankind's dire need for a very unique savior. There has only been one man capable of saving man from this mortality, this certainty of everlasting death.

The first scripture we are going to look at is one that has already been included in previous chapters. However, I bring it up again here because of it's unique emphasis that does not appear anywhere else in the New Testament, other than in the second scripture that we will also look at.

In Luke 20:34-36 Jesus makes a statement that I believe is often overlooked. I think one reason it is overlooked is due to the blinding effect that the traditional view has on the Christian reader. Frequent statements made by Jesus and NT authors that practically scream conditional immortality are ignored, because they fall on deaf ears. It's like God is broadcasting on FM radio, but we are listening to AM, so some things that should be obvious to us, go right over our heads.

In Luke 20, Jesus is talking to the Sadducees. This is a sect of Jewish religious leaders who do not believe in the resurrection from the dead. The Sadducees concoct a bizarre story about successive brothers dying and marrying the same widow over and over again. They devise this scheme to entrap Jesus into denying the resurrection. Jesus turns this scenario around on them, showing that man indeed will have the capability of resurrecting from the dead, never to die again. This interaction focuses on:

- ➢ Death
- ➢ Resurrection
- ➢ Never Dying Again (Eternal Zoe)

Notice the two points that Jesus makes about those who are considered worthy of participating in the age to come and the resurrection from the dead.

First, he points out that they will not marry in the age to come. In my previous background as a traditionalist that is about as far as I got with these verses. I focused on the fact that saved people won't be marrying in the afterlife, and that was it. I thought that was Jesus' main point. As it turns out, that was just his first point, and nearly a moot point compared to what he says next.

Remember, the Sadducees are scheming to force Jesus into denying resurrection from the dead. This prompts his clarification. He is about to correct their misconception on this core issue of resurrection. The mention of marriage is just a side issue.

In Jesus second point, he emphasizes that those considered worthy of participating in the age to come will be like the angels, <u>specifically</u> because <u>they will not be able to die any longer</u>!

257

This similarity is due to the fact that angels are immortal and cannot die. These worthy individuals are made sons (& daughters) of God, and of the resurrection (from the dead).

On the other hand, these verses indicate that if someone is not considered worthy (i.e. because they rejected Jesus) then that person would not resurrect from the dead to eternal life.

> **Luke 20:34-36** And Jesus said to them, "The sons of this age marry and are given in marriage, 35 but those who are considered worthy to attain to that age and to the resurrection from the dead neither marry nor are given in marriage, 36 **for they are not even able to die any longer, because they are like the angels and are sons of God, because they are sons of the resurrection**. (LEB)

Please do not miss the point that Jesus is making here, this is huge! He is speaking specifically about this worthy person being resurrected from the dead, and then not being able to ever die again!! This is called immortality. This is repeatedly referred to in the New Testament as "Eternal Zoe", (being alive unto the ages).

One of the main reasons the traditional paradigm prevents this verse from getting any traction is the traditional belief that man has an immortal soul. So, the idea of never being able to die again is seen as no big deal. In fact, the traditional view cannot make a cogent explanation as to why Jesus even included this statement. Therefore, it is usually just ignored because it makes absolutely no sense from the traditional view.

The next section of verses is possibly even more striking than Luke 20. Taken together this tandem of scriptures are very powerful because they help to explain each other.

The author of Hebrews points out the necessity for Jesus to be made lower than the angels for a short time. In fact, this is such an important point that he repeats this fact a second time. Note: The author quotes the phrase "son of man" from Daniel 7:13-14 as a direct reference to Jesus.

> **Hebrews 2:6-10** "What is man, that you remember him, or the son of man, that you care for him? 7 **You made him for a short time lower than the angels**; you crowned him with glory and honor; 8 you subjected all things under his feet. For in subjecting all things, he left nothing that was not subject to him. But now we do not yet see all things subjected to him, 9 but we see Jesus, **for a short time made lower than the angels**,

Why is this fact so important that the author repeated it? What is the significance of this statement, and even more importantly, what does it mean? Let's continue reading...

> ... because of the suffering of death crowned with glory and honor, **so that apart from God he might taste death on behalf of everyone**.

Let's look at two key points that the author makes here, that are directly connected to the fact that God made Jesus for a short time lower than the angels.

> ➤ First, being made lower than the angels (for a short time) was a precursor that was necessary for Jesus to be capable of suffering death. I believe that the phrase for a short

time indicates the period of time while Jesus took on human form. During this time Jesus was mortal.

➤ The final provision was that Jesus had to be "apart from God" so that he would actually be capable of dying. In John 6:57 we see Jesus say that just as he lives because the Father lives, so also, we will live because of him. We also saw in John 5:26 that God granted that Jesus to have "zoe" (the source of being alive) within himself as part of his intrinsic divine nature.

Therefore, it was necessary for Jesus to be "apart from God, "so that he would be separated from this innate source of zoe. Without this source of life coming from the Father, Jesus would then be capable of dying. We see this take place for a moment of time just before Jesus dies on the cross. Jesus cries out (quoting a psalm by the way), "My God, My God, why have you forsaken me". The sky goes dark for a period while God essentially turns his back on Jesus, so that Jesus can die.

For Jesus to die, he had to "for a short time be made lower than the angels" by becoming a mortal human, and also being separated from God, the source of zoe. These two provisions made Jesus capable of "suffering death".

➤ Finally, the author points out that all of this had to occur because Jesus had to "taste death on behalf of everyone".

The author of Hebrews is not done with this point. Let's continue reading:

Hebrews 2:14-17 14 Therefore, since the children share in blood and flesh, he also in like manner shared in these same things, in order that through death he could destroy the one who has the power of death, that is, the devil, 15 and could set free these who through fear of death were subject to slavery throughout all their lives.

16 For surely he is not concerned with angels, but he is concerned with the descendants of Abraham. 17 Therefore he was obligated to be made like his brothers in all respects, in order that he could become a merciful and faithful high priest in the things relating to God, in order to make atonement for the sins of the people. (LEB)

SEVERAL IMPORTANT POINTS ARE BEING MADE HERE:

1. Since the children are flesh and blood by nature, Jesus was born as a man in order that he could share this same nature. This is specifically pointed out as being necessary "in order that through death Jesus could destroy the one who has the power of death, that is, the devil."

2. By dying, (and then being resurrected) Jesus "could set free these who through fear of death were subject to slavery throughout all their lives."

3. Notice that God was not concerned about angels but rather is deeply concerned about the descendants of Abraham. So, Jesus was obligated to be made like his brothers in all respects. Namely, as we have seen spelled out in Hebrews 2, this includes Jesus being made lower than the angels, apart from God, and sharing in man's nature of flesh and blood, so that he would be capable of dying.

4. Our atonement required Jesus's death. Jesus' death required these precursors, so that he would be capable of dying in our place.

A LOOK AT PHILIPPIANS 2:5-8

There's another verse that also speaks to this requirement for Jesus to be in the likeness of men. This verse does not mention angels but does emphasize the necessity for Jesus to be human. The implication is that it was necessary for Jesus to be in human form, in order that he could die. He humbled himself, emptied himself of some aspect of being equal with God, and took on human form.

Paul understood (evidenced by his teachings throughout his letters) that God is immortal and incapable of dying, and that it is the zoe of Jesus (the source of being alive, that comes through the indwelling Spirit of Jesus) that gives all believers the assurance of resurrection from the dead to live forever, (this is known as eternal zoe).

> **Philippians 2:5-8** Have this mind among yourselves, which is yours in Christ Jesus, 6 who, though he was in the form of God, did not count equality with God a thing to be grasped, 7 but emptied himself, by taking the form of a servant, being born in the likeness of men. 8 And being found in human form, he humbled himself by becoming obedient to the point of death, even death on a cross.

36

Finally, Thank You

I would like to express my gratitude to you for reading all the way through this book. I hope this has been helpful in clarifying Jesus' message and in your accepting the eternal life (*zoe*), which is only available through faith in Jesus the Christ.

Perhaps the day will come in the age of the new heavens and earth, when you and I will meet and have the opportunity to reflect on God's sufficient saving grace through Jesus, as well as his good and sovereign daily grace to each of us through our unique journeys.

Remember John's final words in his gospel regarding *Zoe* . . .

John 20:31 . . . these are written so that you may believe that Jesus is the Christ, the Son of God, and that by believing you may have zoe in his name. (ESV)

37

A Tribute to Edward Fudge & Chris Date

I would like to give tribute to a man who I have come to regard as the vanguard of the Conditionalist movement in this century. (There were others before him, though none in recent decades who are as noteworthy that I am aware of.)

Edward Fudge spent most of his adult life devoted to bringing the truth of the Bible's teaching to this subject. He knew that correctly understanding the truth about Gehenna, Hades, immortality, resurrection and eternal life was not a matter of salvation. He showed grace for those who disagreed with him. He was truly a sweet spirited and tender-hearted man.

However, he knew the importance of having a correct understanding of Jesus' and the Bible's teaching on these topics. His exhaustive biblical research has revealed truth which will hopefully become the new paradigm of Christians in the decades and centuries to come.

Many have said that the Old Testament does not teach much about hell, and they are correct in the sense of "hell" as it is typically understood in the traditional sense.

However, Fudge brings out the overwhelming truth about the numerous instances of the judgment of God toward the wicked, which are foretold throughout the Old Testament. This judgment is the destruction of the ungodly, which is in total agreement with Jesus' teachings on *Gehenna* and John's writings in Revelation about the second death.

I strongly recommend Fudge's latest book, *The Consuming Fire (Third Edition)*, which he completed shortly before his death, in November of 2017.

Fudge was truly the authority on this subject. I regret not getting to know him. After reading much of his work and watching many of his videos, I can only say that he was a child of God, a man fully devoted to rightfully dividing the word of truth, a gentleman, a loving family man, and quite obviously a man who garnered the love and respect of all who truly knew him.

Fudge inspired and mentored several younger individuals (such as Chris Date) who have picked up the torch. One group he was closely associated with is the group of Christians who regularly contribute to the website **RethinkingHell.com**.

I strongly recommend their articles, videos, conferences, and other resources they provide.

There is also the website of **EdwardFudge.com**, which is still maintained by his family at this time. There are many great articles there as well.

You can also do a search on YouTube.com to see several videos of Edward Fudge speaking or debating.

Several of his videos can be seen here:

https://www.truthaccordingtoscripture.com/documents/death/wicked.php#.W-N8aJNKhPZ

https://www.truthaccordingtoscripture.com/hell.php#.YX2XkJ7MLIU

CHRIS DATE: AUTHOR & SPEAKER

As mentioned, Chris Date has carried on the torch that Edward Fudge began decades ago. Chris is one of the foremost scholars on the subject of conditional immortality. He is very active in podcasts with the RethinkingHell.com forum, as well as active with the Rethinking Hell YouTube channel and Facebook page.

There are several other believers who are also biblical scholars that join him in discussion on these venues. While Chris does have some short videos on the YouTube channel, most of his work is quite in depth. Either short or long, I highly recommend his teaching in any of the venues.

Chris did a lengthy video on the Rethinking Hell YouTube channel on the subject of "What Life Means" (Session "LIVE 26"). This is an excellent video and drills deep into the etymology and use of the word "life" in the Old Testament and subsequently in the New Testament. This should be a must view for any Christian struggling with the meaning of zoe. Chris also does a follow up video on "What is Death". Due to the critically important roles of life and death throughout Jesus' teaching, I highly recommend both of these videos.

38

My Primary Resources

I have heavily used certain resources for my own word studies as a basis for this book. I would like to share a few of these, in case you would like to utilize these while conducting your own study.

INTERLINEAR NEW TESTAMENT

One of the most valuable tools online is the Greek-English Interlinear New Testament, which can be found at:

https://www.scripture4all.org/OnlineInterlinear/Greek_Index.htm

Greek-English Interlinear New Testaments have been used as reference material for generations by serious Bible scholars. The online access to this resource is a wonderful study tool.

GREEK DICTIONARY

Strong's Analytical Concordance (book form) is an excellent tool for identifying the use and locations of Greek words in the New Testament.

Some aspects of *Strong's Concordance* are also available online. One of the best online resources for *Strong's Dictionary* that I have found is at this link:

➢ http://Biblehub.com/strongs.htm

ONLINE BIBLE

Another great online resource is the entire Bible, which can quickly be searched by book and chapter. This is an excellent tool for quickly finding verses of interest and being able to read them in various translations.

➢ https://www.Biblegateway.com/

Recommended Resources

RECOMMENDED READING

The Fire that Consumes (Third Edition)

by Edward Fudge

Rethinking Hell: Readings in Evangelical Conditionalism

by Christopher M. Date, Gregory G. Stump and Joshua W. Anderson

The Doctrine of Immortality in the Early Church

by John H. Roller

Immortal, The truth about Heaven, Hell, and the Resurrection

by Lex Meyer

RECOMMENDED WEBSITES

eternalzoe.com

rethinkinghell.com

edwardfudge.com

truthaccordingtoscripture.com (Eternal Torment or Death?)

unlearnthelies.com

YOUTUBE CHANNELS

Eternal Zoe

Rethinking Hell

Unlearn the Lies

FURTHER WORD STUDY

If you are interested in doing more of your own study on *psuche* or *zoe*, please see the webpages below.

The following links will take you to the Strong's definition of both words, as well as provide a list of all the occurrences of the words *psuche* and *zoe*, that you can quickly read through. These webpages are also provided as hyperlinks at www.eternalzoe.com.

PSUCHE

http://Biblehub.com/greek/5590.htm

ZOE

http://Biblehub.com/str/greek/2222.htm

Links Related to Topics

Note: For links to topics discussed in Eternal Zoe, please go to:

www.eternalzoe.com/links

All links are listed without permission. The owners and associates of these websites may not endorse or agree with my views in this book.